# Human Development in the Twenty-First Century

How do human beings develop and function in relation to the human and natural world? The science of dynamic systems focuses on connections and relationships between people rather than on individual actions alone. This collection of engaging, non-technical essays, written by dynamic systems scientists in psychology, biology, anthropology, education, and sociology, challenges us to consider novel ways to enhance human development worldwide in the face of poverty, violence, neglect, disease, and crises in our families. Focusing specifically on how to think about interventions and policies that will benefit human development from a systems perspective, this book brings current research into the realm of application and policy. The authors use real-life examples to propose changes in clinical, educational, and policy-making practices that will be of interest to professionals and the public alike.

ALAN FOGEL is Professor of Psychology in the Department of Psychology at the University of Utah. He has written and edited many books including *Change Processes in Relationships: A Relational–Historical Research Approach* (Cambridge, 2006).

BARBARA J. KING is Professor in the Department of Anthropology at the College of William and Mary. She is the Editor of the *Journal of Developmental Processes*.

STUART G. SHANKER is Distinguished Research Professor of Philosophy and Psychology at York University, Toronto, where he is also President of the Council for Early Child Development and Director of the Milton and Ethel Harris Research Initiative.

# Human Development in the Twenty-First Century

## Visionary Ideas from Systems Scientists

*edited by*

Alan Fogel, Barbara J. King, and Stuart G. Shanker

CAMBRIDGE
UNIVERSITY PRESS

CAMBRIDGE UNIVERSITY PRESS
Cambridge, New York, Melbourne, Madrid, Cape Town, Singapore, São Paulo, Delhi

Cambridge University Press
The Edinburgh Building, Cambridge CB2 8RU, UK

Published in the United States of America by Cambridge University Press, New York

www.cambridge.org
Information on this title: www.cambridge.org/9780521881975

First published 2008
Reprinted 2009

Printed in the United Kingdom at the University Press, Cambridge

*A catalogue record for this publication is available from the British Library*

ISBN 978-0-521-88197-5 hardback

# Contents

# Contributors

BEATRICE BEEBE is Clinical Professor of Medical Psychology in Psychiatry at the College of Physicians and Surgeons, Columbia University, and Research Scientist at the Department of Communication Sciences, New York State Psychiatric Institute

LYNETTE FRIEDRICH COFER is Professor Emerita in the Department of Psychology, University of New Mexico

GEORGE DOWNING is Chief Psychologist at the Infant Psychiatry Unit, Salpetriere Hospital, Paris

GILLIAN EVANS is Associate of the Centre for Child-Focused Anthropological Research (C-FAR) at Brunel University, London, Lecturer in Social Anthropology at the University of Manchester, and RCUK Fellow in the Centre for Research into Social and Cultural Change, University of Manchester

ALAN FOGEL is Professor of Psychology at the University of Utah, Salt Lake City

GILBERT GOTTLIEB (deceased) was Professor at the Center for Developmental Science at the University of North Carolina, Chapel Hill

PETER GOW is Professor of Social Anthropology at the University of St Andrews

ISABELA GRANIC is Assistant Professor at the University of Toronto, and Research Scientist in the Community Health Systems Resource Group at the Hospital for Sick Children, Toronto

STANLEY I. GREENSPAN is Professor at the Interdisciplinary Council for Developmental and Learning Disorders, and the Departments of Psychiatry, Behavioral Sciences, and Pediatrics at George Washington University Medical School

CAROLYN TUCKER HALPERN is Associate Professor in the Department of Maternal and Child Health at the University of North Carolina, Chapel Hill

TIM INGOLD is Professor of Social Anthropology at the University of Aberdeen

JOSEPH JAFFE is Professor of Clinical Psychiatry in Neurological Surgery at the College of Physicians and Surgeons, Columbia University, and Chief of the Department of Communication Sciences, New York State Psychiatric Institute

TIMOTHY D. JOHNSTON is Professor of Psychology, and Dean of the College of Arts and Sciences, University of North Carolina, Greensboro

MASATOSHI KAWAI is Professor and Dean at the Graduate School of Clinical Education, Research Institute for Education, Mukogawa Women's University, Nishinomiya, Hyogo, Japan

MICHAEL E. KERR is Director of the Bowen Center for Study of the Family, Washington DC

BARBARA J. KING is Professor of Anthropology at the College of William and Mary, Williamsburg, Virginia, and Editor, *Journal of Developmental Processes*

BARRY M. LESTER is Professor at the Brown Center for the Study of Children at Risk, Brown Medical School, Women and Infants Hospital of Rhode Island, Providence, RI

MARC D. LEWIS is Professor of Human Development and Applied Psychology, University of Toronto

ROBERT LICKLITER is Professor of Psychology, Florida International University, Miami

GAIL F. MELSON is Professor Emerita in the Department of Child Development and Family Studies, West Lafayette, Indiana

DANIEL S. MESSINGER is Associate Professor in the Department of Psychology and Pediatrics, University of Miami

PEDRO REYGADAS is in the Department of Social Sciences and Humanities, Autonomous University of San Luis Potosí, Mexico

KEN RICHARDSON was Senior Lecturer in Human Development, at the Open University

STUART G. SHANKER is Distinguished Research Professor of Philosophy and Psychology, and Director at the Milton and Ethel Harris Research Initiative, York University, Toronto

BARBARA SMUTS is Professor of Psychology at the University of Michigan, Ann Arbor

STEPHEN J. SUOMI works in the Laboratory of Comparative Ethology at the National Institute of Child Health and Human Development, National Institute of Health, DHHS, Washington DC

CHRISTINA TOREN is Professor of Anthropology, University of St Andrews

# Introduction: Why a dynamic systems approach to fostering human development?

*Alan Fogel, Barbara J. King, and Stuart G. Shanker*

The dynamic systems approach is an emerging interdisciplinary set of principles used by a diverse collection of scientists to help understand the complex world in which we live. The main insight that unites these scientists, despite wide differences in methods and concepts, is a focus on connections and relationships. A relationship between a particular parent and child, for example, is distinguished by the expressions and gestures as well as the words by which they understand each other. A parent's raised eyebrow might mean "pay attention," or "be careful" to their child. This small and subtle gesture has meaning to both parent and child because they have worked it out together by repeatedly learning how to understand each other, negotiating their mutual needs and goals. The raised eyebrow represents that whole history of the growth of the relationship. The relationship is a dynamic system because it changes over time (it is dynamic) and because the mutually understood gestures are the result of both people working together to create something that is more than either one of them alone (it is a relationship system). A dynamic system is a relationship that grows over time, has a history, and is more than the simple sum of its parts.

A more traditional approach to understanding the world treats the parent and child as separate entities, each of which affects the other. The parent's eyebrow raise can be understood, in this approach, to affect the child's behavior, causing the child to pay attention or be careful. This so-called "linear" or "sequential" approach to understanding the world easily leads to principles and policies that assume either the parent or the child is the cause of particular outcomes. Parental behavior is seen in this way to cause children to grow up psychologically well- or mal-adjusted. Or, the blame is placed on the child for being unruly or uncooperative. Policies and public monies are allocated to correct the problems by treating the parent or the child.

These policies and programs can't and don't work out well for anyone, neither the families they intend to help nor the society they were meant to improve. Why? Because the source of the strength or weakness is not in the parent or the child: it lies in their relationship and how it grew. Effective policies and programs, mindful that a problem child usually arises from a series of mis-coordinations and misunderstandings in a parent–child or teacher–child relationship, can harness an understanding of how relationships grow over time to change the course of that growth toward more adaptive patterns. A dynamic systems approach gives us a toolkit of methods and concepts that are relationship-based, oriented toward understanding and enhancing the ties that bind us together.

The dynamic systems approach takes many forms, depending upon the background and training of the scientist. Because this approach originated in physics and mathematics, many scientists strive to find mathematical models that describe complex systems and their changes over time. Mathematical spin-offs of dynamic systems approaches include chaos theory, catastrophe theory, dynamic equations of motion, and fractal geometry. These mathematical approaches are well suited to situations in which concrete measurements can be made of things like time, distance, or speed.

Dynamic systems ideas have also been applied in the biological and social sciences where such precise measurements cannot be made. In these cases, the focus is on the qualitative, rather than the quantitative aspects of the interpersonal relationships that comprise the dynamic social system. Of particular interest to these scientists is the way in which people co-create and when necessary repair mutual understandings in long-term relationships, such as in the example of the parent and child, above. At present less typical, but we hope on the increase, are approaches in the physical and social sciences that bring together quantitative and qualitative analyses of a single relationship system. Such a complementary approach may be particularly apt in attempts to measure and describe change over time in human development.

This book is a collection of essays written primarily by non-mathematical biological and social scientists explaining how their own unique interpretation of the dynamic systems approach constitutes a new way of thinking in their field, and how it contrasts with older methods and concepts. Although we could not include all approaches to applying systems thinking, we strove to collect essays from many different disciplines including psychology, biology, anthropology, primatology, education, and sociology. We, the editors, requested that the authors articulate their use of dynamic systems and relationship principles in non-technical language.

Some of the authors of the chapters in this book endeavor to incorporate explicitly some of the concepts of dynamic systems theory.

For these chapters, the authors explain and apply the concepts in clear and simple language. For other chapters, authors take a more general "relationship" perspective. They show how human development occurs in the context of social systems in which all participants affect each other and in which simple cause-and-effect reasoning is insufficient to comprehend the complexity of the social processes under investigation.

Our main goal in this book is to bring a dynamic systems perspective to the issue of how to enhance and foster human development throughout the life course. It is our hope that these chapters will bring about a novel way of thinking about and solving some of the major hindrances to human development in the world today: including poverty, violence, neglect, and disease. We are also particularly interested in the early years, as the child's experiences during this period may have a large impact on the possibilities for future development. We thus asked each of the authors to think about how their own work may lead to implications for policies and practices related to enhancing and fostering human development.

## The book is divided into four main sections

Part I (Dynamic Relationships between Genetics and Environments) focuses on a new understanding of the complex relationships between genes and environments. Genes cannot be considered to determine physical characteristics or behavior in the absence of their relationships with particular types of supporting environments. If those environments are not present, the genetic potential will not be realized. Dynamic systems thinking helps us to understand the ways in which physical characteristics and behaviors can change over time or remain the same, depending upon feedback transactions in the gene–environment relationship and the way genes manufacture proteins in the cells. The chapters in this section help us to appreciate how changes in the relationship with the environment – in factors related to how the organism responds to diet, education, family communication, and the like – play an essential role in managing genetic disorders and optimizing genetic potentials. They show how no single factor acting in isolation can be held responsible for a developmental outcome.

Part II (The Dynamic System of the Child in the Family) reveals some of the subtle interchanges between children and their families that either promote or restrict healthy development. Dynamic systems thinking – with its focus on change and transformation in relationships – helps us understand how unhealthy and unproductive patterns get stabilized in family relationships, and how they may be changed for the better. The chapters in this section reveal how the emotions, long neglected in people's thinking about what influences healthy development, are a fundamental part of the complex system of inter-individual communication for humans, and also for their closest living relatives, the apes. These chapters also make clear that – just as behavior and thinking does not develop in isolation from the emotions – individuals do not develop in isolation from others in their families. In fact, dynamic systems thinking makes clear that the "individual" is not a useful concept when thinking about creating healthy and nurturing environments. Parents and children co-create their relationships, each influencing the other in a complex system of evolving personal meanings.

Part III (The Dynamic System of the Child in Social and Physical Environment) takes this essential point even farther to include not only relationships in the family but also with the society, culture, and the natural world in which the child is raised. Children become valued and productive members of a society through a complex series of transactions that involve observing the world around them, taking initiatives and receiving feedback, and constructing a view of themselves that is inseparable from the fabric of the social world in which they were raised. The dynamic systems approach shows that it is not possible predictably to change child development outcomes by simply dictating a policy change in the family, school, or any other social institution. The chapters in this section demonstrate that interventions must take account of the complex series of transactions between children and their environments, each affecting the other, and the complex transactions between policies and practices within society.

Part IV (Dynamic Systems Approaches to Mental Health) shows how this theme of complex transaction in the relationship between child and society can be applied to treatment programs that foster child and family mental health. The chapters in this section propose relationship-based interventions that take account of the transactions between children and those around them. Treatment is not focused on fixing the individual but rather on teaching people to communicate more effectively about what is most important to their lives. The dynamic systems approach applied to clinical practice suggests ways to intervene that support not only the child but *also* the social environment in which the child lives day-to-day. Without such whole systems support, interventions are less likely to succeed in the long run.

The book concludes with an introduction to the basic methodological principles of a dynamic systems approach, written in non-technical language. This chapter conveys how keenly we, the editors, believe in the potential for dynamic systems research to shift the ways in which people think about human development. This chapter promises a new approach to scientific research that takes account of the whole system of complex relationships in which the individual is embedded, and how that system changes over time. We currently possess all the necessary scientific tools to carry out such a program of research. Agencies responsible for promoting and planning research can play a crucial role in shaping a more systemic approach to the study of the important questions and challenges facing optimal human development in nurturing environments.

We expect this book to have impact in a number of ways. First, we intend to open a dialogue with policy-makers and to create a platform for future policy-planning debates in such areas as early child development, education, and therapeutic interventions for children and adults. All of the chapters in this book contain ideas relevant for creating policies that are rooted in a dynamic systems perspective on human development. Policy-related ideas involve a wide range of arenas, including clinical practices, making laws that are informed by a broad systems understanding of development, and decision-making about how to allocate funds for research on human development.

Second, we hope this book will serve as a resource for students and scholars around the world who are laboring to master the powerful tools afforded by a dynamic systems approach. For those who want to foster nurturing care and human development in the real world, we offer support for a holistic, dynamic approach and provide a host of new ideas both theoretically and methodologically. Further, each chapter is followed by a list of readings allowing in-depth further exploration of dynamic-systems ideas.

Finally, we hope that this book will make a vital contribution to the study of human development. There is now substantial research establishing the importance of early childhood experiences for the healthy development of the mind and body. What has hitherto been missing, however, is a detailed understanding of what sorts of conditions promote psychological and neurobiological development, and more fundamentally, how these processes operate. The dynamic systems approach provides us with the conceptual and methodological tools necessary to address these critical questions. The better we understand these processes, the better we will be able to understand the diversity of ways that people develop in relation with others around the world, and design social and education policies, and intervention protocols where appropriate, that will enhance the development of all people and better equip them to deal with the formidable challenges of the twenty-first century.

The editors and many of the authors of this book are members of the Council of Human Development, an international group of biological and social scientists who take a systems orientation. The members of the Council believe that research and applied work, as well as policies affecting peoples around the world, need to be informed by the broadest possible dynamic understanding of how human beings develop and function in relationship to the human and natural world. This includes developmental processes that build on the relationships between biological, familial, cultural, and environmental factors.

The Council is guided by the principle that early childhood is the most important time in a human being's development. Growth in these years establishes the foundations for intellectual, emotional, and moral growth; education and intervention regarding nurturing care in these early years can establish long-lasting practices that maintain physical and mental health and prevent unnecessary suffering.

*Primary goals of the Council are*:

- *To promote a "dynamic systems" view of development,* a new science of development that has not yet received widespread attention.
- *To recognize and aid the diverse ways in which people around the world may achieve nurturing interactions and develop safe, caring communities for the future of children.*
- *To initiate and maintain a public education campaign* involving leaders from all public arenas to support a public ethic on the importance of nurturing interactions and safe, caring communities that thrive through a caring relationship with the natural world.
- *To support strategic research and service programs* to further the knowledge base and create the "nurturing infrastructure" to translate these concepts into care for every individual and family.

Eight working groups, each led by a member of the Organizing Sub-Committee, comprise the Council: Anthropology of Human Development, headed by Christina Toren; Biology and Development, headed by Robert Lickliter; Ecology of Human Development, headed by Alan Fogel; Evolutionary Perspectives, headed by Barb Smuts; Geo-Political Contexts of Development, headed by Stuart Shanker and Stanley Greenspan; Mental Health and Development, headed by Stanley Greenspan and Stuart Shanker; Social Developmental Neuroscience, headed by Marc Lewis; and the Latin American Initiative, which is headed by Pedro Reygadas. In addition, the Council co-sponsors publication of the *Journal of Developmental Processes*, edited by Barbara J. King. Please visit the Council's website at www.councilhd.ca

for announcements, new research publications, and new journal issues as they appear.

We are grateful to the many scientists exploring systems ideas in different disciplines that have inspired and informed so much of the thinking presented in this book. We are also grateful to the Harris Steel Foundation, which provided critical support for the creation of the Council and for the meetings that led up to the publication of this book. Finally, we wish to honor the memory of Gilbert Gottlieb, one of the contributors to this book, who did not live to see it published.

*Part I*

# Dynamic relationships between genetics and environments

# 1 Developmental dynamics: the new view from the life sciences

*Robert Lickliter*

James is an eleven-year-old boy who is tall for his age, has blond hair and blue eyes, loves to play baseball, and is the best right-handed pitcher on his little league team. James is easy going, popular among his classmates at school, and excels in math and science classes. What is the source of such traits as athletic ability, temperament, and intelligence? Why are some children outgoing and socially skilled, while others appear introverted and avoid unfamiliar social situations? Why do some children find puzzles of logic interesting and challenging, while others don't seem interested or willing to apply themselves to such mental tasks?

In the first half of the twentieth century, many biologists and psychologists thought that major aspects of behavioral development progressed in an orderly and preordained sequence under the direct control of genes. From this view, genes were seen to guide the nervous system to mature in a predetermined fashion, giving rise to so-called "innate" or "instinctive" behavior. Likewise, human characteristics like temperament, intelligence, or athletic ability were thought to be genetically based and to be relatively unaffected by experience or environment. Thanks in large part to more than half a century of comparative and developmental research, most biologists and psychologists now appreciate that behavior does not simply unfold from some predetermined genetic blueprint or template. Assumptions of genetically determined "innate" or "hard-wired" behavior have gradually given way to the realization that genes cannot, in and of themselves, produce behavioral or psychological traits or characteristics.

This more dynamic view of behavioral development, in which an individual's interests and behavior are no longer seen to be independent of his or her activity, experience, or context, has not, however, been widely extended to other levels of development. While many scientists now appreciate that it is not accurate to speak about genes directly determining psychological characteristics like intelligence or personality, most continue to view the development of an individual's physical traits through the old lens of genetic determinism. Physical characteristics like hair color, eye color, height, or body type are examples of traits that continue to be attributed solely to genetic factors, thought to be directly caused by genes inherited from one's parents. Thus, James's blond hair, blue eyes, right-handedness, and tall stature are thought by many to be caused by the genes he inherited from his mother and father. This view of trait development is both simplistic and misleading, but continues to have a firm hold in the minds of many people.

We now know that all traits, be they behavioral or physical, require the necessary contributions of both genetic and non-genetic factors. Developmental biologists have repeatedly demonstrated that the development of any trait or character is the consequence of a unique web of interactions among an individual's genes, complex molecular interactions within and across cells, and the nature and sequence of the physical, biological, and social environments through which the individual passes during its development. These developmental dynamics must be included in any plausible account of how traits develop and change over the course of infancy, childhood, or adulthood. This shift in thinking requires moving beyond the mistaken idea that genes determine traits and actively exploring *how* traits emerge from genetic and non-genetic factors co-acting over the course of development. This process-oriented approach is often referred to as a "developmental systems perspective" and represents a new way of thinking about human development and behavior that is not yet widely known or appreciated beyond specialists working in the developmental sciences.

An example of the dividends of the emphasis on *how* questions in the developmental systems approach to human behavior is useful here. A common trait widely held to be genetically determined is handedness, an individual's preference to use either the right or left hand to perform such skilled behaviors as using a fork, writing with a pen, or throwing a ball. This assumption probably results from the observation that left-handedness seems to run in families and from the fact that there are no obvious environmental or experiential factors that seem to influence whether an infant or toddler will consistently prefer to use his/her right or left hand to reach for a toy or whether a child will choose to draw or write with his/her right or left hand. Such patterns of cerebral lateralization (in which the left and right sides of the brain specialize in the physical and behavioral functions they support) that result in James throwing a baseball with his right hand have long been attributed to genetic factors, with little concern for how extra-genetic factors, including the specific experiences of the developing individual, might affect such motor preferences.

In recent years, however, a number of animal studies (most using birds like chicks, ducks, and quail) have shown that sensory stimulation present during prenatal development is actively involved in the lateralization of brain and behavior. Like humans, many bird species show strong patterns of lateralized behavior, including foot preferences. For example, of twenty parrot species tested for foot bias, fifteen species showed preferential use of their left foot to hold nuts and other food items. Similarly, 85 percent of newly hatched quail chicks show a left turning bias in the days following hatching.

To the surprise of many, the direction of lateralization in brain organization and behavior has been found to be significantly influenced by the prenatal experience of the developing bird embryo. In the later stages of prenatal development, the embryos of birds such as chicks, ducks, and quail are oriented in their egg such that the left eye and left ear are covered by the body and yolk sac, while the right eye is exposed to light passing through the egg shell and the right ear is exposed to sound passing through the egg shell. As a result of this postural orientation in the egg, different amounts of auditory and visual experience are provided to the two ears and two eyes, which are functional during the late stages of prenatal development. For example, the right eye is closer to the translucent shell and not occluded by the body and yolk, so light stimulation is not equal to both eyes. The right eye (and consequently the left hemisphere of the brain) receives a greater amount of visual stimulation than the left eye (and right hemisphere of the brain) prior to hatching. This differential exposure favors the development of the left hemisphere of the brain in advance of the right hemisphere, significantly influencing the direction of lateralization of a variety of postnatal behaviors, including visual discrimination, spatial orientation, and various motor skills. This finding illustrates that lateralized behavior is not simply genetically predetermined, but rather is due, at least in part, to highly structured and reliably available experiences occurring during early development.

Do similar types of prenatal factors also influence patterns of cerebral lateralization in humans? Can early sensory experience contribute to the organization of brain and behavior in ways usually attributed only to the genes? Does James's preference for using his right arm to throw pitches in his little league baseball games have more to it than simply the genes he inherited from his parents? Several researchers have argued yes, pointing out that, during the late stages of gestation, the majority of human fetuses are positioned with their head facing down and to the left side of the mother's midline, with their right ear facing outward. According to several large-scale European and North American studies, this leftward positioning bias is about 2:1. In other words, during the last trimester of pregnancy approximately 65–70 percent of human fetuses are positioned with the right ear facing out and the left ear facing in toward the mother's tissues and internal organs. As a result of this positioning, human fetuses receive different types and amounts of pre-natal experience to the right and left ears and labyrinths during late prenatal development, probably contributing to cerebral lateralization for a variety of postnatal traits, including speech perception, language function, and limb dominance patterns, like handedness and footedness.

These examples of experience-dependent trait development empha-size the point that all traits (be they physical or behavioral) are always the result of developmental processes involving both genetic and non-genetic factors. These non-genetic factors are often *non-obvious*, in that their effects are difficult to recognize or pinpoint; they typically become visible only when the specific factor is significantly modified or removed from the context of development. Using such research methods, we now know that a wide array of non-genetic factors and conditions that are reliably present during development, including gravity, light, tempera-ture, population density, and sensory stimulation (to name but a few), play significant roles in how organisms develop.

For example, the sex determination of all crocodiles, most turtles, and some lizards depends on the temperature at which they develop. Eggs incubated at one range of temperatures produce males and eggs incu-bated at another range produce females. In other words, the tempera-ture at which the eggs are maintained during prenatal development leads to substantial changes in anatomy, morphology, reproductive physi-ology, and the behavioral traits associated with being male or female. Such dramatic findings from developmental biology have provided a new appreciation of the magnitude of the gap between gene activity and the emergence of specific traits or characters within a given individual.

The complexities of gene–environment interactions are just beginning to be unraveled. It is clear, however, that there are an amazing variety of ways that genes and environment coact to produce anatomy, physiology, and behavior. Genes cannot be characterized as occupying a privileged position in the development of an individual, as they are themselves participants in the developmental process, which includes influences and interactions taking place at many hierarchically arranged levels within and outside the developing individual. These include cell nucleus–cell cytoplasm, cell–cell, cell–tissue, and organism–organism interactions.

Given that physical and behavioral traits are always the complex product of many interacting factors, it is misleading to attribute causal status to any one factor acting in isolation. Researchers working in a number of scientific disciplines are becoming increasingly sensitive to the fact that the functional significance of genes (or neural structures, hormonal levels, or social interaction) can only be understood in relation to the larger developmental system of which they are a part. This idea of *distributed control*, that direction for the emergence and development of our traits resides in the nature of the relationships within and between internal genetic and non-genetic factors and external environmental variables, is a key principle in understanding how development works but is still not widely appreciated by many students of biology and psychology.

The general lack of appreciation of the notion of distributed control is likely due to the fact that, for most of the twentieth century, a major goal of biology was to explain how biological form and function could be reduced down to explanations at the level of the genes. The reductionistic agenda of genetic determinism received strong consensus throughout the life sciences for a number of decades and provided important insights into the molecular and genetic mechanisms of life. While the legacy of genetic determinism persists in the popular press and media, it is now clear that the goal of understanding biological form and function solely in terms of genetic factors is untenable and cannot succeed, despite the significant advances in molecular biology over the last several decades. A wealth of evidence now available from the life sciences shows that the rules and constraints that guide the complex developmental processes that give rise to traits are widely distributed at many levels of the organism and do not reside only in the genes. Biologists now acknowledge that there is not enough information in any genome capable of mapping out the details by which physical or behavioral traits arise in any organism. Clearly, non-genetic factors must also be at play.

Simply put, it is no longer plausible to regard the physical or behavioral traits of a boy like James as simply the manifestation or expression of his genes, or to assert that genetic programs can make us behave in particular ways in particular circumstances, a position still argued by a number of sociobiologists and evolutionary psychologists. These views ignore the known principles of both developmental biology and developmental psychology, including the important idea of distributed control. A strict emphasis on any single domain or level, be it genes, neuroanatomy or neurochemistry, physiology, social interaction, or culture, will simply be too limited to address successfully the dynamic, multidetermined nature of human behavior and development. Unfortunately, few people outside the specialists working in the developmental sciences have been informed of this insight or more generally to the demise of genetic determinism. Contemporary life sciences tell us that there are many gene-dependent processes, but no gene-directed ones.

This revolutionary message effectively eliminates the long standing nature–nurture debate and replaces it with a view that appreciates that organisms and their environments make up a unitary system. What makes development happen is the *relationship* of the components of this amazing system, not the individual components themselves. It is regrettable that many people continue to receive the message that various psychological and biological traits are genetic, as we now know that traits or characters cannot possibly be predicted by factors solely within the genes (or within the environment for that matter). Understanding the fallacy of the nature vs. nurture dichotomy can constructively redirect our thoughts about such basic human issues as reproduction, parenting, and education. While it is still common to hear about the genetic basis of sexual orientation, personality, intelligence, or learning disabilities, there is growing consensus within the biological and psychological sciences that genetic and environmental factors always coact to contribute to any trait development. So, while specific genes and their products certainly contributed to James's blond hair, blue eyes, and tall stature, as well as his athletic ability and temperament, so did a wealth of non-genetic factors. These include cellular, hormonal, dietary, and social factors, to name but a few. Appreciating that genetic factors are necessary but not sufficient to explain the varieties of human development and behavior helps to expand our perspective and points to the importance of identifying the essential resources of normal, healthy development. Defining and providing these resources should be an essential priority for all families, communities, and societies.

SUGGESTED READINGS

Coen, E. (1999). *The art of genes: how organisms make themselves*. Oxford: Oxford University Press.
Gilbert, S. F. (2000). *Developmental biology* (6th edn.). Sunderland, MA: Sinauer.
Gottlieb, G., D. Wahlsten, and R. Lickliter (2006). The significance of biology for human development: a developmental psychobiological systems view. In W. Damon (series ed.) and R. Lerner (vol. ed.), *Handbook of child psychology, vol. 1: theoretical models of human development* (6th edn., pp. 210–257). New York: Wiley.
Johnston, T. D., and L. Edwards (2002). Genes, interactions, and the development of behavior. *Psychological Review*, 109, 26–34.
Keller, E. F. (2000). *The century of the gene*. Cambridge, MA: Harvard University Press.

Lewontin, R. C. (2000). *The triple helix: genes, organism, and environment.* Cambridge, MA: Harvard University Press.

Michel, G., and C. Moore (1995). *Developmental psychobiology: an integrative science.* Cambridge, MA: MIT Press.

Moore, D. S. (2001). *The dependent gene: the fallacy of nature vs. nurture.* New York: W. H. Freeman.

Robert, J. S. (2004). *Embryology, epigenesis, and evolution: taking development seriously.* New York: Cambridge University Press.

# 2    Genes, experience, and behavior

*Timothy D. Johnston*

My aim in this chapter is to provide some guidance for thinking about the ways in which genes contribute to the development of behavior. The more we learn about the science of developmental behavior genetics, the clearer it becomes that every behavior includes some genetic influence – there is undoubtedly no such thing as a completely non-genetic pattern of behavior. The question for behavior is not whether genes are involved in its development, but which genes are involved and how they exert their influence. In the past decade, geneticists have made great strides in identifying genes that affect various forms of behavior and in unraveling at least some of the details of how they do so. As a result, it has become clear that we have to change some of the ways we think about genes and their influence on behavior.

People often write and think about the way genes and environment (or experience) contribute to behavior as if these two influences work separately, sometimes even in opposition to one another. We read of findings supposedly showing that a psychological disorder previously thought to result entirely from experience is in fact partly genetic. Or we hear that the extent to which heredity influences a personality trait is greater than previously thought, the implication being that experience is thereby shown to be less important. Our thinking about this issue seems to be guided by an equation of the following kind:

$$\text{Behavior} = \text{Genetic influence} + \text{Environmental influence}$$

The relation between genes and environment is presented as an additive one in which more of one kind of influence inevitably means less of the other. Since the amount of behavior to be explained remains constant, it appears as if each newly discovered genetic influence implies the loss of some previously supposed environmental influence, so that the equation stays balanced. As hardly a week goes by without the announcement of some such discovery, the balance appears to be shifting inexorably towards an increasingly important genetic influence, and an increasingly unimportant environmental one. We know far more about the genetic contribution to behavior and psychological function today than we did twenty, or even ten years ago, and it is probably fair to say that there is now a broad acceptance among developmentalists that virtually every aspect of our psychological makeup is affected by our genes. But with that acceptance has also come a radically different understanding of how genes make their contributions to development. Developmentalists have argued for a long time that genes and environment do not act independently of one another, that the relationships between these two sets of influences are more cooperative than competitive. What we now know about the molecular details of gene activity fully confirms that claim and shows that the cooperation between genes and environment is even more intimate than previously realized. For example, we have a wealth of evidence showing that learning, generally thought to be a quintessential case of "purely environmental" influence on behavior, depends on changes in gene activity to bring about behavioral change. It has also become clear that genes, far from being the "master molecule" of popular scientific description, must be activated in order to have any effects at all on development and that their activation not infrequently has its origin in the external environment.

## The information metaphor of gene action

The idea that genes and environment act in opposition is supported by an influential metaphor according to which the development of behavior is explained in terms of information, some of it provided by the genes and some by the environment. Scientific metaphors are a valuable way of briefly communicating important features of a complex issue, but sometimes they can be so seductive that we find it difficult to change our thinking about them as new information suggests that they are inaccurate or misleading. The information metaphor describes genes as encoding instructions or blueprints for the organization of behavior and the development of behavior, insofar as it can be attributed to the genes, is understood as a process in which information is read out of the genes to produce behavior. The metaphor is supported by the fact that genes do indeed contain information, in the sense that their molecular structure corresponds directly to specific features of the organism in which they reside. This is the sense in which we speak of the "genetic code" – the one-to-one relationship between the bases that make up the chemical structure of DNA and the amino acids that are the building blocks of protein molecules. Each of the two helical strands of DNA consists of a chain of four different bases (adenine, guanine, cytosine, and thymine) arranged in a linear fashion: A–T–A–A–C–T–G–A–T–T–C–G–G–C, and so on. Read three at a time, the sequence of bases specifies a corresponding linear arrangement of amino acids, and the sequence of amino acids specifies the structure of a particular protein molecule. Although the situation is actually more complicated than this, the genetic code does allow one to speak quite accurately of genes as a source of information for the structure of the organism.

However, this metaphor becomes highly inaccurate and deeply misleading when we consider features of the organism more complex than the sequence of amino acids that make up a protein molecule. Proteins are vital constituents of organisms. Among other functions, they form structural elements of tissues such as bone, muscle, and nerve cells. In addition, proteins play critical roles in almost all biological processes. Some proteins are enzymes, controlling the rate of biochemical reactions within the cells, and others are involved in the transport of substances in and out of cells. The function of proteins in all of these roles is determined by the three-dimensional shape into which they are folded, and that shape depends heavily (though not exclusively) on the sequence of amino acids that make up the protein molecule. Thus, in the nervous system (whose structure and organization underlies all behavior and psychological processes), proteins form structural elements of nerve cells, regulate the movement of substances such as neurotransmitters in and out of cells, and modify processes that occur at the synaptic junctions where neighboring cells communicate with one another. But the linear arrangement of amino acids in a protein molecule, critical as it is to the development and mature functioning of the organism, is far removed from the features of complex behavior that we might try to understand by way of the information metaphor of gene action. There is no useful sense in which the genes "encode" features of behavior such as sexual orientation, personality, cognitive function, or childhood temperament, despite the fact that all of these are undoubtedly deeply influenced by our genetic makeup.

## Genes as resources for development

A more useful way of thinking about genetic contributions to behavior is to view the genes as one of several kinds of resources that contribute to the construction of the organism's behavior as it develops. This view is much closer than the information metaphor to the actual molecular machinery of gene action. We can think of the organism at any point in its development as a dynamic system that may be influenced by a variety of resources: temperature, light patterns, nutrients, sensory stimulation, genes, and so on. Exactly how each of these resources affects the developing system depends on a number of things, in particular on the current state of the system (the same resources may have different effects at different stages of development) and on the availability of other resources (the same resource may have different effects in different contexts). The metaphor of genes as developmental resources encourages us to take a more dynamic view of the developing organism than does the information metaphor. It allows us to recognize that a particular gene product, for example, makes a critical contribution to the development of a certain behavior without encouraging us to suppose that we can identify a feature of behavior that the gene encodes information "for."

The idea that there are genes for complex behaviors is encouraged by the fact that some genetic variants (mutations) cause quite specific and systematic deficiencies in complex behavior. Consider the case of language, certainly a very complex behavior and one in whose development genes must play an essential role. Recent research has shown that a mutation in the *FOXP2* gene on chromosome 7 results in deficiencies in language production and comprehension. The pattern of deficiencies is quite complex but the evidence is strong that they all result from the same mutation in a single gene. The mutation is rare and has been studied in only one extended family in Britain, but let us accept that the mutation would cause the same language disorder in any person who inherited it. Does this mean that the *FOXP2* gene can be described as a gene "for" language? *FOXP2* is a member of a class of genes (the *FOX* genes) that encode transcription factors, molecules that control the activity of other genes and orchestrate the production of proteins involved in the growth of cells and tissues. *FOXP2* is especially active in the developing brain, and it is therefore likely to be involved in the development of circuits in the brain necessary for normal language ability. The mutation results in only one of the two copies of *FOXP2* in each cell being inactive, so that the cell produces only half the normal amount of gene product. The result is that something goes wrong in the development of the circuitry so that the person is unable to produce and comprehend language normally. But those abilities are not encoded in the *FOXP2* gene – the gene encodes a transcription factor. Language emerges as a result of complex interactions between the developing child and the language environment in which he or she is developing. The abnormal gene somehow interferes with those interactions, resulting in an abnormal outcome.

The *FOXP2* gene should be thought of not as a gene for language but as a gene for one of the numerous developmental resources that must be present if language is to develop normally. Normal language development must involve a very complex set of interactions involving the *FOXP2* product, the products of many other genes, and a large number of environmental factors, especially exposure to the sounds of spoken language. Each of these developmental resources is likely to be needed at a specific time during development and, in the case of internally produced resources, at specific locations in the developing brain. Furthermore, it will almost certainly be the case that many of the genes involved must be activated at the right place and time by an environmental stimulus – gene activation does not occur independently of experience.

## The cooperative relationship between genes and experience

This is perhaps one of the most surprising and counter-intuitive findings of molecular genetics. For a long time we have been accustomed to thinking of genes and experience as independent influences on development, whereas in fact there is abundant evidence that many genes require experience in order to be activated, and that one of the first effects of experience in a developing organism is often to modify the activity of a gene. One of the clearest links between experience and gene activation is shown by a class of genes known as "immediate-early genes," or IEGs. Almost always, sensory stimulation results in the activation of one or more IEGs within a few minutes. IEGs, like the *FOX* class of genes of which *FOXP2* is a member, produce transcription factors that control the production of proteins by other genes. Those proteins play a variety of roles in cell growth and development, the processes by which new nerve circuits are built and existing circuits re-shaped. When a child responds to experience with a change in behavior, it is very likely that the modification of nerve circuits that is responsible for the behavioral change is started when the experience activates IEGs in the child's brain. In the development of language, for example, it may well be the case that the child's exposure to language activates IEGs whose products control the activation of other genes, such as *FOXP2*, that we know to be specifically involved in the development of language. Clearly, in a case like this, the development of language cannot be attributed either to experience alone or to genes alone – it is a function of the joint influences of both genes and experience.

## Genes affect behavior throughout development, not just in its early stages

We have tended to think of genes not only acting independently of experience but also acting early in development rather than throughout the lifespan. This temporal priority of genes receives support from the view of genes as a blueprint – the blueprint for a building must, of course, be present before the construction begins, because it specifies (i.e. causes) the entire sequence of events involved in construction. Furthermore, blueprints cease to function after the house is built (i.e. after the organism reaches maturity). If we think of the genes not as a blueprint, but rather as one of many resources for development, then it becomes easier to accept the idea that they may affect development at any stage. Indeed, there is a wealth of evidence showing that gene activity continues throughout life, especially in the nervous system. Gene activity is involved in the changes in neural conductivity that underlie learning (a process that continues throughout life) and indeed virtually every event that elicits a reaction from the organism has some effect on the activity of its genes, especially the IEGs. Once we recognize the continual involvement of genes in a lot of very basic housekeeping activity in the nervous system (and throughout the rest of the body) it becomes harder to sustain the view that they possess some mysterious organizing power and easier to think of them as one among many factors necessary for the development and normal functioning of the organisms.

Genes supply a very important set of influences on behavior. I used the example of language in this essay to illustrate a particular way of thinking about those influences, but the same approach could be applied to any kind of behavior – reading, problem-solving, motor coordination, social behavior, or many others. As we learn more and more about how genes function we may be tempted to conclude that we are learning that more of our behavior is controlled, specified, or encoded by genes, because new genetic influences on behavior are constantly being reported. But these discoveries need to be set in the proper context for understanding *how* genes influence behavior – through reciprocal interactions in which genes and experience cooperate to shape the dynamic processes of development throughout the lifespan.

SUGGESTED READINGS

A number of recent books provide very good summaries of our current understanding of genetics in terms that are accessible to readers without specialized biological training. I particularly recommend:

Lewontin, R. (2000). *The triple helix: gene, organism, and environment.* Cambridge, MA: Harvard University Press.
Moore, D.S. (2000). *The dependent gene: the fallacy of "nature" vs. "nurture."* New York: Henry Holt.

Morange, M. (2001). *The misunderstood gene.* Cambridge, MA: Harvard University Press.

Ridley, M. (1999). *Genome: the autobiography of a species in 23 chapters.* New York: HarperCollins.

(2003). *Nature via nurture: genes, experience, and what makes us human.* New York: HarperCollins.

The various research findings discussed in this essay may be found in the following articles:

Fisher, S.E., C.S.L. Lai, and A.P. Monaco (2003). Deciphering the genetic basis of speech and language disorders. *Annual Review of Neuroscience,* 26, 57–80. (Summarizes research on the *FOXP2* gene and others associated with speech and language.)

Griffiths, P.E., and P.H. Gray (1994). Developmental systems and evolutionary explanation. *Journal of Philosophy,* 91, 277–304. (Introduces the idea of resources for development that include both genes and environmental influences.)

Johnston, T.D. (1987). The persistence of dichotomies in the study of behavioral development. *Developmental Review,* 7, 149–182. (A criticism of the information metaphor of gene action.)

Johnston, T.D., and L. Edwards (2002). Genes, interactions, and the development of behavior. *Psychological Review,* 109, 26–34. (Presents a model for the role of genes in behavioral development and reviews work on the role of immediate-early genes in the organism's response to experience.)

# 3 How dynamic systems have changed our minds

*Ken Richardson*

Laws of physics tell us that all things tend towards states of randomness or disorder. Yet all around the living world we see well-formed structures of dazzling complexity and diversity. How this form and diversity comes about has puzzled thinkers for centuries. When we turn to consider the human mind, the problems of explanation often seem impossibly complex. The depths and intricacies of our knowledge; the logical structures of thought; the acoustic weave of every spoken utterance; the bright new ideas and imaginings of even a five-year-old; the coherence of human cooperative endeavors; all these often seem far beyond any rational or scientific account.

Some philosophers have often wondered whether there may be something within natural laws themselves that explains the complexity of the world, the complexity of living things, and even the complexity of the human mind. The atomists in Ancient Greece certainly thought so. The philosopher Descartes, in the seventeenth century, mused about the possibility. And Alfred Wallace, co-founder with Darwin of the modern theory of evolution, suspected that the same principles of structure-making that create ice patterns on a frozen window are also responsible for the order in living things. In the absence of conceivable mechanisms, however, the main tendency has been to seek explanations in some fundamental agency of design. As with the most recent candidate, the genes, those explanations have almost always implied a fatalism about human nature, and limited, pessimistic views of human potential.

Research over the last twenty years, however, has begun to lift the veil surrounding the origins of structure and complexity in life, including the human mind. New theoretical and methodological advances are creating a coherent perspective on complex natural processes. The effort has involved physicists, cosmologists, mathematicians, chemists, molecular geneticists, other biologists, cognitive psychologists, computer experts, and many others. It has huge implications for the promotion of human development in our social institutions (health, education, employment, etc.) all around the world. It offers plausible remedies for the many contemporary human problems, without the fatalism so often found in the past. And it offers fresh optimism for the future developments of human kind. It tends to be called the dynamic systems perspective, or Dynamic Systems Theory (DST).

So how is it different? The term "dynamic" provides a clue, and suggests it has to do with things changing. But it is not the notion of dynamics popular in physics since Isaac Newton. According to that philosophy, the whole world can be described as mechanical oscillations around fixed points of equilibrium according to fixed rules. Our solar system, the seasons, day/night cycles, and the swinging pendulum are examples of this "vast system of superimposed cycles," as Ian Stewart puts it. From the seventeenth to the twentieth centuries, complex physical systems, and those of bodies and minds, seemed to be best explained as kinds of pre-formed "equilibrium systems" or "mental clockworks."

Those ideas still persist, but they are ultimately disappointing, not least because they still fail to explain the origins of and differences in complexity. The new dynamics, which is neither repetitive nor predetermined in this way, overcomes these problems. Thanks to some simple observations, and then to high-speed computers in which they could be modeled, we now know that novel structures of ever-increasing complexity can emerge from the natural interactions among components even in relatively simple physical systems.

A layer of liquid, for example, can indeed absorb a limited heat input and slowly return to its homogeneous, equilibrium, condition. But, persistently heated from below, the same liquid quickly reaches and exceeds a critical point at which it suddenly appears to form closely packed, intricately structured, convection cells (known as Bénard cells, after the person who studied them). A new organizing factor, based on new "rules," has emerged from interacting forces in response to new conditions: "order for free," as Stuart Kauffman puts it.

Studying such "surprising" effects has now helped explain many of the complex, structured forms and events we see in numerous domains. These include: the formation of the embryo from the egg, the function of immune systems, the rhythms of the heart, ecological systems, organization in insect colonies, the weather, national economies, stock markets, earthquakes, traffic jams, turbulence in hydraulic systems, landslides, and so on. Similar studies explain the origins of patterns in butterfly wings, the spots on the leopard, the intricate structure of the filtration system in the kidney, and so on.

Perhaps above all, this new perspective is beginning to crack the huge mystery about how form and variety in the human mind originate and develop. The primary agent of form and variety in living things, through most of the last century, has, of course, been the gene. Many (perhaps most) psychologists believe that our basic knowledge structures; the way we perceive and think about the world; the grammatical structures of human language; and so on, are somehow formed by our genes.

But, when James Watson and Francis Crick breezed into The Eagle pub in Cambridge claiming to have discovered "the secret of life" – the biochemical structure of DNA – they were engaged in more than a little hyperbole. The complex structure of the gene, together with the vast cellular machinery needed to use it, did not itself just spring into existence out of nothing. We now know that self-replicating living systems existed for millions of years before genes had been "invented." Stuart Kauffman describes how self-organized molecular systems can survive and evolve to a diversity of proto-organisms, without genes as such. As Brian Goodwin, a pioneer in the field of biological complexity, suggests, "Life doesn't need DNA to get started; it needs a rich network of facilitating relationships."

Genes are extremely important, of course. But a dynamic systems perspective explains why development of body structures and functions is not just an assembly line "controlled" by gene codes. There's a serious limitation with such "fixed codes." They would be fine in imaginary, unchanging environments. But if the environment changes, as rest assured it does, modified or different traits, not hitherto coded for, may well be needed. The classic Darwinian solution to this problem is that, in copying the codes from one generation to the next (i.e. in eggs and sperm), accidental errors occur. These mutations may then code for different materials, from which modified traits develop in the next generation, perhaps better suited for the "new" environment. These more favored varieties survive and further reproduce while the masses of others are wasted: hence natural selection.

With this view we get the classic conception of bodily functions as relatively fixed "bundles of adaptations," fitted to the aspects of the environment in which they exist. Could this shaping of functions to the structure of aspects of the world explain both the origins and nature of mental functions like perception, cognition, feeling, and so on? Recent evolutionary psychologists like Lea Cosmides and John Tooby certainly think so when they argue that "Natural selection shapes (mental) mechanisms so that their structure meshes with the evolutionarily-stable features of their particular problem-domains."

There is, of course, abundant evidence for natural selection as a means of tracking environmental change, and it has no doubt been important for many traits. But it is has its limitations, too. These are implicit in

Cosmides and Tooby's reference to "evolutionarily stable" features. That is, natural selection only works for environmental changes that are relatively slow or recurrent. In fact the changes need to be slower than a generation, the time it takes to produce mature offspring with the "new" genes, and associated traits, on which selection can operate.

In chapter 4 of his "Origins" Darwin warned about this limitation: "That natural selection generally acts with extreme slowness I fully admit (and will) depend on physical changes, which generally take place very slowly." If important aspects of the environment change faster than that, as a kind of moving target, then natural selection can't keep up. "Darwinian" genes, that is, are no good (at least on their own) for coding for what's needed for development in aspects of environments that change more rapidly or in more complex ways. Yet, these aspects tend to be far more common than ones that stand still or change only slowly.

Nor does accidental and random mutation of genes tell us very easily why living things and their traits have become more complex during the course of evolution. As Mark Ridley explains in his book *Mendel's Demon*, what really puzzled Darwin is that there seemed no *necessary* requirement for animals to become more complicated. In a letter to Charles Lyell, Darwin said that it seemed impossible to answer the question, how at first start of life, when there were only simple organisms, "how did any complications of organisms profit them?" Such has been the dominance of the perception of essentially stable worlds.

This, in my view, explains the uncomfortable credibility gap in gene-centered accounts of the evolution of complex brains and minds. Change and increased complexity of form are not unrelated. We are now acquiring deeper insights into changeable environments, how changes can be more or less complex, and how these become reflected in evolution of traits. Traditionally, change has been thought of in terms of single variables (e.g. light, temperature, food abundance, etc.) ranging over limited values, and operating as single cues or triggers for responses that best maintain the organism's equilibrium. These cue-response functions may have been important for the earliest, immobile, single-cell creatures passively experiencing external changes. But as soon as animals moved the world became a far more dynamic one of objects and currents in constant flux, in constantly changing patterns and forms. When animals acquired distance senses of vision, audition, and olfaction, these patterns multiplied (a snapshot of a typical visual field may show fifty or more objects), with various degrees of correspondence across senses, and fragmentation of images as objects twist and turn, move in and out of the sensory field, obscure each other, and so on.

This complexity of experience and its structure has snowballed with evolution into more complex habitats. Yet even today, scientific analysis of the environment, especially in psychology, tends to be of stable, independent elements. For example, models of complex perceptual and cognitive processes are based on experiments in which volunteers have been asked to learn simplified images in static, two-dimensional arrays, completely devoid of dynamic structure.

This, then, explains the evolution of complexity like that of mind. Different systems have evolved for dealing with changes of different complexity. As simple habitats became filled, only those living things that could deal with more complex change in new habitats survived. As Darwin put it, "The trend is towards complexity because the simple ways of life are all occupied." Accordingly, he went on, "It is not the strongest species that survive ... but those most responsive to change."

The dynamic systems approach has helped clarify this relationship between the evolution of complex living systems and the complexity of environmental change. Complexity means not just more independent variables to contend with, but also the relationships between them. Changes in one variable will almost always be accompanied by changes in one or more others. Such associations – the simplest kind of structure – are informative for living things because values on one can be predicted from the other, just as distance from the earth's equator might predict food supply. But the association may depend upon (i.e. change with) values on one or more other variables: e.g. the association just mentioned may vary over time, or season (itself associated with length of day and other things). This "deeper," or interactive, structure actually improves predictability for animals that have evolved ways to register it, making the complex doubly informative. Thus, animals that migrate or hibernate have physiological systems that have adapted to this more complex environment.

Experience of objects, especially animate ones with many parts, and of events in which they are involved, present many more variables with far deeper interactions, often reflecting changes over fractions of seconds. The world becomes a stream of bounding, looming, and lurching objects, moving themselves, or perceived to be moving through the viewer's own actions. Animals have obviously found ways to adapt to these far more complex environments, using the dynamic structures within them. For example, it has frequently been shown that moving objects, which exhibit that kind of structure-in-time, are much more recognizable than static ones, that minimize it. Since changing experience is such that objects and events are often presented in fleeting, obscured, or partly hidden ways, such structure can be crucial if organisms can somehow "represent" or attune to it.

Finally, variables and their interactions may be related in non-linear ways, rather than simple incremental ones: that is, small changes in one may be associated with uneven changes in another. In interactive relationships this means that the system can potentially respond in surprising, unusual ways, beyond that of a pendulum-like equilibrium behavior. In a natural world that is constantly changing, processes of living things may be frequently pushed into such "far from equilibrium" states, often inducing responses other than simple linear, incremental, ones. These novel responses may be adaptive in changed environments. For example, many relationships between components in enzymes, the molecules that enable thousands of the metabolic processes in cells, are intrinsically non-linear. Unusual changes in the environment can often result in surprising responses from them, changing whole patterns of metabolism, and introducing new adaptabilities for the organism. In these ways, rather than passive, equilibrium "machines," self-organizing living systems can respond creatively to events, in turn affecting development and evolution.

These creative processes probably started from the first proto-organisms. Dynamicists studying the origins of life have shown how assemblies of interacting, self-regulating, and self-replicating molecules like nucleotides and amino acid chains constituted the first units of life. Structural genes – those that code for structural proteins that make up the body – came later, more as valuable resources than precise architectural blueprints. As with production and reproduction in any domain – say in a car factory – it's nice to have a "bank" of raw materials that are going to be needed over and over again. But keeping a separate warehouse is obviously a difficult strategy for living cells. How much simpler to just have "codes" for the production of those materials as and when needed. These codes can also be copied from one generation to the next, so their usefulness goes on. Structural genes, that is, are codes for resources needed for development. They are not codes for the course and end-points of development itself.

In fact, in keeping with the need to deal with changeable environments, the vast majority of genes have evolved as "regulatory," rather than structural, resources. For every gene that codes for some bodily raw material there are up to eight or nine others coding for proteins that regulate how and when that gene is used. The products of the vast majority of genes are, therefore, regulatory proteins. Correspondingly, up to 90 percent of the DNA (the genetic material) on genes functions as receptors for regulatory factors from elsewhere. Those factors determine when a structural gene is transcribed, and with how much product. They often snip and rearrange the products; and sometimes rearrange the code (the DNA structure) itself. These self-organizing activities are informed by vast signaling networks detecting changes inside and outside the cell. These are all evolved ways of dealing with changes more rapid and complex than Darwin's slow and ponderous ones. They can even ensure that whole "regulatory states," corresponding with environmental states, are transmitted from parent to offspring, as a form of "epigenetic" inheritance, with no change in genes as such.

Because of their increasing adaptability to change, it is these regulatory networks, with their emergent properties, that have marked the course of evolution, rather than structural gene changes as such. A myriad specific cases have now been described. For example, a gene called Hoxc8 is involved in the development of thoracic vertebrae. Subtle changes in regulation of its transcription alters the numbers of vertebrae: seven in chickens, two hundred in snakes.

Because of this primacy of regulatory over pre-determined processes, genomes are surprisingly constant in content from worms to humans: vertebrates have, on average, only twice as many genes as invertebrates, like worms and flies. It is now generally accepted that it is such tinkering with the dynamics of developmental pathways that has (ultimately) made species different and more complex.

If we are really to understand the origins and nature of complex mental functions, therefore, we need to identify them within the context of systems dealing with change, and their evolving, emerging levels. Genetic codes alone do not provide an answer to complexity in living things: there is no known independent "genetic" system operating as a fundamental "recipe," "controller," or other determinant of form and function in living things. From its very origins, life has existed as a dynamic system of self-regulations with emergent properties, later using genes as codes for resources recurrently needed. So level one consists of those intricate "epigenetic" systems that can be adaptable to change in various ways.

In some cases the task is one of buffering the development of a critical structure against environmental bumps and shocks, as well as internal genetic variation, maintaining it on a reliable course. This is called "canalization" of development. Take, for example, the eye of the fruitfly, which has been studied in some detail. This is an organ crucial for fly survival, obviously. It's a highly complex structure consisting of 800 little facets, each facet consisting of eight light receptors and various other cells, all put together in a very precise pattern. Quite wide variation has been revealed in the genes utilized in the development of the eye. And different individual embryos can experience widely different environmental bumps and shocks. Yet the intricate pattern of the eye that develops is virtually invariant from individual to individual. Only an interactive, self-organizing developmental system can achieve this. Only relatively rare extremes of genetic or environmental variation disrupt it.

Alternatively, the epigenetic system underlying other traits may be tuned to create developmental "plasticity." This is appropriate when offspring can find themselves in environments significantly different from that of parents. For example, water flea larvae may find themselves in ponds inhabited by a predator (signaled by some excreted chemical). They develop prominent defensive "hoods" that are otherwise absent. So different are the results of such plasticity in some cases – even in genetically identical individuals – that the individuals were once thought to belong to different species. Examples of this kind of developmental plasticity are now legion. In each case, the epigenetic system can be said to exist in two or more "metastates," switching from one to another as appropriate.

Maintaining the individual in a living state after early development, though, requires plasticity throughout life. These are functions attributed to physiological and behavioral processes. In single cells, both sets of functions respond to signals from the outside world through surface receptor systems that have been greatly elaborated in the course of evolution. In multicellular organisms, most of the signals come from other cells. So important are such signals that it is now clear that little goes on within individual cells without signals from others, some close, others quite remote and transmitting signals in the circulating fluids.

Traditionally, physiological and behavioral (psychological) functions have been treated as being largely homeostatic (equilibrium) processes – i.e. maintaining some constancy of internal milieu in the face of disturbances from inside or outside. As Steven Rose points out in his book *Lifelines*, "No modern textbook account of physiological or psychological mechanisms fails to locate itself within this homeostatic metaphor." Yet, in the case of physiology, closer analysis has recently shown that many physiological functions often cope with "far from equilibrium conditions," in creative ways. For example, heart rate variability exhibits deep interactive properties, rather than shallow reflex ones. Hector Sabelli notes how such variation in heart rate reflects the totality of our physical, mental, and emotional state as we interact with changes around us.

This approach has produced new insights into the adaptability of regulation to unusual conditions, as well as the nature of disease. As Ary Goldberger and colleagues explain, "A defining feature of healthy function is ... the capacity to respond to unpredictable stimuli and stresses," whereas "highly periodic behaviors ... would greatly narrow functional responsiveness." It is the breakdown in this adaptability to changing conditions that seems to produce disease states. As Rose says, the metaphor of "homeostasis" needs to be replaced with one of "homeodynamics." Note that, in producing further adaptability to change, physiological functions do not supplant the epigenetic systems, described above. Rather they work with, and amplify them, sending out appropriate signals to cells and tissues, further regulating gene transcriptions, and so on, but extending them to shorter term responses.

Behavior, too, is a set of functions for dealing with environmental change, either by moving the individual to or from favorable conditions, or responding to nullify the changes, or to utilize them. In the earliest living things behavior simply involved slow movements towards light, food, and so on, or away from noxious chemicals, or obstacles. Being forced out of simple habitats, however, brought experience of increasingly complex, changeable environments. And behavior itself increasingly became a cause of environmental change. Again, these changes have consisted less in variation in single variables, but in the patterns of interaction among them. Adaptability to these more complex patterns has increasingly required cognitive systems.

Cognitive systems evolved very early in the evolution of behavior. Traditional models have described them in very simple terms, such as the learning of linear, one-to-one associations among variables. But recent research shows cognitive functions to be far more complex, even for those that evolved early. For example, it is known that honeybees will fly from the hive in, say, a northwesterly direction to one pollen source, and then in a northeasterly direction to another. Then they can be observed to fly back to the hive, not by retracing the original trajectories, but in a more direct southerly route. In order to do this, they must have somehow represented deeper relations between what we now know to be many variables – landmark constellations; position of the sun, polarized light pattern of the blue sky – and then performed a kind of algebra on that representation to compute the final track home. That is, even insects are not reflex automata, but need to adapt to a constantly changing scene, especially in their foraging.

A number of more recent studies have revealed the amazing cognitive abilities within a brain having only 0.01 percent of the neurons of a human (around 960,000), 1 cubic mm in volume, and weighing less than 0.1 mg. They all illustrate the essential function of cognitive systems. That is to induce the "deep" structural patterns from complex, changeable environments; patterns that themselves change over time, in ways too fast and/or too radical to be coped with by epigenetic or physiological systems alone.

As those changes have become more complex, so have the brains and cognitive systems needed to abstract them. Moving among objects (imagine birds flying through trees), chasing novel prey or escaping from novel predators, requires induction of new "rules," and response decisions very rapidly. The distinctive feature of cognitive systems, as opposed to other adaptable (epigenetic, plastic developmental, and physiological) systems, is precisely that they can rapidly update "rules" throughout life. In the most advanced cognitive systems, every thought or new idea, every new concept or conceptual scheme, is the equivalent of a new "genus" or "species" in more primitive animals. Darwinian natural selection needs generations to realize new "responses" to a changing world. The developmental systems mentioned above can create them in the course of a single generation. But cognitive systems can do it in seconds or even milliseconds.

How the remarkable abilities of cognitive systems "work" has, of course, baffled philosophers and scientists for thousands of years. Numerous models, based on a wide range of principles, have been proposed, but still attract little agreement. It may be too strong to suggest, as does Guy van Orden, that "not one cognitive mechanism exists on which cognitive scientists can agree about its boundaries, its empirical shape, or details about its function." But he has a point. Most recent models have assumed the cognitive system to operate as a kind of computer. But attempts to model even the very simplest aspects of cognition, like categorizing static stimuli, have only been achieved in slow ponderous steps, taking lots of time. And they have required complicated programming, and data preparation, such as perfectly formed static images. They fail strikingly in the most distinctive aspects of cognition: the ability to deal with rapidly changing, fragmentary experience; the depth of knowledge formed; and the incessant creation of novel ideas, and novel behaviors.

A dynamic systems view of cognition stresses that, as Ichiro Tsuda puts it, "inputs and parameters change relentlessly." No doubt, the very structure of brain, and its system of vastly interconnected neurons, is crucial in dealing with them. The distinctive property of the networks is their sensitivity to the deeper structure in changing patterns of input, rather than independent values. This property is, in fact, an evolutionary emergence (restructuring) of the cell–cell signaling pathways found in earlier systems, as mentioned earlier. The difference is that the structure in patterns of signals between vast numbers of neurons itself reorganizes and modifies the individual connections. It is through this synergy between individual connections and patterns in the whole that the network is being constantly updated in response to the changing structure of experience. This updating is the proper definition of learning. Knowledge resides in the way networks are tuned to reflect the deeper spatio-temporal relations in experience. Memory is not composed of images in a file, but patterns of activation that may be resurrected given appropriate interactions between knowledge and current inputs.

The system has remarkable properties. One result is an amazing power of predictability from often skimpy data. It means the system can "fill-in" missing aspects of scenes from fragments of information: a dog's tail protruding from behind a wall creates an image of a whole animal. Much of perception, indeed, seems to be designed to direct sense organs to pick up such structure, often across sense modes. Just probing with a fingertip can produce complex visual images of objects. A blind person can induce the surface structure of a manhole cover or roadside curb from probing with the tip of a cane.

Other cognitive functions of thinking, decision-making, and action formation also come from this dynamic nature of the network and its adaptability. The ever-changeable nature of sensory input ensures that the network is constantly operating in far from equilibrium conditions. A network in such a state (called "criticality") is able quickly to reorganize and swiftly adapt to new situations. As a result, instead of taking one or a few states, as with epigenetic systems, self-organizing neural networks exist in a myriad possible states, with rapid state transitions between them, often producing entirely new ones. This means that responses are often created, not just "selected" from a limited range of options.

In studies of mouse olfaction, Walter Freeman has shown how perceptions are created as novel patterns in the brain, not just copied or repeated from old. It is not external smells *per se* that animals respond to, in a direct way. Rather they respond to internal images created by the dynamics within the olfactory center, involving interactions with numerous other brain centers. These interactions mediate between external inputs and the tuned internal networks, and generate the most compatible "images." As Freeman says, the capacity for exceedingly rapid creative behaviors is thus not that of an "equilibrium" system, which cannot create novel patterns, but only of a self-organizing dynamic system.

In a similar way, thought processes can be envisaged as dynamically constructed neural activity patterns, finding the most compatible form, then rapidly transmitted and dissolving, to move on to the next one. These explore the predictabilities in percepts in the context of a lifetime's experience, rapidly creating the best conceptions and actions. The pay-off, in terms of adaptability to changing environments, is that the system exceeds even the flexibility of the epigenetic and physiological systems, so that the individual becomes, in effect, a whole population of responses. Note again, also, that these rapid adaptive responses arise with no ultimate "controller," or separate executive system, within it. Only a dynamic systems perspective can even begin to approximate these distinctive properties of cognitive systems.

This dynamic quality of cognitive systems seems to apply from the simplest of cognitive systems in bees, flies, and worms, to the far more sophisticated ones of monkeys and apes. But the cognitive system became vastly more complex when our ancestors started to cooperate in their perceptions and actions two or three million years ago. It is now thought that cooperation was itself an adaptation to more changeable environments. Humans constitute the first genuinely cooperative species among advanced animals, and it is no simple matter, because, by itself, it creates new cognitive challenges. Two individuals cooperating just to lift a rock, say, must have "metaperception" (perception of others' perceptions); metacognition (cognitions about others' cognitions); and meta-action (action with others' actions).

If you have any doubts about these demands consider helping someone move a wardrobe downstairs – an activity mundane to us, but impossible in any other species. In the joint attentions and actions, pains and curses, a whole new (social) world is created. We certainly needed bigger brains (three times bigger than our nearest animal relatives) for handling this new mass of rapidly changing data. But it also needed a new system of regulations. Just as the activities of individual neurons have to be coordinated by the patterns emerging between them, so coordinating individual attentions and actions can only be done by new *interpersonal* regulations.

These social regulations have now been well studied within a systems perspective. They include shared conceptions of the world; the myriad rules and procedures through which we organize our joint activities; the language through which these are mediated; the hardware tools, technologies, and skills through which they are implemented. This is what we mean by human culture, and it is their manifestation through these cultural tools and devices that makes human cognitions so distinctive. They "take over," and extend and amplify, the previously evolved cognitive system of the monkeys and apes.

Take memory, for example. As Lev Vygotsky pointed out, in other species it remains a very individual function. But the cultural invention of shared written symbols and numerals, and then books, libraries, and computers, has transformed memory in humans into a vastly more expansive form. From the moment of birth, and throughout life, a myriad such inventions transform human perceptions, cognitions, and actions, and give structure and predictability to our personal knowledge and our thinking. The system still operates in response to rapidly changing, multiple inputs in the dynamic ways described above. But the activity patterns are ones refracted through and among countless other minds. Especially in the scientific field, human cognitions become the expression of patterns of activity between minds, just as much as of those within them.

This activity on different levels also creates another distinctive property. The constant interaction between social regulations and personal histories (as reflected in tuned networks) can create a continuing stream of conflicts or disequilibria. These, in turn, generate new, unique patterns of activity that can then be communicated back into the social level. In the theories of Vygotsky and A.R. Luria, it is this kind of conflict – peculiar to humans – that has continually driven the new ideas and technological innovation that have so characterized human history.

A system that operates by "plugging into" external implementation systems, either as technology hardware or social rules, extends and amplifies the cognitive systems of our ancestors. And the process is obligatory. The vast increase in brain size, and extension of neural networks, in human evolution only took place within the context of the emergence of cultural tools and regulations; the former would now be simply redundant without the latter. As Clifford Geertz once put it, "Rather than culture acting only to supplement, develop and extend organically based capacities ... it would seem to be ingredient to those capacities themselves ... the Homo sapiens brain, having arisen within the framework of human culture, would not be viable outside of it."

As well as allowing us to deal with the complexities of social life, this also means that we now deal with the demands of the physical world on a completely different plane relative to other animals. We don't have the biological regulations that equip us with wings. But we fly better than birds. We can travel through water better than fish; dig better than moles; and through the cultural invention of things like x-rays, infra-red cameras, radar, ultrasound detectors, and so on, we see and hear far beyond the biological limits of our eyes and ears. Vastly expanded brain networks and cultural tools, working in tandem, have allowed us to predict and anticipate change on a new scale, so that humans largely adapt the world to themselves, rather than vice versa.

Understanding that living systems evolved to deal with increasingly complex kinds of environmental change helps explain the amazing properties of the human brain/mind. But that understanding would not be possible without a dynamic systems perspective. Although its bearing on cognitive science is still in its infancy the new perspective already suggests many applications. Indeed it might be said that the ideas within it put cognitive and brain sciences on the edge of an exciting new era in which they may, at last, become advanced sciences. And it has huge implications for understanding and promoting human development. I will suggest just a few of these.

First, it promises a new, optimistic view of human developmental possibilities. It provides a response to Robert Robinson's (probably legitimate) complaint that "Until now, a psychological paradigm could only be scientific by severely limiting its view of human beings and their potential." For example, it rejects prevailing, fatalistic, ideas that humans come into the world with fixed cognitive functions, in the form of innate knowledge or processes, genetically selected for stable or recurrent circumstances. In the extremely changeable world of human social activity, such restrictions would be hugely dysfunctional. They reflect an impoverished analysis of the dynamic nature of experience, especially among cooperating humans.

Related to this is the idea that human abilities have fixed limits, reflected across individuals as an easily identifiable "range of ability" (a term regularly used by educators). As we have seen, evolution itself has depended on regulatory, developmental systems frequently breaching such limits, by numerous devices, to overcome new challenges. And cognitive systems are specialized for rapid, creative responses to ever-changeable environments. As a result, the mental limits of early stone-age humans have been surpassed many times over in the course of human history, even though our biology is essentially the same. This is not to suggest that "anyone can do anything": early developmental outcomes, at various levels, can themselves present constraints on later development. But it is important to recognize the essential unpredictability of what might be possible at both individual and group levels. Present cognitive states may be very poor guides to what is possible in the future.

Another implication is that, having evolved to deal with the deep dynamic structures in experience, cognitive systems – and the brains that support them – can only develop fully with sufficient exposure to such structure. This applies even to simple cognitive systems, as in the honeybees, but increasingly so in the course of evolution. Among humans the most crucial form of structure is that arising in social contexts as cultural tools. For a long time it was thought that infants and children simply needed lots of "stimulation" or "experience" to foster cognitive development. However, it has been difficult to find strong relationships between simple, independent, indices of environmental experience (e.g. number of toys in the home) and cognitive development. Research within a systems perspective has shown that what really fosters cognitive development is experience within dynamically structured social contexts.

This problem may be increasingly acute in class-structured Western societies, and impoverished parts of developing countries. Lower-class people do not enjoy the employment and financial security, the persistence of structure, nor the sense of control of their environments or their activities, enjoyed by middle and upper classes. Instead, they and their children have continually to adjust to less cohesive, inconsistent, conditions, devoid of deeper social structure, forcing short-term strategies, stress, and anxiety. Research has shown that such adaptations, and their effects on self-esteem and aspirations, are transmitted psychologically from parent to child, suppressing cognitive development.

Dispelling mythical limits on human development, then, would be a major policy advance. These practical implications are no more important than in education systems. Traditional and many contemporary practices impose largely meaningless curricula (Jerome Bruner calls them artificial, "made-up" subjects) on what are presumed to be essentially passive minds mostly of fixed learning potential. This assumes that learning is an essentially personal shaping of individual brain networks, and that these limitations lie in specific components like genes or in the brain networks themselves. Consequently, the first steps to suitable intervention in cases of difficulty in school learning are increasingly being seen as those of genotyping children and performing brain scans. For example, the possible availability of such information in future has urged Michael Posner and Mary Rothbart to suggest "menus of intervention" providing "material to teachers, administrators, parents and children," to "change the underlying network."

On the contrary we have seen that specifically human learning takes place through the acquisition of a myriad cultural tools in the context of socially shared goals. Under these conditions complex cognitive skills, such as creative thinking, language, and productive action, develop naturally, rapidly, and easily. Problems of learning rarely lie in individuals, but in a curriculum that divorces them from the basic conditions of human learning.

Accordingly, a major policy implication of DST, at least in the later grades, is to find ways of associating educational processes with genuine cultural activities. For example, genuine problems can be taken from factories, farms, and distributive outlets, and health, legal, political, and other institutions, for school students to work on. Within such "live" cultural contexts, reflecting the constant challenge of change, all aspects of a suitable curriculum, including language, math, science, arts, and so on, could be pursued. This would help activate and develop the intelligence of all, in ways consonant with the dynamic cognitive systems we have.

SUGGESTED READINGS

Buller, D. (2004). *Adapting minds.* New York: Bradford Books.

Davidson, E.H. (2001). *Genomic regulatory systems: development and evolution.* New York: Academic Press.

Dushek, J. (2002). It's the ecology stupid! *Nature,* 418, 578–579.

Freeman, W.J. (2001). *How the brain makes up its mind.* London: Weidenfeld & Nicolson.

Karpov, Y.V. (2005). *The neo-Vygotskian approach to child development.* New York: Cambridge University Press.

Kauffman, S. (1995). *At home in the universe: the search for the laws of self-organization and complexity.* Oxford: Oxford University Press.

Minugh-Purvis, N., and K. J. McNamara (2002). *Human evolution through developmental change.* Johns Hopkins University Press.

Muller, G. B., and S. A. Newman (2004). *Origination of organismal form: beyond the gene in developmental and evolutionary biology.* New York: Bradford Books.

Oyama, S., P. E. Griffiths, and R. D. Gray (2001). *Cycles of contingency: developmental systems and evolution.* Cambridge, MA: MIT Press.

Pigliucci, M. (2002). Buffer zone. *Nature,* 417, 627–630.

Prigogine, I., and N. Gregoire (1998). *Exploring complexity: an introduction.* New York: W. H. Freeman & Co.

Richardson, K. (2006). *A mind for structure: exploring the roots of intelligent systems.* Boca Raton: Brown Walker Press.

Rose, H., and S. Rose (eds.) (2001). *Alas, poor Darwin: arguments against evolutionary psychology.* New York: Harmony Books.

# 4 Individual development as a system of coactions: implications for research and policy

*Gilbert Gottlieb and Carolyn Tucker Halpern*

Viewing individual development as a system of coactions means that human behavior, personality, intelligence, and so forth are a consequence of multiple "hidden" influences in addition to the obvious ones in the external environment. The "hidden" influences come from the brain and nervous system, hormones, the activity of genes, and the like, which operate beneath the skin. None of these influences, including the environmental ones, are primary or act independently; they are all necessary and thus "coact" in a systemic way to produce developmental outcomes. This is in contrast to the way we usually think about how organisms develop.

When we think of how living things grow and change, we typically tend to think in terms of one cause and one effect. For example, a certain gene causes brown or blue eyes, punishing someone for a behavior lessens the likelihood that they will repeat the behavior, or supportive, loving parents help to create a sense of self-worth in their children. This one cause–one effect approach is straightforward to think about and to study scientifically. In fact the traditional scientific method of experimentation is based on the idea of holding everything in a situation constant except for one factor, the purported "cause" of interest, which is allowed to vary. In a well-designed experiment, changes in the outcome of interest are attributed to the changes in the one factor that was allowed to vary. However, these ideas and traditional methods assume that the many factors affecting individual development act independently of each other and that it is possible to isolate these independent factors and their effects. This assumption is most evident in the classic nature–nurture controversy, wherein some may argue that "nature" (biological factors) is more important and others argue that "nurture" (experiences and learning) is more important in determining how an individual will develop in terms of personality, temperament,

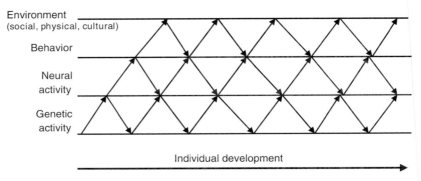

Figure 4.1 Bidirectional influences in a developmental systems view
*Source:* After Gottlieb, 2002

intelligence, psychological health, and so forth. Even views that recognize the importance of both biological and social factors often assume that their contributions to development can be isolated and that their total effect represents an *additive* process (that is, a summation of independent nature and nurture factors). In this view, a certain amount of variation in development is caused by biology and an additional amount of variation is caused by social influences.

More and more scientists are explicitly recognizing that the idea of influences operating independently represents a false dichotomy, and that components of a "developmental system" do not act in isolation, nor do their effects proceed in only one direction. In a developmental systems view, the cause of development – what makes development happen – is the *relationship* or "coaction" between two or more components, not the components themselves. This idea is illustrated in the accompanying figure, which depicts four levels of developmental analysis (genetic activity, neural activity, behavior, and the cultural, social, and physical aspects of the organism's environment). The process and outcomes of relationships or coactions between components of a developmental system can be at the same, at lower, or at higher levels of the system. However, studying development from a coactional perspective is not as straightforward as simply incorporating factors measured at several levels of the developmental system, or investigating potential cross-level pathways in one direction. Many coactional relationships are bidirectional, so they are subtle and complex and, therefore, not easily recognized. For example, although genetic activity plays a role in the development of the nervous system, hormones produced by the nervous system can turn genetic activity on or off, thus illustrating a bi-directional, or two-way, relationship between genetic and neural activity.

A study using a strain of rats called "spontaneously hypertensive" (SHR) provides a clear example of coactional developmental processes. When SHR rat pups are suckled and reared by normal (i.e. non-hypertensive or normotensive) mothers after birth, the rat pups do not develop hypertension. In addition, when normal rat pups are suckled and reared by hypertensive mothers after birth, the normal rat pups do not develop hypertension. However, when SHR rat pups are suckled and reared by hypertensive mothers, the SHR pups **do** develop hypertension. So the cause of hypertension in this strain of rats is not just nature (e.g. genetic predisposition) and not just nurture (e.g. how the mother behaves toward the pup); the cause of hypertension is in the nursing *relationship* between the SHR pups and their mothers. To call the SHR rats spontaneously hypertensive is to obscure the necessarily relational (coactive) nature of their disorder.

There are many examples of how biological factors may contribute to behavior and experience, that is, how biology may have "upward" effects on higher levels of the system illustrated in the figure. There are also many examples of how behavior and experience, in response to biological influences, differ in individuals of different personality make-up. For example, increasing levels of the male hormone testosterone contribute to increasing sexual interest during puberty. However, behavior toward potential romantic partners is different in shy versus outgoing individuals. So, we have a difference in behavioral expression in different individuals, even though the testosterone surge may be about the same. This difference in behavior illustrates the relational point of view – it is not just the testosterone change or just the personality trait, it is the combination of the two (plus other factors) that leads to behavior.

Moving in the other direction, or downward in the developmental system, social experiences can change biological factors that may, at first glance, seem stable and unlikely to change. Two studies, one done with rats and one done with humans, illustrate how experiences can change biology. In the rat study, groups of baby rats were exposed to different types of experiences. One group was separated from their mothers for brief periods (two to five minutes); a second group was separated from their mothers for much longer periods of time – a much more stressful experience for baby rats than brief separation. These different kinds of early experiences were later associated with very different biological and behavioral responses to stress. Rats that had been separated from their mothers for long periods reacted much more strongly to later stressful experiences, as indicated by the release of stress hormones and other biological changes, as compared to the briefly separated rats that had gradually become accustomed to new experience. These different early life experiences actually changed the way the infants' biological systems operated in response to stress in adulthood.

A conceptually related study looked at how adult women reacted to stressful situations. Some women had, as children, been exposed to physical abuse, a stressful experience that is perhaps analogous to long-term maternal separation in the rat study. Like the rats that had experienced the very stressful condition of long-term maternal separation as young pups, those women who had been abused as children reacted more strongly to experimental stressors in adulthood than did women who had not been abused as children. Thus, as in the animal experiment, an early, extremely stressful experience was associated with a change in the way that their bodies reacted to stressful situations later in life. In both cases those extreme earlier experiences made the rats and the women more sensitive to stress and less able to cope behaviorally and biologically. In other words, the early very stressful experience (environmental factors) acted in a "downward" direction to affect the biological level of function in the women and the rats. This change at the biological level later acted in an "upward" direction to affect the behavioral level; the adults in both cases became highly sensitive to subsequent environmental stressors. (The earlier figure shows the upward and downward directions in the development of behavior.)

So, to further exemplify "coaction" with reference to the levels shown in the figure, in these studies an early and stressful experience coming from the environment changed the nervous system and brain (neural level) such that, when later exposed to a different stressor from the environment, both the human and the rat nervous systems were altered in their sensitivity to stress hormones. Further, in the rat studies it was also possible to demonstrate that, in the briefly separated animals, gene activity was affected by the early experience. These animals became less responsive to later stress through a series of genetically activated hormonal changes in the brain. Thus, changing genetic activity in the rats participated in the establishment of a well-regulated stress response system, which became apparent later in development. It is possible that positive life experiences for humans, analogous to the brief separation period for the rats, would also buffer human response to stress through changes in genetic activity. However, it's difficult to conduct a parallel study for humans because of the invasive nature of measuring genetic activity in the brain.

### Research implications

Although it is clearly possible to use a multi-level coactional framework to study human development, it is admittedly difficult. For example, longitudinal studies – studies that follow the development of the same individuals over time – are better suited to this perspective. Such designs allow for observation of continuity and change within the trajectory of individual development. They also provide a prospectively measured history of the individual's experiences and social contexts. However, such studies require more time and money to conduct than do studies that examine different age groups at the same time (cross-sectional study) in order to "construct" a picture of development. It is also difficult to examine factors and processes from different levels of the developmental system. Studying multiple levels requires expertise in multiple disciplines, such as molecular biology, psychology, and sociology. Because few scientists have the necessary expertise in all these areas, transdisciplinary teams of researchers who have different skills are needed to implement the coactional developmental systems model in humans as well as in animals. Collaborative work can be daunting, as the scope of expertise that is needed to address multiple levels of the developmental system is both a strength and weakness of collaboration. Researchers from different disciplines ask different questions, apply different theories, use different statistical tools, and even speak different scientific languages. Truly collaborative work requires some degree of blurring of these disciplinary boundaries, a requirement that is not supported by the typical structure (i.e. by discipline) of academic organizations.

### Policy and practice implications

What are the implications of a developmental systems model for policy and public health? In light of the rather considerable "hype" attendant to the completion of the Human Genome Project, we think it is especially important to recognize the multiple levels that must be traversed to get from genetic activity to overt behavior during the course of individual development – genes, in and of themselves, do not make behavior happen. Further, it is important for the public and policy makers to know that genes are inert unless acted upon by signals from the internal and external environment, so the traffic of information surrounding genes necessarily crosses all the levels of the developmental system in both normal and abnormal development, as shown in the accompanying figure. Finally, the overemphasis on genes as determining factors in disease has perhaps blinded otherwise reputable and conscientious scientists to the fact that numerous developmental psychological disorders for which it is said "putative genes have been isolated" are disorders that involve gene deletions (gene *inactivity*). When, in the usual course of events, these genes are activated, normal development ensues, provided that things go as usual at the other, higher levels of organization. The developmental disorders in which gene inactivity plays an important role are Prader-Willi syndrome (unremitting food seeking), fragile-X syndrome (mild to severe mental retardation), Williams syndrome (severe visual–spatial perception deficits), and lissencephaly (severe mental retardation). When the "putative genes for" these disorders are active, there are no disorders! Also, it has been shown in animal models that when the "usual genes" are not operating, enhanced rearing conditions can activate other genes and the outcome of development is normal (i.e. "rescued"). In summary, the medical disease model is not applicable to the development of mental and behavioral disorders.

These same developmental systems considerations are applicable to prevention and intervention programs. We will use adolescent health as an illustration because risks are largely a function of the adolescent's own behavior. Because of the failure of many brief, narrowly focused prevention programs in adolescent populations, there has been a theoretical shift in programmatic rationales away from a "one technique to target one behavior" approach (e.g. education about the health effects of drugs as a sole means of preventing drug use) to a more holistic approach that acknowledges the complexity of development, the complexity of the systems in which adolescents are embedded, and the capacity of adolescents to affect those systems as well as be influenced by them (i.e. bidirectionality).

As in basic research, the keys to successful programs are comprehensiveness, coordination, and sustainability over time. Joy Dryfoos' synthesis of what we have learned about effective prevention and intervention programs for adolescents illustrates the programmatic shift to holistic approaches well. In her book, *Safe Passage: Making It Through Adolescence in a Risky Society*, Dryfoos discusses success factors at the level of the individual, the family, the school, the community, and at a state and national policy level. At the level of the individual, continuity in mentoring/guidance, acquisition of basic cognitive and social skills, and developmentally appropriate approaches (i.e. taking into account a child's history and current status) to teaching those skills contribute to a successful transition through adolescence. At the level of the family and school, parental involvement, sustained programs such as Life Skills Training, and access to school-based resources (e.g. mental health clinics) can facilitate positive developmental outcomes. Perhaps most difficult of all is the cultural and policy level, which clearly has the potential to affect all other levels of the system, yet is plagued by disagreement and controversy. For example, although there is general consensus that the postponement of sexual initiation promotes adolescent health in multiple ways, there is significant disagreement about the best strategies (e.g. comprehensive sex education versus abstinence only approaches) to achieve postponement. Policy that focuses on a single factor (e.g. a decision to say no) without consideration of other aspects of the developmental system (e.g. physical and cognitive maturity, reproductive health knowledge, access to health resources, social context) ignores the interplay of biological, social, and cultural/historical factors in determining complex behavior.

In sum, we believe a developmental systems view of human development is pertinent not only for basic research but for applications in the real world of children.

SUGGESTED READINGS

Brodsky, M., and P. J. Lombroso (1998). Molecular mechanisms of developmental disorders. *Development and Psychopathology*, 10, 1–20.

Cierpial, M. A., and R. McCarty (1987). Hypertension in SHR rats: contribution of maternal environment. *American Journal of Physiology*, 253, 980–984.

Dryfoos, J. G. (1998). *Safe passage: making it through adolescence in a risky society.* New York, NY: Oxford University Press.

Gottlieb, G. (2002). *Individual development and evolution: the genesis of novel behavior.* Mahwah, NJ: Erlbaum.

Plotsky, P. M., and M. J. Meaney (1993). Early, postnatal experience alters hypothalamic corticotropin-releasing factor (CRF) mRNA, median eminence CRF content and stress-induced release in adult rats. *Molecular Brain Research*, 18, 195–200.

Rampon, C., Y. Tang, J. Goodhouse, E. Shimizu, M. Kyin, and J. Z. Tsien (2000). Enrichment induces structural changes and recovery from nonspatial memory deficits in CA1 NMDAR1–knockout mice. *Nature Neuroscience*, 3, 238–244.

# 5 Gene–environment interactions and inter-individual differences in rhesus monkey behavioral and biological development

*Stephen J. Suomi*

Billy seemed overly fearful and shy almost from the day he was born. As an infant he usually would avoid touching novel objects, including new toys that most others his age would eagerly grab, preferring to play instead with familiar objects. He seemed uncomfortable whenever he was brought to a new place, especially if there were strangers present. When he was a toddler he seldom sought out other youngsters as playmates, and he was often reluctant to respond when they tried to play with him. These tendencies persisted throughout his childhood, and when his male peers began leaving home to start new lives after puberty, Billy remained with his family, almost as if he were afraid to leave his familiar physical and social settings.

Fletcher, by contrast, was seemingly fearless when he was a toddler and continued to be so throughout his childhood years. However, he also appeared to be highly impulsive, even reckless, in many of his interactions with family, friends, and especially strangers. When he played with others his age he often started fights that sometimes turned out to be physically violent. Not surprisingly, he was not very popular among his peers, and by late childhood many adults from other families were already treating him as if he were a menace to their community. Once he ran away from home and was gone for six weeks. During that time he swam halfway across a big river several miles away, camped out for two weeks on a small island in the middle of the river, begging or stealing food from fishermen who had docked on the island, and then swam to the other side, crossing a state line in the process, where he stayed until he eventually was apprehended by the authorities.

Billy and Fletcher are not the product of contemporary American culture or, for that matter, any other human culture. Nor are they bonobos – or members of any other great ape species (see Barbara King essay in this volume). Instead, they are rhesus monkeys (*Macaca mulatta*) who were born and raised in a large captive group that is maintained within a five-acre outdoor enclosure located in the Maryland countryside, approximately thirty miles from downtown Washington, DC (the river that Fletcher swam is the Potomac and the state that he entered is Virginia).

Rhesus monkeys are members of the genus *Macaca*, whose common ancestors diverged from those of apes and humans over 25 million years ago. Their natural habitat extends over most of the Indian subcontinent, encompassing a larger geographic area and subject to a wider range of climatic variation than that of any other living nonhuman primate species. There they reside in large, distinctive social groups (troops), each comprised of several different female-headed families (matrilines) spanning several generations of kin, plus numerous immigrant males. This pattern of social organization derives from the fact that rhesus monkey females stay in their natal troop for their entire lives whereas virtually all males emigrate from their natal troop around the time of puberty, usually in their fourth or fifth year, and then join other troops. These troops are also characterized by multiple social dominance relationships, including distinctive hierarchies both between and within families, as well as a hierarchy among the immigrant adult males. Any given monkey's dominance status within its troop depends not so much on how big and strong it is but rather on who its family and friends are – and the latter is clearly dependent on its development of complex social skills during ontogeny.

Rhesus monkey infants spend virtually all of their first month of life in physical contact with their biological mother, during which time they form a strong and enduring specific attachment bond with her. In their second month of life, they begin exploring their immediate physical and social environment, using their mother as a "secure base" to support such exploration, and they also begin interacting with other troop members, especially peers. In subsequent months play interactions with peers increase dramatically in both frequency and complexity and thereafter remain at high levels until puberty.

The onset of puberty is associated with major life transitions for both males and females, involving not only significant hormonal alterations, pronounced growth spurts, and other obvious physical changes but also major social changes for both sexes. Adolescent females never leave their natal troop. For them, puberty is associated with increases in social activities directed toward maternal kin, especially when they begin having offspring of their own. These females' ties to their own families and, to a lesser extent, to their natal troop remain strong throughout the rest of their natural lifespan.

Adolescent males, by contrast, experience far more dramatic social disruptions: when they leave home they sever all social contact not only with their mother and other kin but also with all others in their natal social troop. Virtually all of these males soon join all-male "gangs," and after several months to a year most of them then attempt to join a different troop, usually composed entirely of individuals largely unfamiliar to the immigrant males. The process of natal troop emigration is exceedingly dangerous for these young males – their mortality rate from the time they leave their natal troop until they become successfully integrated into another troop is typically between 30 percent and 40 percent depending on local circumstances. Moreover, there appears to be striking inter-individual variability in both the timing of emigration and in the basic strategies followed by these males in their efforts to join other established social groups. There is comparable inter-individual variability among rhesus monkey females in the patterns of social activities they direct toward both family and non-family members, as well as the manner in which they rear their offspring throughout their adult years.

My colleagues and I have long been interested in documenting these inter-individual differences and understanding the factors that contribute to such differences not only during major life transitions but indeed throughout the whole of development. We now know that approximately 15 to 20 percent of the rhesus monkeys we have studied longitudinally in both captive and field settings appear to be unusually fearful and shy (like Billy), whereas another 5–10 percent of our study populations grow up to be impulsive and excessively aggressive (like Fletcher). These differences in temperament or "personality" appear early in life and, in the absence of major environmental change, remain remarkably stable from infancy to adulthood. Moreover, they have biological correlates that are similarly stable throughout development. For example, whenever monkeys like Billy encounter novel or mildly challenging circumstances, they typically experience profound arousal in those physiological systems traditionally associated with stress. In these circumstances fearful monkeys consistently secrete greater amounts of the stress hormone cortisol, they exhibit higher and more stable heart rates, and they metabolize their brain supply of the stress-sensitive neurotransmitter norepinepherine more rapidly than do most other monkeys. In contrast, individuals like Fletcher consistently show deficits in their metabolism of serotonin, an important inhibitory neurotransmitter, throughout multiple regions of their brains.

What is the basis for these dramatic inter-individual differences in rhesus monkey behavioral and biological functioning – are they attributable to differences in the monkeys' genes or are they a product of the monkeys' individual experiential histories – or both? Traditional heritability analyses carried out on several different populations of captive rhesus monkeys have shown that the differences in some of the above-mentioned biological measures, most notably plasma cortisol concentrations and cerebrospinal fluid (CSF) concentrations of 5-hydroxyindoleacetic acid (5–HIAA), the primary metabolite of the neurotransmitter serotonin in the brain, are highly heritable. Thus, several major aspects of these inter-individual differences can be attributed at least in part to genetic factors.

On the other hand, experiences also appear to play crucial roles in shaping any given monkey's behavioral and biological development. For example, longitudinal studies of differentially reared captive rhesus monkeys have revealed dramatic, ubiquitous effects on measures of behavior, neurobiological functioning, brain structure and function, and even gene expression. Rhesus monkey infants reared in the absence of mothers but in the continuous presence of peers for their first six months of life exhibit both more fearful and more aggressive behavior and both higher plasma cortisol and lower CSF 5–HIAA concentrations throughout development, than their mother-reared counterparts. Clearly, many heritable characteristics, behavioral and biological alike, are also subject to significant postnatal modification via differential early experiences.

In sum, *both* genetic and early experiential factors can affect a monkey's behavioral and biological development. Do these factors operate independently, or do they actually interact in some fashion? Recent research has demonstrated several significant interactions between specific genetic and experiential factors in shaping developmental trajectories for rhesus monkeys. For example, one particular gene, the serotonin transporter (5–HTT) gene, is thought to be involved in regulating the metabolism of serotonin in the brain. In both humans and in rhesus monkeys (but, surprisingly, not in most other primates) there are two different versions (alleles) of this gene – some individuals possess a "long" (LL) version of this gene, whereas others possess a "short" (LS) version of the same gene. Genetic researchers have hypothesized that in humans the "short" allele may be associated with deficits in serotonin metabolism relative to the "long" allele, although evidence for this hypothesis to date has been decidedly mixed.

In contrast, several studies have now demonstrated that the consequences of having the LS allele differ dramatically for peer-reared monkeys and their mother-reared counterparts. Peer-reared monkeys with the "short" allele exhibit deficits in measures of attention during their initial weeks, heightened cortisol reactivity in late infancy, excessive aggression as juveniles, and reduced serotonin metabolism as adolescents, compared with peer-reared monkeys possessing the "long" 5–HTT allele. In contrast, mother-reared subjects possessing the "short" 5–HTT allele are characterized by normal early patterns of attention and cortisol reactivity, as well as equivalent levels of aggression and serotonin metabolism as their mother-reared counterparts with the "long" 5–HTT allele. One interpretation of these interactions between 5–HTT allelic status and early social rearing environment is that being reared by a competent mother appears to "buffer" potentially deleterious effects of this "short" allele on serotonergic function and behavioral responsiveness. Indeed, it could be argued that having the "short" allele of the 5–HTT gene may well lead to heightened risk for developing behavioral and biological abnormalities among monkeys with poor early rearing histories but might actually be adaptive for monkeys who are being raised by competent mothers.

The implications of these recent findings could be considerable with respect to the cross-generational transmission of specific behavioral and biological characteristics, in that the particular maternal "style" characteristic of any given monkey mother is typically "copied" by her daughters when they grow up and become mothers themselves. If similar buffering were to be experienced by the next generation of infants carrying the "short" 5–HTT allele, then having been raised by mothers might well provide a non-genetic basis for transmitting its apparently adaptive consequences to their own offspring.

This possibility seems especially intriguing given recent findings that in free-ranging settings, excessively aggressive rhesus monkey males with low CSF 5–HIAA concentrations (like Fletcher) are far more likely to be expelled from their natal troop prior to puberty and less likely to survive to adulthood than the other males in their birth cohort. Moreover, those few excessively aggressive males who do survive the emigration process are subsequently unlikely to engage in successful reproductive behavior ... and equally unlikely to pass their genes on to the next generation. On the other hand, young females who have chronically low CSF concentrations of 5–HIAA also tend to be impulsive, aggressive, and generally rather incompetent socially. However, unlike their male counterparts, they are not expelled from their natal troop but instead remain with their families throughout their lifetime, and most eventually become mothers, passing their genes to the next generation. However, recent research indicates that the maternal behavior of these low 5–HIAA females is often grossly incompetent – and their offspring are disproportionately likely to turn out to be like Fletcher.

In sum, gene–environment interactions provide a possible means whereby a specific allele (like the "short" 5–HTT allele) that is associated with highly maladaptive outcomes under certain early social rearing conditions but not under others can theoretically remain in the gene pool for generation after generation, as long as females carrying that allele are competent in their maternal behavior, essentially buffering their offspring from any potentially deleterious consequences of carrying that same allele themselves. On the other hand, if contextual factors such as changes in maternal dominance rank, instability within the troop, or changes in the availability of food were to affect a young mother's ability to care for her infants in a way that compromised any such buffering, then one might well expect any of her offspring carrying that particular allele to develop some of the behavioral and biological problems clearly exhibited by monkeys like Fletcher. What those relevant non-genetic mechanisms might be – and through what developmental processes they might act – are questions that my colleagues and I are currently investigating in ongoing studies being carried out in both laboratory and field settings.

To what extent can studies of behavioral and biological development in rhesus monkeys enhance our understanding of how genetic and environmental factors might contribute to inter-individual differences among developing humans? To be sure, rhesus monkeys are *not* furry little humans with tails but rather members of a different primate species, and one should be particularly cautious when making comparisons between humans and other species, especially with respect to expressions of excessive fear and/or aggression, given that there exist obvious age, gender, and cultural differences in what might be considered excessive or abnormal for humans. Nevertheless, there are some general principles that emerge from the research with rhesus monkeys outlined above that might be relevant for considerations of human development. In particular, these findings clearly demonstrate that the social context in which a rhesus monkey infant is reared can have far-reaching consequences throughout the whole of its development – not only at the levels of behavioral functioning and emotional regulation, but also at the levels of hormonal responsiveness, autonomic reactivity, neurotransmitter metabolism, brain structure and function, and even gene expression. Thus, the social context in which development takes place clearly matters a great deal for rhesus monkeys. It is hard to imagine how it could be otherwise for developing humans.

SUGGESTED READINGS

Bennett, A. J., K. P. Lesch, A. Heils, J. C. Long, J. G. Lorenz, S. E. Shoaf, M. Champoux, S. J. Suomi, M. V. Linnoila, and J. D. Higley (2002). Early experience and serotonin transporter gene variation interact to influence primate CNS function. *Molecular Psychiatry*, 7, 118–122.

Champoux, M., A. J. Bennett, K. P. Lesch, A. Heils, D. A. Nielson, J. D. Higley, and S. J. Suomi (2002). Serotonin transporter gene polymorphism and neurobehavioral development in rhesus monkey neonates. *Molecular Psychiatry*, 7, 1058–1063.

Fairbanks, L. A. (1989). Early experience and cross-generational continuity of mother–infant contact in vervet monkeys. *Developmental Psychobiology*, 22, 669–681.

Suomi, S. J. (1999). Attachment in rhesus monkeys. In J. Cassidy and P. R. Shaver (eds.), *Handbook of attachment: theory, research, and clinical applications* (pp. 181–197). New York: Guilford Press.

(2004). How gene–environment interactions shape biobehavioral development: lessons from studies with rhesus monkeys. *Research in Human Development*, 1, 205–222.

Williamson, D. E., K. Coleman, S. A. Bacanu, B. J. Devlin, J. Rogers, N. D. Ryan, and J. L. Cameron (2003). Heritability of fearful-anxious endophenotypes in infant rhesus macaques: a preliminary report. *Biological Psychiatry*, 53, 284–291.

*Part II*

# The dynamic system of the child in the family

# 6 Relationships that support human development

*Alan Fogel*

When Susan was one-and-one-half years old, she had been playing the "lion game" with her mother for the past few months. With a lion puppet on her hand, Susan's mother made the lion roar, tickle, bite, and tease Susan, who seemed delighted to be aroused and frightened. Susan and her mother first concocted this curious blend of happiness and fear, approach and withdrawal, when they discovered tickling games. Susan was only six months old at the time. As her mother loomed in for the tickle, Susan would pull away, turn her body to the side, and at the same time reach out for her mother, look at her, and laugh heartily with her mouth wide open. From early in the first year, simple games create emotional challenges – such as a conflict between approach and withdrawal – that are negotiated in the long-term parent–infant relationship.

Emotions are good for us, a kind of psychological workout. Joy, fear, surprise, and sadness move us internally, shifting our body chemistry and lighting up our brains. Babies are more emotionally alive than most adults: they feel and respond to everything. As people leave infancy behind, however, they learn not to feel as much or as intensely. People who are repeatedly left alone as children, for instance, experience powerful fear and sadness during the separation. Without someone present to whom a child can turn to relieve them, these emotions had to be suppressed because they would be too overwhelming. People who were abused have to put their spontaneous joy and love away because there was no one with whom those feelings could be shared.

Families cannot protect children from feeling loss or fear, and they cannot indulge all their needs. Families can, however, provide a place where such feelings are permitted, talked about, and resolved. A family atmosphere of love and acceptance allows children the safety to really feel fear or sadness, for example, without running away and hiding.

The tension between the fear and joy of tickling is emotionally healthy so long as it remains safe, so long as the child can catch her breath, so long as it is done with love and surrender, so long as it is part of an ongoing relationship in which all the emotions are welcomed. Play mixing fear and joy became a permanent part of the relationship between Susan and her mother, finding its way into new games as Susan got older, like the lion game. When Susan was eighteen months old, she tried for the first time to put the lion puppet on her own hand and she pretended to scare her mother. Here is a description of that moment of change.

Mother and Susan are sitting on the floor. Mother hides the lion and Susan follows the lion, looking for it. Suddenly, the lion comes out of his hiding place and roars! Susan screams and steps back, a little more frightened than usual. She stares at the lion for a few seconds. She then abruptly grabs the puppet from the mother's hand and tries to pull it off. The lion resists and screams, "No! No!"

After a short and playful fight, Susan is able to slip the puppet off mother's hand. She smiles victoriously and explores the puppet. She turns it around looking for the opening to put her hand in. The mother comments, "Oh, *you* are gonna do it!" Mother helps her to put the lion on her hand. Susan smiles with confidence and says, "Roar!" Mother laughs and comments, "Scare mom." Susan then carefully observes the lion. She turns the lion toward her own face and makes it open its mouth. She first smiles and then watches the lion. She looks surprised and a little confused. The mother intervenes: "Ahh! You scared me!" Susan then moves the lion toward mother a little more tentatively and says, "Roar!" while smiling. Mother pretends to be scared, screams, and then comments, "Scare mommy."

During this episode, Susan is experimenting with being frightened and being frightening. There is something compelling about having the puppet she is herself holding for the first time stare back at her. There is still some fear yet Susan herself is the agent. It is confusing and yet fascinating. Susan also begins to realize that she can be the lion, that she can scare her mother, yet pretend is not quite real and real is not quite pretend. Still, she bravely gives it a try, not sure if she can really scare mommy even as she is being invited to do it.

## The importance of relationships for human development

Susan's emotions in this episode can only be understood with respect to the long-term relationship she has with her mother and in the context of their experiences playing games together. During the first two years of life, children acquire ways of relating, of being-in-the-world, that are foundational to every later experience of relationship.

- Children establish a connection with themselves, with their physical bodies, senses, and feelings including emotions.

- Children establish a connection with the important other people in their lives.
- Children establish a connection with the natural world.

All living systems are dynamic networks of relationships both within the organism and between the organism and its surround. Relationships are integral systems in which individuals develop. An example is the relationship between plants and animals. Plants have receptors for carbon dioxide. They are waiting to be completed by an animal's exhalations. Animals need the oxygen given off by plants. Animals cannot be complete as living beings without oxygen. They would die but it's not that trivial. We animals have a blank spot, an incompleteness that must merge with something from our planetary companions. Flowers and bees, grazing animals and grasslands: these are relationships whose inherent processes (large herds allow only grasses to survive and grasses sustain the herd size) define the evolution of individuals through time. Human interpersonal relationships are sustained for long periods because each person provides what is needed to help their partner feel more complete.

When we use the word "relationship" we are talking about a living, developing system. To say that people are inherently relational means that they are inherently incomplete. People must find themselves in the other, become who they are through the other. Because people require something from other people to complete themselves, people are inherently open to being altered in the company of others. The act of communication changes the other and the self. The person one began to get to know is not the same person later but rather the composite of their history of relationships with others. This is true not only in parent–child relationships but also in romantic relationships, friendships, and professional relationships.

The conventional viewpoint is that relationships are linkages of individual entities. There are senders and receivers who exchange signals. There are innate and acquired characteristics. There are mothers and children who have endowments to reach out toward the other. In this perspective, the entities are primary and the relationships are an afterthought, a way of connecting these autonomous parts. Each person is complete in itself and could be fully described and known if enough time and effort were expended to exhaust its list of characteristics.

A dynamic systems viewpoint, on the other hand, emphasizes that people are inherently connected and that development occurs through creative communication. When one approaches the other with an acceptance of their own and the other's incompleteness, however, both people change. All such communications are inherently creative. People make discoveries about themselves and about the other person. Call it creativity, or emergence, or discovery: something new arises when people approach each other with acceptance and a willingness to be affected.

The lion game between Susan and her mother shows how change can occur in relationships in which both partners are open to being changed by the other. The moment Susan put the puppet on her hand is an instance of personal self-discovery, an "ah-ha" experience. It led to a creative process in which she discovered that she too could pretend to be a lion, and this moment will lead to further discoveries as Susan explores what is possible with this new way of relating to her mother.

How did this change happen? First of all, notice what did not happen. Susan did not go off in the corner and think about this on her own. Her mother didn't just hand her the puppet at some point and say, "Here, let's see what you can do with this." The discovery, in other words, did not occur in an isolated mind that spends time alone thinking about an abstract problem.

What actually did happen is considerably more complicated and it has taken my research team years to decipher this sort of complexity. Perhaps this seems odd. After all, what is simpler than a mother and child playing an innocent little game. It is a perfectly ordinary, everyday occurrence. Scientists, however, have a habit of looking in ordinary places for extraordinary things. Indeed, we found that locked in this apparently everyday exchange is the secret to understanding individual differences in human development, the secret to understanding why some people grow up successfully and others do not.

Susan gets the puppet. That seems simple but it isn't. Mother had frightened Susan more than usual, which seemed to precipitate what followed. Susan pulled back a bit from the game, which was unusual for her. Perhaps in that moment of relative distancing that was created between her and her mother, she decided, and this was a spontaneous insight, that she wanted the puppet. Notice that Susan stood and looked at the puppet for a few seconds but even here, the mother is part of the process. She had the grace to wait and to observe quietly. Suddenly, Susan grabbed the puppet but her mother didn't give it up so easily. Why not? Because she knew from their history together that there was something engaging about an emotional dynamic between them that heightens the tension: release is combined with a struggle, enjoyment with conflict.

During the playful tug of war, it may have been obvious to both of them that Susan would get the puppet. But the game transforms a simple grabbing of the puppet into something much more meaningful for Susan: a victory for herself, for her initiative taking, a new sense of self as the protagonist of the game, which her mother quickly reinforces by helping her with the puppet and asking to be scared.

Conventional scientific approaches want to isolate cause and effect. Thinking along these lines, one would search for a sequence of prior maternal actions that can be said to cause or to lead to Susan's newfound sense of initiative. Alternatively, one might presume that something internal to Susan, such as her brain development, is the cause of her advances in self-understanding and initiative taking.

In dynamic systems approaches, on the other hand, it is fruitless to attempt to separate cause and effect in these kinds of communicative sequences. A more descriptive metaphor is co-creation. Mother's behavior is just as responsive to Susan as Susan's is to hers. But in addition to responsiveness, there is a constant creation of emotional meaning and interest that heightens the salience of the newly emerging sense of self. Susan's mother waits or withholds, not in order to respond to Susan, but in order to *play* with Susan so that Susan may come to feel herself in the process of growing.

### Understanding successful and unsuccessful developmental pathways

Other infants we have observed have relatively little play and creativity in their relationships with their mother. Our observations show that under these conditions, the infant loses touch with his or her own body, sensations, and emotions. One mother did not like her infant son, Jimmy, to suck on his hand. Even when he was as young as three months of age, she used strong prohibitions and pulled his hand out of his mouth. This was not playful. The infant resisted and pulled away but without any signs of accompanying joy, such as might occur in the normal conflicting emotions of a tickling game.

By five months, this form of interaction evolved into the mother grabbing toys from Jimmy and teasing him by pretending to give back the toys and pulling them away at the last minute. Jimmy never had a chance to participate equally. When his mother finally did return the toy, he grabbed it in anger and withdrew into himself. Jimmy showed severely restricted and tense facial expressions. His smiles were strained and brief, lacking evidence of joy and spontaneity. His infrequent attempts to resist were subdued and barely visible, very unlike the ready availability of Susan's active defiance. Jimmy's affect was flat and his behavior often seemed aimless, as if he was not aware of having his own intentions.

How can we explain the different pathways of emotional development and sense of self between Susan and Jimmy? From the conventional perspective, one or the other person is thought to have an unchanging characteristic of non-responsiveness or responsiveness. Susan's mother would be called responsive and Jimmy's mother would be called insensitive. There is good parenting and bad parenting. Good parenting produces joyful, spontaneous, and self-assured children and bad parenting does not. Or one might explain the difference by saying that Susan was temperamentally happy and Jimmy temperamentally withdrawn.

From a dynamic systems perspective, however, different types of people can develop relationships based on mutual creativity and fulfillment. Mothers with relatively low levels of responsiveness and infants who are relatively withdrawn can still meet each other as equals, share emotions, and use their relationship to expand the range of their emotions with each other.

According to dynamic systems thinking, all interpersonal relationships tend to evolve or grow into a number of recognizable patterns, some of which lead people into a fuller and more creative relationship with the self and others of which lead to a more constrained and apparently painful relationship with the self and others. The two different patterns are characteristics of the relationship – what actually occurs between the partners over a long period of time – and not of the individuals per se.

Notice, for example, that after a few months, both Jimmy and his mother continue to co-create this emotional dynamic. The more withdrawn Jimmy becomes, the more the mother feels the need to invade his space in order to make contact. This makes Jimmy even more unreachable and confines him inside a shell of self-protection. The relationship system creates an emotional trap in which both people are caught or it can create an emotional aliveness that inspires both people toward creative advancement.

But where does it all start? Dynamic systems of relationship evolve into patterns that stabilize over long periods of time but it may not be anything big that predisposes a couple to one or another developmental pathway. It could be something barely noticeable at the start, like the way the mother and infant play the opening moves of their games with each other.

It may have been that Jimmy was temperamentally difficult to reach from the beginning. Coupled with a mother who may have interpreted Jimmy's withdrawal as a rejection of her mothering, little by little they evolved a pattern of communication that was not playful, one in which mutual tension escalated rather than being metabolized by the kind of joy and creativity shown by Susan and her mother. Research on patterns that form in nature, everything from the shape of galaxies to different forms of mental health and illness, shows that big differences may begin with very tiny differences that over time become amplified into seemingly permanent structures.

The dynamic systems approach and the conventional approach offer different perspectives on treatment and intervention. The conventional view may try to teach mothers to be more sensitive to the unique characteristics of their infant, who may have turned out differently than she wanted. Or, it may prescribe individual psychotherapy for the mother or child to help resolve their conflicts about the other person. Conventional approaches to working with families may intervene in the relationship, suggesting activities to facilitate the couple to heal themselves together. Making a videotape of a mother playing with her baby and then discussing the communication process with her has been shown to improve the relationship radically. Introducing simple games that balance tension with enjoyment can also result in dramatic changes.

A dynamic systems approach, on the other hand, may use any of these traditional interventions with an additional crucial element: opportunities for mutual creativity. Parents can be encouraged to engage in activities with their children that are playful. When there is a specific goal or outcome, spontaneity is lost. In the conventional approach, Jimmy's mother, for example, might be taught not to pull his hand out of his mouth and to give Jimmy a chance to explore his hand. A dynamic systems intervention would not give the mother a specific directive (don't pull your child's hand away from his mouth). Instead, she could be told how self-exploration is a creative activity for infants and taught to observe Jimmy's behavior in a way that allows an appreciation for Jimmy's growing abilities. She could be encouraged to invent playful games that inspire creativity in both herself and her baby, such as imitating Jimmy's sucking on his hand, giving him objects to explore with his mouth and hand, and sharing that experience with her. Finally, she could begin to notice that with this kind of creativity, children will naturally and spontaneously develop away from habits or patterns that may initially seem undesirable. Once a relationship system recovers the possibility for play, even for play with negative emotions, it is enough to set each person free to discover themselves through the other.

SUGGESTED READINGS

Beebe, B., and F. Lachman (2002). *Infancy research and adult treatment: co-constructing interactions*. New York: Analytic Press.

Bowlby, J. (1969). *Attachment and loss: vol. 1. Attachment.* New York: Basic Books.

Buber, M. (1958). *I and thou.* 2nd edn. (R. G. Smith, trans.). New York: Scribner.

Fogel, A. (1993). *Developing through relationships.* University of Chicago Press.

(2001a). *Infancy: infant, family and society* (4th edn.). Belmont, CA: Wadsworth.

(2001b). The history (and future) of infancy. In G. Bremmer and A. Fogel (eds.), *Handbook of infant development.* Cambridge: Blackwell Publishers Ltd.

Fogel, A., I. deKoeyer, F. Bellegamba, and H. Bell (2002). The dialogical self in the first two years of life. *Theory and Psychology,* 12(2), 191–205.

Greenspan, S., and S. Weider (1998). *The child with special needs: encouraging intellectual and emotional growth.* Perseus Publishing.

Panksepp, J. (2001). The long-term psychobiological consequences of infant emotions: prescriptions for the twenty-first century. *Infant Mental Health Journal,* 22(1–2), 132–173.

Piaget, J. (1952). *The origins of intelligence in children.* New York: International Universities Press.

Schore, A. (2001). Effects of a secure attachment on right brain development, affect regulation, and infant mental health. *Infant Mental Health Journal,* 22(1–2), 7–66.

Stern, D. N. (1985). *The interpersonal world of the infant: a view from psychoanalysis and developmental psychology.* New York: Basic Books.

Winnicott, D. (1971). *Playing and reality.* New York: Basic Books.

# 7 The impact of emotions and the emotional impact of a child's first words

*Stuart G. Shanker*

Can a five-year-old child who has never said a word still learn how to speak? What about a five-year-old who can't look people in the eyes and seems locked in his own private world: is he still able to become an active social being? Or a child who is unable to control his emotions and erupts into tantrums or withdraws into himself at the slightest provocation: can such a child still learn how to self-regulate and engage with others? How about a child whose thinking is highly fragmented or who has trouble distinguishing between reality and fantasy: can such a child still become a reflective, logical thinker?

These are questions that philosophers rarely if ever address; but philosophical thinking from the past has profoundly influenced the way scientists think about these questions. There are a large number of psychologists and psychiatrists today who believe that children with the above kinds of deficits have suffered some genetic malfunction that has rendered them incapable of acquiring these capacities. And if a particular child should, through intensive therapy, develop one of these higher abilities, that doesn't mean, according to these scientists, that we have to rethink this genetic hypothesis; rather, it means that we have to rethink how to characterize whatever the ability is that the child may have acquired.

In other words, regardless of how much therapy may benefit a child with any of the above problems, the hard-line "nativist," as this school of scientists is called, because of their belief that human capacities are innate, cannot be dislodged from their position. Thus we see nativists go to extraordinary lengths in order to persuade us – and themselves – that the child who had no language at the age of five but is happily jabbering away at the age of ten only appears to have acquired language. Or the child who was diagnosed at a young age with autism and, at the age of ten can be seen happily playing with peers in a normal school setting, only shows how easy it is to misdiagnose a young child. Or the child who goes from catastrophic emotional reactions to developing warm and stable friendships, or who goes from telling incoherent stories to writing long involved narratives with wonderful character development, is testament to the effect that training and drill can have on a child's long-term memory.

That is not to say that nativists are committed to holding a negative view about the benefits of administering therapy; on the contrary, the nativist may be more than ready to concede that some wonderful results can be obtained in this manner. *But*, the nativist will insist, these results should not be construed as somehow validating the view that children *develop* their higher linguistic, cognitive, and social abilities as a consequence of the environment in which they are raised and the kind of nurturing interactions that they experience in the first years of their life; for the nativist believes that, when therapy is successful, it *must be* because it has enabled an alternative component of the mind to perform the task of the system that was knocked out.

This sort of dogmatic thinking is a sure sign of a philosophically driven theory. The theory in question was inspired by the views of the great seventeenth-century Philosophe, Nicholas Malebranche. Malebranche argued that, if we look closely, we can see how a mature tree is contained within the "germ" from when it springs. That is, the seed determines in advance all the features of the mature tree: given, of course, that the seed receives the proper sorts of nurturance. And Malebranche was convinced that, once science had developed sufficiently powerful tools, we would see that a chicken or a frog is contained within its eggs, and indeed, that even humans are contained in miniature form within their "germs" (Malebranche 1674).

Enlightenment philosophers quickly seized on the point that what holds true for the human body also applies to the human mind. Medieval philosophers believed that the mind is composed of a number of autonomous "faculties." Enlightenment philosophers added to this view of "faculty psychology" the idea that each of these "mental organs" grows out of some innate germ. Of course, a proper environment may be necessary to nourish each faculty – an assumption that many philosophers were more than happy to put to the test! But the actual structure of the faculty, the way that the faculty develops and works, was thought to be contained within its germ.

As Robert Lickliter shows in his contribution to this volume, "genes" have replaced "germs" in the modern version of this nativist doctrine. For example, according to one of the most influential thinkers of the twentieth century, Noam Chomsky, language – which has long been regarded as the paradigm of the faculty psychology outlook – literally *grows* in a child's mind in the same way that a physical organ grows.

Indeed, Chomsky argued that the idea that a child *learns* language is one of the great confusions perpetuated by empiricist philosophers (see Chomsky 1980). Rather, language, according to Chomsky, *maturates* in the same way that other biological phenomena maturate. Hence a five-year-old who is developing typically in all other respects (e.g. has age-matched IQ, doesn't have hearing problems, is socially adept), but doesn't speak, must have suffered some damage to his "language germ"; for each of the systems of the mind is autonomous, and each "grows" out of its own unique seed.

As with plants, there is said to be a window of opportunity in which the information that is stored inside a "mental seed" can be released: what psychologists now refer to as a "sensitive period." By the age of five this window of opportunity is said to have closed; hence all a therapist can do is to try to recruit some other faculty to do the job of the failed system. Thus, the ten-year-old jabbering away on the playground who didn't have language when he was five is seen as proof of just how much can be accomplished by training the child's memory system. But this, according to the nativist, isn't really *language*: at least, not language as Chomsky defined it, as an innate system that gets activated in a child's mind unconsciously, automatically, and without effort. For such a child has had consciously to memorize each of the rules that he has mastered in order to pass himself off as a competent speaker. Such a child is like one of those champion scrabble players that spends hundreds of hours memorizing the dictionary, who knows how to spell countless words, but doesn't actually know what many of them mean or how they are used.

To understand how this argument works, consider how, in English, there are two kinds of verbs: regular and irregular. The regular verbs, like "add" and "look" and "talk," form the past tense by adding "ed." But the irregular verbs, verbs like "break" and "creep" and "feel," have their own special rules for forming the past tense. What the nativist wants to argue is that an infant's brain is "primed" to extract the rule in English for forming the past tense for regular verbs. That is, a child is said to be born with innate knowledge of the most general principles of language, which enables her to extract this rule of grammar automatically and unconsciously, simply by being exposed to spoken English. But the child has to memorize, one by one, the endings for each of the irregular verbs.

Thus, when a nativist talks about our knowledge of language as being innate, what he means is that the brain is equipped with a couple of processing "super-rules" that enable it – i.e. the brain – to formulate the basic grammar of whatever the language that is spoken; memory then does the rest (e.g. mastering the vocabulary of the language, its grammatical peculiarities, the sorts of social acts involved in speaking, etc.). But when we look at the sorts of children described above who have only acquired language skills through intensive speech-language therapy, what we discover, according to the nativist, is that the way their minds work, there is no distinction between "regular" and "irregular" verbs. For them all verbs look the same, and the child has to memorize every single one of them individually. And if you examine very closely how such a child uses verbs you'll notice some anomalies that you don't see in a child who has acquired language naturally: for example, you'll see very subtle pauses in their use of verb endings, which, according to the nativist interpretation, suggests that it's the memory system that is doing all the work and not the innate "language system."

This view of speech-language therapy is based on a form of behavioral modification that was and still remains widely practiced. On this form of therapy the child is induced, through constant repetition and positive reinforcement, to memorize the sounds and then the rules for using words on a case-by-case basis. Over the past two decades, however, new forms of interactive speech-language therapy have been developed that have had some startling results. The following is one such example:

Pete is a withdrawn little five-year-old boy suffering from the sorts of problems outlined at the start of this chapter. He rarely looks anyone in the eye and spends most of his time in highly repetitive activities. He vocalizes a little, primarily grunts and cries, but has no words. When he was four years old he was diagnosed as having Pervasive Developmental Disorder. He has been undergoing behavioral modification ever since, with no positive results, so his parents have decided to try the interactive style of therapy known as "Floortime" developed by Stanley Greenspan.

At their initial meeting the parents explain how the behavioral therapist has been trying to get Pete to pronounce the sound "m" by making the sound over and over, sometimes by itself and sometimes in simple syllabic combinations. She would force Pete to sit quietly in a small chair in front of her and attempt to ensure that he watched her face: with various sorts of treats and occasionally forcibly holding his head. But no matter how many times she has tried to engage his attention Pete has refused to make the sound.

After digesting all this, the therapist watches Pete for a while as he plays by himself on the floor. Pete has gotten hold of a toy truck and he is sitting quietly, staring intently at the wheels of the truck as he spins them over and over. He doesn't make a sound and is oblivious to the three adults around him. The therapist slowly starts to become intrusive, asking Pete to allow him a chance to play with the toy truck. Pete ignores him completely and continues to focus on the toy and tune out the therapist. He even turns his back in order to shield the toy. The therapist becomes even more animated in his pleas to allow him a chance to play, and repeatedly attempts to block the path of the truck. Finally

Pete puts the truck down for a moment and the therapist makes as if he is going to grab the toy. This provokes Pete's very first word: a loud shout of "MINE." The therapist then asks Pete's mom to leave the room and slowly close the door behind her. Pete immediately follows her and starts banging on the door. The therapist acts as if he doesn't understand what Pete wants. He starts looking around the room and asks whether Pete wants the toy truck. Pete ignores this and continues to bang on the door. The therapist points to a doll in the corner and asks if that's what he wants. Does he want a glass of water? Through all this Pete's banging is getting even more intense: suddenly he stops and makes the sound "o." A look of understanding comes over the therapist's face: "AH, you want me to open the door," which he immediately does to end the session.

At their next session the therapist repeats the same scenario. Pete again plays with the toy truck, rolling it back and forth while ignoring those around him. Again the therapist becomes playfully obstructive and, this time, blocks the movement of the truck with his hand. Pete makes a whining sound of annoyance and moves the truck away, blocking the therapist with his back. But now, as he continues to roll the truck back-and-forth, he watches the therapist out of the corner of his eye. The therapist again blocks the truck with his hand and begs for his chance to play. There ensues a sort of cat-and-mouse game between the two of them, with Pete pausing, almost as if he is daring the therapist to try to block the truck. After a couple of minutes of this interactive game the therapist once again asks mom to leave the room and slowly close the door behind her. This time Pete follows her and, with his hand on the doorknob, he looks directly at the therapist and says "open."

Pete had clearly taken his first steps towards speaking. In fact, five years later he has become a remarkably articulate and affectionate little boy. He has no trouble looking people in the eye and delights in conversations and swapping jokes. He has become a good student and has lots of close friends. Apart from some lingering problems with his motor coordination, one would never dream that, just five years ago, he had been diagnosed with a crippling developmental disorder.

In the excitement of hearing Pete say his very first word – that defiant declaration of "MINE" – nobody noticed that he had spontaneously produced the very sound that hours of behavioral therapy had failed to elicit. What was it about this interactive format that enabled Pete to produce, spontaneously, the very behavior that hours of forced training had been unable to elicit? As a result of seeing the same phenomenon over hundreds of times with different children, Stanley Greenspan has shown that the critical factor involved is the mobilization of the child's emotions (see Greenspan 1997). A case like Pete's is particularly interesting because it is clear from his first dramatic utterance that his language comprehension was more advanced than was previously suspected. But in order for Pete to start speaking his emotions had to be strongly engaged. His desire to communicate what he wanted had to overcome whatever the forces were that were inhibiting him from speaking. Once Pete had taken this momentous emotional step he developed age-matched language skills fairly quickly. He continued to receive interactive speech-language therapy sessions on a regular basis for several years; but whatever the theme of the session, they were first and foremost designed in such a way as to maintain Pete's interest and enjoyment.

Pete's story has been told countless times by many different people who have developed language at a relatively late age. Probably the most famous example is Helen Keller's moving description of the thrill she experienced when she suddenly grasped that Miss Sullivan was spelling out the word "water" on her hand (see Keller 1990). To be sure, Keller was driven throughout her life by powerful emotions. But the epiphany that she described could not be more common: indeed, it is one that every single child experiences on their way towards talking. It is a giddy experience for a child when she takes this momentous step into speaking: one that has an extraordinary emotional impact on everyone in the family, but most of all, on the child herself. Yet the grip of the determinist picture of the mind is so strong that this simple fact has been completely overlooked by generation after generation of scientists who study language development as if it were a mechanical phenomenon, somehow overseen by the genes.

When we look carefully at the kinds of cases as those presented at the start of this chapter we realize just how impoverished is this determinist picture of child development. Such children aren't giving the false appearance of having overcome the challenges that they faced when they were five; and it isn't simply by boosting their memory that we help them to develop their cognitive, linguistic, and social capacities. By looking for a purely mechanical explanation for why therapy enables such children to make the sorts of advances that have been observed, one that holds fast to the basic hypothesis that the design of our higher cognitive and linguistic capacities is contained within our genes, nativists have either ignored the role of emotional development on these higher capacities, or else, regarded a child's emotions as *extrinsically* related to her language development. But emotions appear to play a far more significant role than simply operating as a motivational factor that may enhance or impede the linguistic, cognitive, or social-communicative processes at work; rather emotions appear to serve as the very architect of language development.

A child's first words, her early word combinations, her first steps towards mastering grammar, and later, to learn how to read and to write creative stories, are not just guided by, but, indeed, are imbued with emotional content. A child's capacities to speak fluently and freely, to form deep and meaningful relationships, to become a competent member of her socio-linguistic community, to use her burgeoning language skills to master more complex aspects of language, and to enter other domains of knowledge, are all the consequence of intrinsically emotional processes. Thus, language is not acquired as some sort of abstract system for transmitting one's private thoughts; nor is language development simply the result of mapping words onto concepts that a child has constructed in the sanctum of her mind. Rather, language, on the dynamic systems outlook sketched in this chapter, is first and foremost a *lived experience*: much more complex than, but fundamentally similar to and growing out of the smiles and frowns, the gestures and head nods, the cries of joy and shouts of anger, whose meaning a child learns through shared emotional experiences with her caregivers. It is these shared emotional experiences that underpin the growth of a child's mind.

The implications of these discoveries for research funding priorities are clear. The current rise in social, communicative, cognitive, mental, and developmental problems among young children is having a profound impact on our families, our schools, and society at large. By developing new models based on dynamic systems principles, we can not only deepen our understanding of how the minds of children develop but also create educational programs that incorporate these latest findings and dramatically improve our intervention methods for treating children with developmental, learning, or mental health disorders. Our ultimate goal is to better the lives of all children; dynamic systems theory is presenting us with precisely the tools that we need for this vital task.

SUGGESTED READINGS

Greenspan, S. I. (1997). *The growth of the mind.* New York: Addison-Wesley.
Greenspan, S. I., and S. G. Shanker (2004). *The first idea: how symbols, language and intelligence evolved from our primate ancestors to modern humans.* Boston, MA: Da Capo Press, Perseus Books.
Malebranche, N. (1674). *De la recherché de la verité*; quoted in C. Pinto-Correia, *The ovary of Eve*, Chicago: University of Chicago Press, 1997.

# 8 Emotional habits in brain and behavior: a window on personality development

*Marc D. Lewis*

As an infant, Lucy was active, easy to soothe, interested in everything, and able to spend long periods playing by herself. She was happy and energetic, though not as cuddly as some babies, and she soothed herself by sucking and babbling when she became tired or anxious. Her parents of course knew Lucy better than anyone. But they could not have predicted that, at the age of sixteen, she would be outgoing yet slow to make friends, talkative and creative, a follower rather than a leader, prone to feelings of shame but not guilt, and irritability rather than depression, self-centered as are most adolescents, but also eager to please her parents and teachers. What connection was there between Lucy as a baby and Lucy as an adolescent? Where did Lucy's teenage personality *come from*, if it wasn't there already in infancy?

Her brother Max was a more active and fussy baby, less capable of self-soothing and more reliant on his parents, but sweet and personable when he wasn't distressed. By the age of three, Max would be described as "difficult" in temperament, excessively demanding and prone to anxieties, night terrors, and temper tantrums. At this age his mother alternately became distant or angry when she could not be there for him. By four he was mischievous and sneaky, and by six he was avoided by his peers because he was aggressive and unable to share. One could not predict this sad outcome from Max's demeanor as a baby. But even at the age of six, Max's personality was not carved in stone. Max actually remained isolated and friendless till the age of fourteen or so, and then he quickly blossomed into a funny, gentle, and popular adolescent, known for his warmth, honesty, and easy-going manner. Where did this new personality pattern *come from*?

Parents sometimes say that their children's personalities were fully formed in infancy. "Jenny's always been outgoing – since she was six months old." There may be lasting qualities that were present early on, such as fascination with other people, shyness, difficulty facing frustrations, or determination to achieve goals. But much of personality has yet to grow from these basic qualities. Even when they enter school, we cannot yet predict or even imagine what kinds of adults our children will become. The emergence of personality patterns from their early origins has remained a mystery to psychologists. We know from everyday observation that personalities grow and change the most in childhood. And, when we meet an old high-school friend after several decades, we find that personalities often don't change much after adolescence – although there are points in adult development (e.g. having children) when further changes are likely. It is obvious that early experience has a big impact on personality development. Having a younger sibling steal the limelight at age two or three gives rise to jealousy or competitiveness that may last a lifetime. This is why the Jesuits said to give them the boy for a few years and they would return the (well-formed) man. And why Freud, though wrong about some things, was right to emphasize the impact of early frustrations on character formation. What isn't obvious is *why* personality changes with some experiences and not others, *how* personality patterns eventually become relatively fixed and immutable, and *when* they remain open to change or reconstruction.

While personality development is impossible to predict, it is not impossible to explain. Personality development follows certain rules: it is more easily shaped by early experience, more stiff and resistant to later experience; it solidifies over time, yet there are certain points along the way – early adolescence being one of them – when it heaves and buckles like the earth's crust in an earthquake and then settles once more into a lasting mold. These "rules" may be visible to anyone who examines personality development up close. Your grandmother probably knows them as well as you do. But our job as psychologists is to look beneath the rules and try to understand how they work. Dynamic systems ideas, a focus on emotion, and an in-depth understanding of the developing brain, provide the tools that can help us to do so.

### Dynamic systems and emotions

Dynamic systems are systems that change or remain stable due to the interactions of their own components. Many natural systems can be described as dynamic systems, including climates, ecosystems, species, societies, families, and individuals. All of these can be thought of as wholes composed of interacting parts. Individuals are systems too, because, like societies and families, they consist of interacting parts: cells that depend on one another, bodily organs and their interconnections, muscle groups communicating with eyes, ears, and nose, psychological processes such as emotions, and the massively complex interactions among the parts of the brain that keep these processes going. In our own research, we look at the individual child as a system (though we also recognize the larger system of the family), and we try to examine the psychological processes and brain processes that are fundamental to the growth and consolidation of this child-system. We are particularly interested in the growth of *emotional habits*, such as anxious vigilance, avoidance, perfectionism, or blamefulness – we consider these habits the anchor points of personality.

The "parts" of the child's psychological system include thoughts and emotions that interact to produce "wholes" such as intentions, behaviors, attitudes, and personality itself. As with any dynamic system, the inter-action of the parts not only creates particular wholes in the moment; it also forges stronger links among those very parts, making it easier for the same interactions to take place again. This is crucial for understanding development. The more often the same thoughts and feelings interact with each other (e.g. anger at an interfering parent, jealousy toward an "adorable" sibling) the more linked they become over time, and the more *likely* they are to interact on future occasions. According to our dynamic systems approach, this is *how* personality develops from day-to-day psychological events. Thought and feeling components link up to form the psychological habits of childhood: I'm mad because it was my turn! I'm scared that nobody can protect me from bad things. I'm excited about being the center of your attention. I'm ashamed at being dirty, or selfish, or mean to my little sister. We call these repetitive patterns of thought and feeling *emotional interpretations*, or, with ongoing entrench-ment, *emotional habits*. The more they repeat, the more they become strengthened, and the more difficult it is to replace them with other possible interpretations (e.g. it's not so bad that I'm selfish, everyone is selfish, so I have nothing to be ashamed of). Whether they are accurate or inaccurate, benign or damaging, it is the entrenchment of these interpretations that yields a lasting personality structure.

## Measuring behavior and brain patterns

To study the development of emotional interpretations, the first thing we measure is children's behavior. We videotape a child and parent having a play session or a discussion (depending on the age), and then we break down the videotape into codes. Some codes represent emo-tional components: smiles, frowns, a hostile tone of voice, lowered gaze. Other codes represent the more cognitive aspects of interpretation: the meaning of words, knowledge about a situation. Then, we look at how the codes link up from moment to moment. What goes with what? Does an anxious tone go together with talk of manners, bedtime, or many different topics? Does anger usually follow anxiety? Or does anxiety lead to avoidance and isolation? By seeing behavior codes link up the same way or different ways, from moment to moment and occasion to occasion, we can estimate when emotional interpretations are fairly fixed and when they are changeable. In other words, we can watch personality *develop*.

For example, angry situations may call up the same combination of codes over and over, until the child reaches school age, or adolescence. And then, different codes begin to converge. Anger may now link up more with self-reflection, less with blame, and finally, perhaps by the age of sixteen, we see a very different kind of angry interpretation, one that is indignant toward others but then denigrating toward the self. Max would *always* blame others when angry until about the age of fourteen: he could not think about his role in a conflict. Then, over the next few months, he began to see himself as part of the problem, and his anger was now mixed with guilt and remorse. That brought about a real breakdown in his habitual brand of emotional interpretation. It was the beginning of a transformation that has brought him friends, comfort, and popularity for the first time in his life.

The second thing we study is the patterning of brain activity. Behavior may look clear to the outside observer, but it is not a direct readout of what a person thinks and feels. That's why we so often misread other people's intentions. Of course we can never know exactly what someone is thinking or feeling – especially a young child whose words are not precise enough to describe inner feelings. Also, behavior doesn't really explain anything: it is an outcome of many internal processes. For these and other reasons, psychologists have become increasingly interested in moving beyond behavior and studying the brain processes underlying it. Patterns of brain activity are at least as intricate as patterns of behavior, and they change with behavior from moment to moment. The brain is the part of the body where thoughts and emotions take shape, leading to changes in behavior, even while behavior is continuously picked up by brain processes, contributing to further adjustments in thought and feeling. So studying brain processes gives us an independent and very intimate window on emotional interpretations and the personality patterns that crystallize around them.

When Max acted out as a young child, his brain was alive with electrical activity patterns. From inside Max, these were experienced as anxiety and anger, accompanied by thoughts, perceptions, and plans, forming and dissolving in an effort to get the anxiety under control. From outside Max, these brain patterns could have been measured by a net of sensors on the surface of the scalp, called an electroencephalogram or EEG. As scientists, we are interested in measuring these unique patterns of brain activity while children like Max are trying to get hold of their emotions. When we do so, we might find that the parts of Max's brain that try to control emotion are on overdrive for minutes or hours when he's anxious, but this pattern of activity melts away when he is soothed and made to feel safe. The parts of Lucy's brain that control emotion might show a different pattern when she gets distressed, with a brief period of high activation followed by a spread of energy to different brain systems – for example, those that are concerned with switching plans rather than defending against harm.

By looking at the brains of different children while they are struggling with their emotions, we can see how biology and psychology are enmeshed. And we can glimpse another dynamic system at work, buried under skin and bone yet critical to our being. The brain itself is composed of hundreds of billions of cells, arranged in many different parts and subsystems, and the interactions of these cells lay down patterns that become entrenched over time. It is no accident that the entrenchment of brain patterns corresponds with the entrenchment of behavior patterns as children develop, because brain patterns direct behavior and, at the same time, behavior sculpts connections in the brain. But how do brain patterns become entrenched, and how do we use this knowledge to further our understanding of personality development?

## Personality development and the brain

As mentioned earlier, the parts of a dynamic system become linked together more tightly simply because they interact with each other. This is much like the widening of a ditch caused by the flow of water along it. When we're talking about brain cells interacting, there are specific physiological processes that are responsible for this strengthening of connections. Brain cells communicate with each other constantly through nerve fibers. Each time a brain cell "fires" it releases a bit of chemical down a nerve fiber, and this is picked up by other cells through connections called *synapses*. Every cell that receives that chemical contribution is then a little closer to firing itself. If one brain cell activates another one repeatedly, or at a high enough level of intensity, the synapse between these cells changes in structure. The membrane of the second cell becomes more sensitive to the chemicals that cross over the synapse from the first cell. That means that the second cell becomes more likely to fire when the first cell fires. Think of two people at a dance club. They are surrounded by many other dancers, but they happen to share a glance or a comment at some point in the evening. If the event makes both feel some degree of liking for each other, they may move a little closer together, or glance at each other more often. Now, it takes less for communication to occur. Before long they are dancing in synchrony to each other's steps.

In personality development, patterns of firing produce lines of communication between some brain cells and shut down communication between others. As a result, just living life day-to-day forms networks of interacting cells that work together. Firing patterns in these highly connected networks are repeated over many occasions, and it is these patterns that come to underlie habitual thoughts and feelings. In fact, firing patterns specific to each of several interpersonal situations (e.g. sharing, aggressing, nurturing, defending) create islands of interpretive habits, each of which is repeated more easily when a similar situation comes up again. As particular networks or pathways are sculpted by experience, they become the familiar routes for activity patterns that join the components of thought and emotion in an emotional interpretation.

One of our primary research goals is to study the solidification of personality patterns, measured behaviorally, in parallel with brain activity patterns that become entrenched concurrently. This is an ambitious, long-range goal. But what will it give us? Being put on the spot in front of strangers will trigger anxiety for most preschool children. For three-year-old Lucy, this anxiety may have generated neural activity patterns in areas responsible for self-control. However, when Max was three, his neural activity patterns may have migrated instead to areas that fixate attention on danger cues. Let's say we observed these differences at bedtime – a time of day when Max became difficult, whiny, easily upset, and stubborn, and when Lucy became highly engaging and sociable. These observations would inform us that certain brain networks dominate others during particular emotional states *differently* for Max and Lucy. If these children were studied at the same time (and we ignore their age differences for now), we would infer that Max gets stuck on the features of the situation when Lucy doesn't, and that he necessarily sees things at their worst when Lucy sees several options open to her. Max gets angry and anxious at the same time, and his brain activation patterns lock him into a preoccupation with vigilance and defense. Lucy gets angry too, but snaps out of it quickly, based on entirely different brain processes. Studying these brain differences tells us much that we didn't know about *why* and *how* these children's characteristic emotional interpretations come about. The dynamic system of the brain has its own habits, and we have the tools to measure them.

## A sample study

A few research studies have allowed us to take initial steps toward the goal of linking brain and behavior in personality development. In one of these, we had parents bring their four- to six-year-old children to the EEG lab, and we taught the child to press a button each time he or she saw a white frame appear around a face on a video screen. Many faces appeared and disappeared during the experiment, some happy-looking, some neutral, and some angry-looking. We were particularly interested in how the children reacted to the angry faces. Angry-looking faces often cause anxiety, and, as noted with Max and Lucy, children deal with anxiety in a variety of ways. So we hoped to find differences between the brain patterns of anxious and non-anxious children, especially in the presence of angry rather than happy faces. These brain differences might be characteristic of children's developing emotional interpretations – or developing personality. We asked mothers to fill out a personality questionnaire for their child, and compared these descriptions with the brain results. What we discovered is that all children had more activation in a particular brain region when seeing the angry faces. That region is called the *anterior cingulate cortex*, in the center of the front part of the head, and it is responsible for controlling behavior in challenging situations. But children who were described as more anxious by their mothers showed activation in that region *more quickly* (e.g. by one-tenth of a second or more) than the others did. For these children, the dynamic system of the brain fell into its "anxious" pattern more immediately, perhaps denoting a habit that was further crystallized, whereas the brains of more secure children took longer to gravitate to this particular "interpretation." It will be important to find out at what age such neural habits consolidate and to what degree they remain malleable as children develop.

## Conclusions and policy implications

The study of brain and behavior changes in relation to personality development may seem to be a far stretch from the day-to-day problems of developing children and the research needed to help them. But while this line of work is still at an early stage, it has broad implications for our understanding of development. Different personality patterns are the templates for different pathways of problem behavior. Anxious children can develop anxiety disorders, blameful children can develop conduct disorders, and so forth. Understanding personality development is crucial for discovering where these emotional habits first appear and when they cross the line from normal to pathological. As well, psychological theorizing can get "soft" without the backbone of biology to connect it to concrete bodily processes. Biology, including neurobiology, helps us understand the causes of behavior. That is why neuroscience and psychological science are becoming increasingly unified. The more we know about the brain, the more precisely and accurately we can talk about emotions, development, and personality. Dynamic systems ideas provide an excellent bridge for connecting our knowledge of psychology with our study of the brain. Looking at neural networks as dynamic systems, where habits grow and stabilize through interacting cell groups, gives us some purchase on mysteries that have proved intractable to more conventional approaches. In fact, looking at the brain as a dynamic system helps us to see it as a highly sensitive, developing system in its own right. This understanding is crucial for devising techniques to minimize problematic developmental pathways.

Although we have just begun to understand how brain and behavior are linked in development, our research program already points toward a number of policy implications:

1. The brain is more plastic – and behavior more malleable – earlier in development and at several transitional stages throughout the childhood years. Understanding when neural networks are most plastic, sensitive, and modifiable will help us target the timing of efforts to prevent problem outcomes and to intervene once they have appeared.
2. Individual children interpret the same situations very differently, just as they react with different emotions when those situations arise. Identifying the brain processes that correspond with these psychological differences will help explain why some interventions don't work for some children. It will also help us devise interventions that do work, based on the capabilities and habits anchored in brain and expressed in behavior.
3. Particular kinds of situations have specific effects on brain regions where emotional habits are activated. As we learn more about these relationships, and how they differ with different children, we can design educational practices and educational technologies that influence the whole biopsychological system more effectively, eliciting cooperation and interest rather than anxiety and disengagement.
4. Finally, the brain processes that underlie emotion and interpretation are never fixed completely. Understanding how neural connections

change with experience will open new doors to our conceptions about parenting, teaching, and caring for children with psychological problems.

SUGGESTED READINGS

Harkness, K. L., and D. M. Tucker (2000). Motivation of neural plasticity: neural mechanisms in the self-organization of depression. In M. D. Lewis and I. Granic (eds.), *Emotion, development, and self-organization: dynamic systems approaches to emotional development* (pp. 186–208). New York: Cambridge University Press.

Lewis, M. D. (2002). Interacting time scales in personality (and cognitive) development: intentions, emotions, and emergent forms. In N. Granott and J. Parziale (eds.), *Microdevelopment: transition processes in development and learning* (pp. 183–212). New York: Cambridge University Press.

Magai, C., and J. Hunziker (1993). Tolstoy and the riddle of developmental transformation: a lifespan analysis of the role of emotions in personality development. In M. Lewis and J. M. Haviland (eds.), *Handbook of emotions* (pp. 247–259). New York: Guilford.

McAdams, D. P. (1994). Can personality change? Levels of stability and growth in personality across the life span. In T. F. Heatherton and J. W. Weinberger (eds.), *Can personality change?* (pp. 299–313). Washington, DC: American Psychological Association.

Siegel, D. J. (1999). *The developing mind: toward a neurobiology of interpersonal experience*. New York: Guilford.

# 9 Creating family love: an evolutionary perspective

*Barbara J. King*

- One day after her birth, infant Elikya gazes up at her mother, who holds her. Elikya moves her head down, then again gazes up at her mom, then moves her head down once more. Her mother, using her whole hand, moves Elikya's head back up, and gazes into her eyes.
- Once in a while, Elikya's mother needs a break from caring for her. One day when Elikya is a bit over two months old, her mom hands her over to an older sister. As she is transferred, Elikya makes a facial pout towards her mother. While held by her sister, Elikya extends her arm three times in succession toward her mother. Although Elikya is close enough to touch her mother if she chooses, she instead makes this gesture, slowly and deliberately. As Elikya is making the third gesture, her mother takes Elikya back. As Elikya relaxes against her mother's body, her sister pats her gently.
- As she matures, Elikya becomes more independent in terms of movement and locomotion. At nearly a year of age, Elikya moves far away from her mother. She comes upon her older brother, who is reclining, on his back, in an old suspended tire. Elikya extends one leg, with toes spread slightly apart, toward her brother. As he extends his own leg toward hers, Elikya proceeds forward and climbs onto his chest. The brother gives her big, broad, pats on the back as he clasps her in an embrace.

The mutual adjustment, affection, and protection that suffuse these three vignettes from the life of Elikya might characterize a family in the United States (or Argentina or Ghana). Depending on the culture and customs involved, parents and older siblings may communicate their love for young children via an engulfing hug or warm gaze; by joking banter or more somber guidance and teaching; by playing joyfully with their children or supervising their safe play with other youngsters; and in a hundred other ways, large and small, every day.

Elikya and her mother, however, are not humans; they are bonobos, great apes of Africa (a fact that explains the toe-spreading in vignette number three!).[1] Together with chimpanzees and gorillas, bonobos are humans' closest living relatives. Watching family interactions unfold in Elikya's small family – or in any group of African great apes, whether in captivity or in the wild – can tell us much about the long evolutionary history of our own parent–child interactions. Specifically, they can help us recognize what may be difficult to see in attempting to turn a scientific gaze upon our own lives: that much more is going on than the unilateral response of family members to children's needs. Caretakers and children create opportunities together in which the children's needs are met. In short, *parents and children act together to create love.*

## Co-regulation

Elikya's movements, linked from day one in a very bodily way with those of her mother and other kin, took on meaning *as* they became part of an interaction with a cherished social partner. Only as her mother, sister, or brother noted and participated in them did the movements become what we might want to call social gestures. Elikya's arm and leg extensions, then, became social requests only in the context of the unfolding social interactions. Her mother chose to take Elikya back when Elikya expressed distress at their separation; her brother chose to invite Elikya to approach, then embraced her. In each case the older partner took the responsibility for shifting the interaction, from an either distressed or hesitant one, toward a loving one. The older partners *might* have chosen differently, and if they had, Elikya could have been ignored or even rejected.

Another way to express these ideas is to say that Elikya and her social partners participated in co-regulated communication. In co-regulation, social partners actively (and continuously) adjust their movements to each other during social events that are unpredictable and contingent. Coined by Alan Fogel in describing actions of human infants and their caregivers, co-regulation is a very useful term for describing great ape social communication. The notion of co-regulated social communication differs strikingly from the typical terms in which Elikya's behavior would be described by primatologists. On the conventional

---

[1] Elikya was born in June 1997 at Georgia State University's Language Research Center. I am grateful to Sue Savage-Rumbaugh and Duane Rumbaugh for enabling me to conduct research on these apes, and to Erin Selner, Heather Bond Poje, and Dan Rice for assistance in data collection.

model, Elikya would be said to produce signals that transmit information to her intended receivers. In other words, what's of primary importance on the traditional view is the vocalization, facial expression, or gesture itself, plus what sort of information and meaning it might carry. By contrast, in co-regulation it is the social relationship that is of paramount importance, plus the meaning created by the partners as they enter into a social event. A focus on co-regulation recognizes that the older, more experienced partner may take more responsibility for shifting the outcome of the interaction, even when both partners are fully engaged with each other.

## Co-regulation and socio-emotionality

The basis for great ape co-regulation is, I believe, that these creatures are not just social but socio-emotional. Great apes, slow to mature with relatively long lives in the animal kingdom, form social groups in which shared histories and close emotional bonds are paramount. They express love, grief, empathy, and jealousy in their dealings with others in their social network.

Starting at birth, great apes enter gradually into a complex web of social interactions among kin, close associates, coalition partners, rivals, and enemies. As they grow up, youngsters become increasingly adept at negotiating these relationships. More than other primates and probably more than almost all other mammals,[2] they are primed by their participation in socio-emotional bonds to be well-suited for co-regulated communication.

Let's consider other examples, from both wild and captive great apes, in order to illustrate the nature of this socio-emotionality:

- An eight-year-old chimpanzee named Kakama, living with his community in Uganda, East Africa, carries around with him a small log. He cradles the log; retrieves it when it falls; and even makes a small nest for the log similar to the nests these apes fashion for themselves to sleep in. The tender quality of Kakama's actions and the fact that they occur during his mother's pregnancy – when she may be tired and is about to produce a "rival" younger sibling for

---

[2] My intent here is not to put great apes among all non-humans in an exclusive club. Rather, I wish to suggest that the quality of great ape co-regulated social communication is closer to that of humans than are other primates (monkeys and prosimians) and most mammals. Dolphins, elephants, and other mammals may in fact equal or approach great apes along these lines, but because I am interested in evolutionary questions, I engage primarily with the primate lineage.

Kakama – are both noteworthy. Though we cannot tell from this rare observation exactly what this young ape intended, Kakama's behavior is consistent with the suggestion that he has powers of imagination, and it certainly attests to his emotional needs. (Observation by the researcher Richard Wrangham)

- Chimpanzees living in the Ivory Coast, West Africa, act in intriguing ways when a member of their community dies. Four months after the death of her mother, Tina, a ten-year-old female, was killed by a leopard. For six straight hours, other chimpanzees attended her body. They swatted away flies, but interestingly, did not lick her wounds, although they sometimes do this for chimpanzees who survive severe injuries. They also kept young chimpanzees away from the body, with a sole exception. Tina's five-year-old brother, Tarzan, was allowed to approach and inspect the body of his sister. We have little under-standing of awareness of death in these apes, but observations like this one indicate that chimpanzees feel empathy (research by Christophe Boesch; see also my book, *Evolving God*).
- Three-month-old Kwame, a western lowland gorilla housed with his family in captivity, sits with his mother. His older sister approaches. She touches Kwame and puts her face near him, clearly desiring contact with her little brother. Immediately, the mother gathers up Kwame protectively and moves away. The sister follows and touches the mother from behind. The mother sits and pulls Kwame's head in toward herself, with a cupping motion. The sister approaches closely again about two minutes later. Immediately, the mother blocks her own breasts. The sister reaches towards Kwame. The mother blocks this reach with her hand, but Kwame reaches out so that he and his sister touch. (My ongoing study at the Smithsonian's National Zoological Park[3])

Experts at reconstructing primate evolutionary history tell us that the African great apes and humans shared a common ancestor at about seven million years ago, after which time the two lineages began evolving in different directions. As a result of this lengthy period of shared evo-lution, great apes and humans have highly elaborated versions of the primate "hallmarks": grasping hands, overlapping fields of vision that allow depth perception, and enlarged neocortical areas of the brain. The

[3] I thank Lisa Stevens and the National Zoo staff for research support at the zoo, Charles Hogg for technology support, and Christy Hoffman, Margie Robinson, Rebecca Simmons, and Kendra Weber for research assistance. For funding I am grateful to the Wenner-Gren Foundation for Anthropological Research and the Templeton Foundation.

ability to move the fingers independently and to grip fur or objects opened up a new niche for primates in evolution, one based upon infant clinging, hand-feeding, manipulation of objects and tools, and communicative gesturing. Depth perception enabled visual acuity of a new order. Neocortical expansion underwrote the abilities to relate complicated stimuli to each other, and to think abstractly.

Most important from a developmental perspective, however, is the *interactive effect* of these three features with a fourth: single births marked by a long period of infant dependency on the mother. As we have seen, it is this intense mother–infant bond that "sets up" the web of sociality that we have been discussing. And, this bond is intensely realized in the great apes. Great ape infants living in the wild are barely out of infancy at age six, and still quite emotionally dependent on their mothers. Sexual maturity and reproduction are years away yet. Fifi, daughter of the famous chimpanzee Flo studied by Jane Goodall, had her first infant at about age fourteen, for instance. Twenty years later, she gave birth to her fifth offspring.

### The dynamics of infancy

For decades now, primatologists have recognized that infant primates play active roles in their own development. Rather than talking about a process of socialization – which implies that infants are relatively passive creatures waiting around to grow up – they describe infant development in interactive terms. Emerging more recently, however, is a picture that goes beyond interactivity to recognize the fully *dynamic* nature of the social relationships in which all primate infants, especially great ape and human infants, participate. By using the word "dynamic," I return to the idea (already noted in discussing co-regulation) that social partners transform each other's behavior *as* they interact. That primate social relationships are unpredictable and contingent, and that caretakers may use this situation to the benefit of developing youngsters, is a critical point for understanding the evolution of human development.

Anyone who has cared for a human infant will already have recognized continuity between what happens in great ape mother–infant and human mother–infant pairs. Like Elikya and other great ape babies, human babies too gradually become more active in gesturing and vocalizing as they participate in co-regulated communication with their social partners. Think of any number of so-called "interactional routines" between baby and caretaker: baby being fed cereal with a spoon, or being bathed in a tub, or simply engaging in play with an adult who holds a stuffed toy. In such interactions, babies routinely babble, utter a variety of other sounds, and make gestures, and their caretakers join in with words, simple sentences, and gestures of their own (and both partners preserve turn-taking conventions!). Though referred to as "routines," in reality events vary in myriad small ways from instance to instance, depending on the child's and the caretaker's emotions, moods, level of energy and health, and so on.

Of course, human babies participate in social events dynamically in ways that at times differ from what great ape infants do. In humans, mutual gaze, mutual pointing, and other examples of joint attention between social partners occur routinely rather than exceptionally. The capacity for genuine intersubjectivity, for understanding the social partner's perspective and possible emotions, develops fully as human infants mature. Many psychologists (including Jerome Bruner, Alan Fogel, Stuart Shanker, and Stanley Greenspan) have documented the development of these uniquely human traits that characterize our species' infant–caretaker interactional routines. What anthropologists wish to add is the *evolutionary depth* that study of our closest living relatives can bring to the understanding of human development.

### Evolution and our children today

An evolutionary perspective can point us in two helpful directions as we nurture our children, and the world's children, in the twenty-first century. First, we can recognize *and learn from* our deep connection to other animals, perhaps especially the African great apes, with whom we share this planet. We humans are fond of noting that our capacity for higher reasoning, emotional expression, language, art, and technology is unmatched by any other animal on Earth. We typically ascribe this to the fact that we are cultural beings, shaped primarily by our long childhoods that are in turn marked by social learning. We often consign other animals to the "biological" category, assuming that they are guided primarily by instinct to respond to stimuli in the environment, with some limited social learning thrown in. But as I hope I've shown already, contenting ourselves with this conclusion amounts to a missed opportunity. That great apes are profoundly socio-emotional allows us to identify the true nature of the "evolutionary platform" that they represent.

Second, we can recognize *and learn from* the fact that we humans have evolved to be exquisitely sensitive to unpredictabilities and contingencies in our social interactions. When we meet our families at the dinner table at the end of a day, or out in the back play-yard on a weekend morning, we bring to our interactions millions of years of socio-emotional relating.

The lesson for caretakers of children – that is, for all of us – is that as we interact with children, we can work with the social unpredictabilities and contingencies, and use them to create love. The quality of our movements and tone of our voice as we choose which of the youngster's actions to participate with lovingly, and which to ignore or discourage, make all the difference. How readily we adjust our postures to a child's; offer a reassuring touch or word as a child tentatively smiles at us or starts a mumbled apology; and how gently we move to deflect a tendency toward frustration or aggression, all give us the chance to create love together with that child – and to create a world in which others will create love as well.

SUGGESTED READINGS

Fogel, A. (1993). *Developing through relationships*. Chicago: University of Chicago Press.

Goodall, J. (1990). *Through a window*. Boston: Houghton Mifflin.

King, B. *The roots of human behavior* and *Biological anthropology*. Audio- and video-courses available from The Teaching Company at www.teachco.com

(2004). *The dynamic dance: nonvocal communication in the African great apes*. Cambridge: Harvard University Press.

(2007) *Evolving God: A provocative view on the origins of religion*. New York: Doubleday.

Rumbaugh, D., and D. A. Washburn (2003). *Intelligence in apes and other rational beings*. New Haven: Yale University Press.

*Part III*

# The dynamic system of the child in social and physical environment

# 10    The tempest: anthropology and human development

*Peter Gow*

> Humans make their own history, but they do not make it as they please; they do not make it under self-selected circumstances, but under circumstances existing already, given and transmitted from the past.

The truth of this statement is obvious to anyone who reflects on their own childhood, for we do not select for ourselves where we were born nor who our parents are. We come into a world already given to us, and we have to find our place within it. Our developmental possibilities are constrained by the world as we find it. Equally, however, our developmental possibilities, as they take shape, create new worlds for others, new circumstances that will already exist, given and transmitted from the past, for other people. If the world is given to us, then important aspects of it become, as we develop, what we in turn give to others. Anthropologists who have spent time studying people whose experience of the world is markedly different from their own necessarily understand these gifts in a particular way. I want to explain how I understand these gifts through a story about my time living among the Piro people of the Bajo Urubamba River in Peruvian Amazonia, and what they have taught me.

I want to explain how I understand these gifts in the form of a story because this is what Piro people insistently taught me to do. Piro people dislike overt statements of personal opinions, however well-founded, for these inevitably focus attention on the opinion-holder and his or her differences to the audience. To focus on such differences leads, as they have noticed, to unproductive social conflict. "I think that we should do X" inevitably elicits a corresponding "Well, in my opinion, we should do Y," and so on. Piro people far prefer to address complex and troubling problems, problems that face us all, through the medium of stories about their own experiences, of the form, "This happened to me ..." The audience is thus invited to think about the appropriateness of the narrator's response to such a situation, and to formulate, for themselves,

91

their own responses to situations in which they might equally find themselves, as life unfolds. So, here is my story ...

The late Pablo Rodriguez, his nephew Juan Mosombite, and I were traveling up the Bajo Urubamba River by canoe in 1988. It was late in the dry season, and the river was very low. We were heading for Pablo's aunt's house in Bufeo Pozo, and night had fallen. We came to a set of rapids caused by the low water, and we could not go forward. Pablo steered us to the beach, turned off the outboard motor, and started to walk backwards and forwards, stopping and gazing attentively into the darkness. I asked him what he was doing and he asked me to be quiet. He said, "I am trying to hear where the main river channel is, to find out where we should go." I was incredulous. I could hear the rushing water, the sounds of the forest at night, the distant thunder, and the rolling of rocks in the river bed. Pablo could clearly hear something else. He continued to walk back and forth, stopping and listening intently. Finally, he shook his head and came over to Juan and me and said, "I think it is over there but there are three channels at least and in this darkness we won't be able to find the right one." I was completely stunned that my friend Pablo, whom I thought I knew so well, could use his ears to visualize a landscape that he could not see.

Over to the east, a massive thunderhead had gathered. It was a harbinger of the rainy season, and sheet lightning flashed through it, briefly illuminating us. It, and the torrential rain that it contained, was headed directly for us. Pablo said, "Well, we will have to sleep here on this beach and tomorrow when we can see we will find the right channel." This was a typical Piro canoe journey: we had no food, no shelter, no means of making any, and we were about to have to sit out the coming tempest on that beach. Pablo and Juan looked resigned to their fate, for such a situation was an ever-present possibility within the wider joys of canoe travel. Doubtless they had lived through the experience I had often seen undergone by their younger relatives: a child shivering and whimpering softly in a canoe in the rain, as an adult says, "Now you see? I told you not to come with us, but you wouldn't listen!" I remembered similar scenes from my own childhood, with the difference that these took place on Scottish hillsides, and the child was saying, "See, we shouldn't have come!" and the adult was saying, "Och, it's just a wee drop of rain!" My childhood adventures had always ended up tucked up in bed safe inside, while Pablo's and Juan's probably often had not. So while Pablo and Juan gloomily accepted their fate, I refused mine. Shelter, and food, must be found. We had to get inside.

In the pitch darkness, the only light was from the stars and the storm, but there was also a house light burning across the river to the east, below the lightning. I asked who lived there and Pablo said it was the ranch of a white man he did not know. I said, "We must go to that house. We cannot sleep on this beach with that storm coming." Pablo said, "They will not welcome us." Piro people are extremely reluctant to take risks with the hospitality of unknown white ranchers because they know that the humiliation that they will experience is much worse than a bad night's sleep and a good soaking. I was desperate and I told Pablo, "This is ridiculous. I am a white man and those people will have to welcome me and they will have to welcome you and Juan because you are with me. We must go there!"

Piro people fear white people, the ones they call *kajine*, and they fear them for very good reasons. The Summer Institute of Linguistics missionary Esther Matteson lived among Piro people for many years and learned *yineru tokanu*, "human words," the Piro language. She recorded the following about this process of learning, as she tried to find the full meaning of the Piro word *salewakchi*, which can be translated as "affliction." A Piro man explained it as follows,

Yes, it is an affliction that my little boy was born blind. And then again, when a white comes to live in one of our villages and we cannot get rid of him, that's affliction.

Piro people experience affliction as something that happens to them and which must be endured, as one must sometimes endure a tempest on a beach at night. White people came to settle on the Bajo Urubamba river in the late nineteenth century and have never left, and Piro people have been enduring them ever since.

This fear of white people, and the endurance it generates, was one of the most difficult aspects of my ethnographic fieldwork among Piro people. Initially, I thought that they had been scarred badly by racism, and I tried to use my anthropological training and my knowledge of anti-racism to overcome that scarring. I remember in the early days showing a group of Piro people some photographs of Asháninka people I had met in the neighboring Ene river area a couple of years before. I thought that by showing these photographs of other indigenous people I had met, people far more traditional in appearance than them, Piro people would see that I approved of their being indigenous people and hence could speak at ease about their traditional culture to me. But as these Piro people looked at my pictures of the Asháninka people, they would then look at me and then silently hand the photographs back. I could see instantly that they were thinking, "This white man thinks that we look like that!" They were not amused, and I never showed anyone those photographs again.

This very unpleasant event had one interesting outcome, however. These Piro people, sensing that the Asháninka people interested me and that this might be a good way to start a conversation that would let me tell them more about myself, started to talk about Asháninka people. "The Asháninka people eat frogs!" they would say, taunting me and laughing. I once made the mistake of saying, "I've eaten frogs with them too!" The Piro people reacted with disgust and incredulity, then with laughter. They said, "We do not eat frogs, they are not food. Only the Asháninka people eat frogs. How disgusting!" I found this troubling. On the one hand, we were now talking and laughing, which was good. But we were talking disrespectfully about the Asháninka people, whom I liked, and I didn't think that the best way for Piro people to overcome their fear of me, based on their experience of racism, was by being racist about another ethnic group.

Piro people kept this up with me for months. Constantly they would criticize their neighbors for doing and eating things that they did not. The Amahuaca eat uncooked food, the Yaminahua eat snakes, the Ticuna eat bats, and so on and on and on. This appalled me, and I would much rather that they had told me other things, nicer things, nice things about themselves. It was ugly and unpleasant but at least I was learning about what Piro people do and do not eat. Then it finally dawned on me why they were doing all of this. They were telling me about themselves and what they expected me to be like if I wanted to live with them. If I wanted to eat frogs, indeed if I even thought that eating frogs was a good idea, then why was I there and not off living with Asháninka people? After all, they were enduring the affliction that I had brought to them by moving into their village, and they were telling me their conditions for my continuing to live there.

So, I discovered that there are certain kinds of white people that Piro people can grow to like and to trust. These are those white people like Esther Matteson and myself who come to live with them for a long time, who learn to understand them as they speak in their own language, and who can show Piro people their intelligence, their *nshinikanchi*. This Piro word is hard to translate into English, for it covers our concepts of memory, respect, love, thinking, and more. It is what Piro people value in other people, and if a white person goes to one of their villages and attends to the affliction that they have brought to those Piro people and attends carefully to what they say and do, then those Piro people will respond to this evidence of mindfulness. They will say, *Wa tye yinerni*, "This one is human."

Piro people treated me exactly as they treat newborn babies. When a baby is born, the first question is, "Is it human?" If, as almost invariably happens, the answer is "Yes," then the cord is cut, and the long process of eliciting the child's *nshinikanchi*, its mindfulness, begins. We might see the care given to the baby as evidence that the child is its parents' child, but Piro people do not put it that way. They say that they care for the child because it is lonely and suffering, and they feel sorry for it and so console it. Child care is not a duty towards a young relative, but rather compassionate help for this little person who cannot help itself. Piro people extend the same compassionate help to their pets, especially young captured birds and mammals. Pets can respond with apparent expressions of love, but only babies start to respond with mindfulness, and slowly begin to mark the beginning of social relations by using kin terms like *mama* and *papa*. Piro people hold that it is impossible to teach a child to speak or to specify its social relations. Children do this for themselves, and the relations they elicit with others are respected by these latter. Piro people seldom praise their children, but they take seriously the evidence of their growing mindfulness and respond in kind. At the same time, they give them nicknames that correspond to any unhuman attributes, and mercilessly tease them when they show themselves to be unmindful.

It was the same with me. Piro people decided that I was human, and saw my loneliness and suffering. They fed me and cared for me. Piro people also responded with their own characteristic manner of being friendly to strangers, joking. Piro joking is both very subtle and very robust. Piro people give strangers they are befriending nicknames, *rumotikolu giwaka*, "names of affection." These names define a specific characteristic of the named and commemorate an aspect of his or her relation with the namer. Juan's impish younger brother calls me "Murderer," in commemoration of what his older kinspeople told him they thought I was when he set about befriending me in his adolescent defiance of their worries. Another man calls me "Brother" because his wife once announced, when drunk, that she wanted to have sex with me and I was embarrassed that she had said this in front of her husband and then he was embarrassed by my embarrassment. These nicknames commemorate moments of emotional danger to both the namer and the named and celebrate the warm texture of the friendship by endlessly drawing attention to the fragile moment of its inception. Constantly called to mind, the difficult memories of the beginnings of a growing friendship steadily transform in their emotional tone. I went on to discover that while Piro people often say very unpleasant things about other people, and while they often say very unpleasant things to other people, the fact of saying these unpleasant things bears no relation to how they actually treat other people.

On a hot dry season afternoon, Pablo Rodriguez, his wife's oldest sister Lucha Campos, and I were idling in Pablo's mother-in-law's house. The village was deserted, and we felt no compulsion to look busy, so we were just enjoying each other's company: two ebullient young guys and an attractive middle-aged woman having some fun. As we talked and teased and laughed, two men appeared on the far side of the village coming from the direction of the next village upriver. Something about the clothing and carriage of these men suggested that they were Asháninka people from the Tambo River to the west. I asked my companions, "Who is that arriving? Are they from the Tambo?" Lucha said, "Pablo, here come your relatives from Impaniquiari," an Asháninka village on the Tambo where Pablo's brother worked as a schoolteacher. Pablo replied, "Oh, come on! I bet they're called Campos!", the surname of Lucha's Asháninka father. Slowly the two men approached the house, as Lucha and Pablo ridiculed their clothing and haircuts, and I laughed too. When they got within earshot, Lucha greeted them, and asked where they were from. The older man told us they were from Impaniquiari. Lucha then said, laughing, "Surely you must be Rodriguez!" He replied, "No, Campos." Pablo and I burst out laughing, while Lucha kept a relatively straight face, and said to them, "Then you are my kinspeople. There is nothing in this house for you so come to my house to drink beer." Lucha did not ask Pablo or me to join in, and we later heard the sound of their laughter resounding across the village, Lucha's very clever punch line.

Piro people do not hold that statements imply opinions. One of the first Piro words I ever learned was *kayloklewakleru*, "liar." This word flies regularly between Piro people, and it is not an insult. This always surprised me, with my childhood spent being constantly told never to tell lies, and I was amazed by the casual manner in which Piro people would accuse their children of lying, but never punish them for doing so, or even suggest that it was a bad thing to do. "Liar!" is even often said by women to a baby that gropes for the breast but refuses to suck. Piro people feel no pressing need to tell the truth, nor do they expect others to do so. Indeed, they hold that spoken language is primarily a vehicle for lying. Instead of trusting words, they trust deeds, and in particular they trust to acts of generosity. The good person, in their eyes, is not the truthful person, for how on earth would they know if that person was telling the truth? Virtue cannot lie there. In Piro people's eyes, the good person is the generous person. They are people with very long memories for acts of generosity or ungenerosity. That is what *nshinikanchi* is. Even old people will talk of specific meals that they were given by their parents, and adults regularly evoke their childhood experiences when talking of older people, saying, "She is my aunt, when I was a child, she fed me. She was good to me, so now I always remember her."

And that is why Piro people fear white people, and why they experience white people living among them as an affliction. White people are not, on the whole, generous in the kinds of ways that Piro people value. As they say,

Go to the white man's house and see if he will feed you! That's where you will learn how to suffer!

White people either do not notice other people's hunger, or they do notice it and do not care. I strongly suspect that the latter is true, and that this is as good an example of racism as one could find. Racism is not simply injustice, it is a social relation. Here, the social relation is the active refusal to see another's suffering and then do something about it. We might prefer to think of this as the absence of a social relation, but we would be very wrong.

In the prospect of that tempest, as I stood on the beach with Pablo and Juan, I activated the one resource I possessed that might have spared us a very cold wet night on that beach: the obvious fact of my being a white man. Pablo could not find the way ahead, so I stepped into the breach. In the gathering tempest, I offered a new possibility. Let's go to that white man's house, because he will have to welcome me and be generous to you too. Pablo and Juan didn't argue and indeed seemed relieved. They didn't want to sit out that storm on that beach either. In Piro terms, I was the initiator of this new plan, I was its owner, and hence I was fully responsible for its ongoing consequences for myself, for Pablo, and for Juan. Pablo said, "OK, let's go." We got back into the canoe and Pablo started up the motor and we headed for the ranch's port. We got out, and started walking along the path towards the house with the light. I walked in front, where the owner of a plan walks, the position of responsibility towards others.

I could sense that people were coming towards us along the path. Suddenly a torch was switched on and we were dazzled by the bright light. A voice said, "Halt! Who goes there?" Simultaneously, there was the eerie trak-trak sound of the bullets being loaded into the firing chamber of a high-velocity rifle. The strangers in the dark were preparing to kill us. Pablo stepped in front of me and said to these men we could not see and did not know, "I am Pablo Rodriguez, the uncle of the schoolteacher Celia Mozombite from Bufeo Pozo, and this is Juan Mozombite, her younger brother. Do you have anywhere we can sleep? That storm is coming and we do not want to sleep on the beach." The lamplight was lowered as was the rifle. Finally we could see two very frightened men. Gruffly they told us we could sleep in an outhouse, which they led us to. Feeling responsible for Pablo and Juan, I asked if they had any food that they might sell us. They said no. "Not even some manioc flour?" I asked. "We have nothing," they replied.

So we went to bed quickly, and hungry. I fell asleep. The storm broke and it poured with rain, soaking our beds. Pablo woke me up to get me to move from where I was sleeping. We then slept very badly. At the first hint of light, Pablo roused me and said, "Let's go." Pablo and Juan packed up their beds quickly and quietly, and I followed their example. We walked past the main house, and I asked Pablo if we should thank the residents before we left. He said, "No. Let's just go." We arrived in Bufeo Pozo, at Pablo's aunt's house. She fed us a good breakfast of salted *boquichico* fish and plantains. Pablo told her what had happened to us the night before, talking with quiet intensity. His aunt listened closely and told us that the "terrorists" had just told the owner of the ranch that they would kill him. She said,

The owner is not there, he ran away. He is afraid. He left those men there to watch out for his house and his cattle. They must have thought you were the terrorists. That must be why they greeted you at gunpoint.

Pablo, Juan, and I whistled in horror, and our fear made us cold. Pablo's aunt suggested that we sleep. We slept there.

A few years ago, visiting the Bajo Urubamba, Juan called me to his house. Juan is a very shy man, a little tongue-tied, and seldom says much even when he is drunk and merry. He is happily married to his Asháninka wife and the mother of his children who, although she did not know me, fed me as I sat in their house. I was happy and grateful, and thought that Juan and his wife were just being kind to me. Suddenly, and to my utter astonishment, Juan started to tell us about the journey in 1988, with force and energy and detail. He told us, his voice straining with emotion,

Remember when we were stuck on that beach. Remember how you said, "We must go to that house!" Remember how we went to the house and heard the bullet going into the chamber, trak, trak! How afraid I was, oh, how afraid! Then we slept in the outhouse, and the rain fell on us. How much we suffered, remember!

I was amazed to hear Juan talking so animatedly and at such length. He said to me,

Often, in the evening, I tell my children about that journey with my late uncle Pablo and with you. And my children listen to me and ask me, "What happened next?" I will never forget that journey! Never!

Juan's young children peered at me shyly, this man who they had heard so much about from their father. I was a white man to them, an object to fear, but I was also that white man, the one in this amazing story of their father's.

As I have said, Piro people hold that spoken language is primarily a vehicle for deception. Often, I am sure, Juan's wife and children must have doubted the veracity of his story of this journey. Did these remarkable things really happen or did Juan just make them up? His uncle Pablo was dead, and so Juan could not appeal to him. Then suddenly I appeared again, and Juan could tell the story again, in a new way. For I did remember what he told, and could say, "Yes, that is how it was!" I could remember all of the incidents, I could remember the emotions we went through, and I could also tell Juan's wife and children that this remarkable story was true, for I had been through these things too. Juan's children listened, and looked at me with curiosity, as they went through the process of realizing that not all white people are frightening, even although most are.

As humans, we have the fact of once having been children in common: even as children, we have all once been younger. But if childhood is universal, each childhood is particular, fashioned out of the unique gifts given to us by others, the circumstances that already existed for us. An adult who learned as a child that telling the truth is more important than being generous is a very different adult to the one who learned the opposite, and this is true even although none of the adults around us as children would have explicitly stated these hierarchies of ethical values. Similarly, the adult who endlessly remembers the Scottish calls to "Behave yourself!" is a different adult to the one who endlessly remembers the Piro call, "¡Ptuplashatanu!", "Sit still and don't move!" The fact that the former may strike many readers as acceptable and even desirable, while the latter may seem bizarre or even unnatural, reflects the fact that humans differ. It has become customary to refer to these differences as cultural, as traditional, but I believe this to be inadequate, for I think that these differences reflect specific adult knowledge of the world as it actually is. To "behave oneself" and to "sit still and not move" are ultimately the same thing, admonitions by adults to children to teach them how they should live in the world correctly. What differs between these statements is what the world looks like to the adults, their specific takes on the circumstances they too have received from the past. That Scottish children can no more behave themselves than Piro children can sit still and not move is not the issue. Both are being pointed out into an unknown future as adults when they will have to rely on what they can remember of advice given in childhood, a future that might well contain being stuck on a beach as a tropical storm looms. What to do? Sit still or behave oneself?

Two things stand out to me about this story of the tempest. The first is an ethnographic question about Piro people and about the men defending that ranch. When Pablo realized that I had inadvertently led us into danger as we heard the man call, "Halt, who goes there!", and as he seized the initiative back from me, and when he then told those frightened men who he and Juan were, he never mentioned me. Nor did those men ask who I was. Why not? I have very little idea. I was rendered totally invisible, even although, in the circumstances, I rather stood out. I was too tall, too pallid, and totally out of place. I suspect that Pablo and the armed men, in the very dangerous moment that we were in, decided simply to ignore me as an irrelevance, a problematic detail of a situation that would take far too long to address. It was better to ignore me completely.

The second thing that stands out to me about this story is that when I said to Pablo and Juan that I was a white man, I felt a little uncomfortable. It seemed like a statement not simply of my difference from Pablo and Juan but more importantly that I was somehow both different and special. I was brought up to hold that even though humans vary, they are all equal, nobody is special by virtue of their differences. My childhood also led me to hold that many people in the past, and in the present, did hold that difference is linked to special-ness, and had caused and cause much human suffering. It continued to be held true by many white people on the Urubamba. So I was a little afraid that I had not been behaving myself, and that I had offended Pablo and Juan. But my comment did not offend them, for had it done so, they would have let me know it. I can imagine it with utter clarity. Either Pablo or Juan would have told the story, "And then he said, 'I am a white man,' and then we nearly got killed!" Everyone would have laughed long and loud, and I would have been firmly put back in my place. Even although I felt uncomfortable in saying this thing, I know that Juan and Pablo did not. They simply heard me suggesting another solution to our collective predicament, on that beach as the tempest approached. That my solution, in the gathering storm, was a very stupid and dangerous one in those precise circumstances was never held against me by Pablo or Juan. I had simply acted out of my ignorance, an ignorance I shared with them, and then we all had to endure the new affliction that we entered.

As I sit and remember these things, I think that I am culpable of one thing, which I suspect is general to people like me: I always try to solve problems like being stuck on a beach as a tempest approaches. I would prefer to be more like Piro people, and learn to endure afflictions that I can do nothing to avoid. I should have listened to Pablo, this man who could use his ears to visualize a landscape that he could not see, and had a bad night's sleep on that beach and gotten a good soaking. The alternatives, as I discovered, can be very much worse. But I suppose this too is an inevitable product of my own childhood, all those endless exhortations to do things, to be active, to solve problems: "Well, don't just sit there! Do something!" And, of course, my foolish plan was the long resounding echo of the desperation kindled by suffering in the rain on Scottish hillsides, the thought that we should not have come, and the imperative to be safe inside. A Piro person would end the story there, leaving the listeners to draw out its wider meanings for themselves. Their unwillingness to draw out deeper lessons and wider implications lies in the value they place on endurance of suffering. After all, any personal story about affliction has a very obvious lesson: the teller clearly survived to tell the tale. However, as I pointed out, people like me, people raised to "behave themselves" and always, in a crisis, to "do something," are unlikely to be easily satisfied by that. What, we must ask, is the point of this story, what is its lesson? What is its implication for the policy decisions that professionals who make accepted claims to expertise in this field should advocate? What, in short, should we do?

I can think of two things we might profitably do. Firstly, we should try to do something about our self-imposed moral imperative to "do something." While doubtless often very helpful, this imperative has led to much well-meaning folly. I give an example. In the year 2000, I traveled down the Urubamba River and was appalled to see that every Piro village was ruined with what looked like portable toilets raised along the banks of the river. Most Piro villages are handsome lines of palm-thatched houses aligned to the river bank, and to see their beauty defaced with blue plastic latrines was devastating. Piro people were aesthetically less offended than I was, but they were still bemused. They explained that a German non-governmental organization had provided the money and material to install a latrine for each household in each village. Knowing that Piro people have a strong aversion to the smell of urine and feces, and avoid defecating in the same place twice, I asked them what these latrines could possibly be for, since they clearly did not and would not use them. They explained that they were for the "foreigners" to use when they came to visit Piro villages, because, as they had noticed, "foreigners" are afraid of defecating in the forest, where feces are recycled with awesome speed. I am sure, however, that many Piro people had also picked up on the message that the German

NGO workers, like local white people, considered them to be dirty. I was angry. Of all the things that Piro people needed, plastic latrines were very far down the list. And it was a spectacular waste of money. The moral imperative to "do something" should always be carefully scrutinized by those who experience it, and very often must be resisted.

Secondly, we should rethink what we call "culture." Following from a tradition of anthropological usage, we tend to imagine that a culture is an inventory of how people customarily do things as members of communities in which they grow up and live. We further imagine that we could come to a reasonably complete inventory of such customary modes of doing things for any given human community. Experienced ethnographers know that this is impossible. As my story about the storm shows, Piro people react in a manner to new situations, such as being stuck on a beach at night with me, in ways that are clearly of a piece with other things they do, but which I could still never predict. The complexity of their motives for action in a complex world will always outstrip my abilities to comprehend, far less describe, either. Anthropologists always know this feature of their ethnographic knowledge, but non-anthropologists often complain that anthropologists should have something clearer, simpler, and more useful to say about their knowledge. Anthropological knowledge, incapable of being reduced to a "variable" or "factor" of any given human situation, ends up looking too obscure and complex to have any use.

In fact, the lesson of anthropological knowledge is remarkably simple to grasp, as long as it is accepted that it is about how to know something about people, rather than about what to know. This point is evident in the story about the tempest, which hinged on my inability to discriminate between Pablo's general fear of unknown white people and of that specific house, and presumably his inability to discriminate between my bright plan and its empirical groundlessness. The key anthropological point is about listening carefully, and asking ever more refined questions. We do not yet know, when we ask a question, how other people will interpret what we have asked, nor when they reply, do they yet know what we meant by the question or what we will understand by their answer. Indeed, initially, they have no idea why we would even ask that question, and we have no idea why they bothered to reply. It takes a very long time, and many turns in speaking, to begin to clarify both sides. Anthropological knowledge raises doubt even for what might seem its greatest possibility, the "consultation" of local people, for here the meanings of the questions are not transparent to those who are asked them, and neither are the replies they receive. Instead, anthropological knowledge points towards a very different mode of knowing, that embedded in conversation, where people seek to get to know each other better. For Piro people, stories are always embedded in conversation, and especially those that are longest and most open-ended. So, this is my story about anthropology and human development, and what Piro people have taught me about them.

# 11   An anthropology of human development: what difference does it make?

*Christina Toren*

As the reincarnation of a specific ancestor, a Beng baby of the Côte d'Ivoire is enticed into staying alive by virtue of the mother's care in looking after it and especially in keeping it clean and fed and beautified with bracelets and skin paint; by these means the infant is persuaded to detach itself from the invisible ancestral realm and recognize its kinship with the living. Infants are understood to desire to return to the ancestral realm, so it is not until a child is walking and speaking that it is known to be surely desirous of remaining with the living – a desire that is only fully accomplished when, at the age of six or seven, the child is able to understand and express in speech its knowledge of the difference between dreaming and waking or of death. This brief and unexamined example suggests the possibility that people's ideas of themselves, of kinship, of bodily substance, of what a child is and can be, may be manifold and varied. As indeed they are. Thus a child of the Amazonian Araweté is solely the product of its father's semen for which the mother is the receptacle, but children of the same mother assert their closeness to one another as successive occupants of the same place. In Fiji a child is born a member of its father's clan, but its relation to the people of its mother's father's clan entitles it throughout life to take what it wants from them without asking. In the Canadian north, kinship is not taken for granted. Not only does an Inuit child have to learn the moral obligations that kinship entails but also that it can make its own kinship ties on the basis of an emotional relationship with one who shares the same name; having the same name as another person makes one substantially like them irrespective of any genealogical connection. By the same token, a daughter may be addressed by her father as aunt (for instance) because she carries his sister's name and as grandmother by her own mother because she carries too the name of her mother's mother. In Bermondsey, London, a child born to parents who were themselves born and bred there, knows its kin ties to be as much a matter of place, as of biological relatedness; the child's sense of self is bound up with the locality: having kin who are themselves "Bermondsey born and bred" makes one "real Bermondsey" and by the same token these kin ties are the more recognized and nurtured.

We may know for a fact that people hold markedly different ideas about themselves and the world, but we rarely consider that these differences *really* make any difference. Why so? Precisely because the developmental process that makes us what we are produces in every one of us, everywhere in the world, the certainty that our own ideas and practices are self-evidently right and proper – at least for ourselves, if not for others. To the extent that we know about other people's perhaps very different ideas we may tolerate them, we may even say we understand them, but even so we tend to feel that, when it comes right down to it, we're the ones on the right track. And this is so even though we know that our own ideas about ourselves and the world have changed over time. The point is that, at any given time, we hold to our own current understandings: by and large we're pretty certain they're the right ones. What then are the implications of these prevailing different certainties for how children make sense of themselves and the world?

From birth, babies are immersed in relations with caregivers; indeed psychological studies show that newborn babies have capacities which have the effect of facilitating social relationships and which, through functioning, become ever more highly differentiated or, in other words, developed. That babies find other humans extraordinarily interesting is clear enough: for example, newborn babies prefer pictures of faces over other attractive pictures, they can discriminate and imitate certain facial gestures of others, can discriminate language sounds from other sounds, and at four days have learned enough to differentiate their native language from others. At three months they are matching heard speech sounds to speakers' lip movements and by six months they are following the gaze of others and paying attention to objects others use. By nine months, they can not only perform simple actions with objects that they see others do, but can also communicate about those objects by, for example, pointing.

A comparison of the range of people's ideas and practices across the world in respect of domains of everyday life such as religion and political economy (in short, comparative ethnography) suggests that infants' capacities to facilitate social relationships are brought to bear on the particular conditions in which any given child comes to knowledge of itself and the world. Every infant and young child has to come to know its own place in relation to those others who care for it – its parents and other caretakers. The infant and young child is fed, handled, carried about and/or left to lie, played with, cleaned, cuddled, talked about and/or talked to, and in all cases these activities are given particular meanings by adults and the child itself accorded certain attributes. In Fiji, as among the Beng, an infant has multiple caretakers and girls aged seven or eight years old are responsible and efficient baby-carriers and minders; an English infant cannot by law be left without adult supervision. In Samoa, young children learn that it is up to them to understand what is said to them by an older person; an adult has no duty to explain. By contrast, middle-class mothers in Australia are constantly giving answers to toddlers' and young children's questions beginning with "why." Thus, in the very process of being looked after and learning to speak its own language, the infant and young child is at the same time learning who he or she is, and how to behave, in relation to those others. In other words, the child is learning what a person is, what a relationship is, what sociality is, and how to understand him- or herself and what he or she is, in the eyes of those others.

The point here is that *what* a child learns has everything to do with *how* it learns and, in every case, this what and how are embedded in social relationships. From an anthropological point of view, the infant and young child cannot be a more-or-less passive object of socialization, if only because we know that no human being holds exactly the same ideas as any other (even where they are identical twins). This observation alone suggests that the process of arriving at highly differentiated complexes of ideas about the world is not merely developmental: it's not a simple unfolding along a pre-determined trajectory, but a process that transforms existing concepts and may give rise to new ones. At the same time it is manifestly the case that for all they differ from their parents, and from one another, Beng babies grow up to hold ideas about the world and to follow practices that are identifiably Beng and likewise what English or Fijian adults say and do makes it clear that they are a product of their upbringing. So an older Fijian child is likely to have an idea of him- or herself as operating within a complex of relations with many kin to whom different obligations are owed; who I am as a Fijian child has everything to do with what I am *given to be* at particular times in particular relations with particular kin – senior sibling, junior sibling, cousin and prospective spouse, uncle and prospective father-in-law, or aunt and prospective mother-in-law, grandchild, child. By contrast, an Anglo-American child (whether from a blue-collar or middle-class family) is likely to hold an idea of him- or herself as an individual whose relations with others, even with kin, contain a large measure of choice. This is because here individuality tends to be foremost in ideas of self, and the idea that one chooses to be who one is, is a crucial aspect of holding oneself to be an individual. It follows from these examples that child development provides at once for continuity and transformation. How can this be so? Well, the process is straightforward enough.

Put simply, making sense of the world entails that each of us makes meaning out of meanings that others have made and are making. This is a microhistorical, rather than developmental process: it is not a pre-determined unfolding whose blueprint is given in the genes, it is always as much a process of change as of continuity, and it is always personal even while it bears on the world we have in common with others. So each one of us becomes who we are by virtue of engaging the others alongside whom we live in making our own sense of the world; this process is microhistorical because each of us continues to change over time in the course of our relations with others and each of us, at any given time, is the unique product of the past we have lived. This is the past that we each carry about with us, that we literally embody, that lengthens and becomes ever more complex as we age – the past that we cannot help but bring to bear upon every one of our successive engagements with people and things. It is also the past that allows us to take for granted what we may have in common with others when we assert ourselves to be, for example, English or African-American or Iranian.

Each one of us is born into a world in the making that is already rendered meaningful in all its material aspects and, over time, we make these meanings anew. To take just one example, the design and use of the space in which a child spends its early life – be it a one-room house in a Fijian village, an apartment in Manhattan, or the felt tent that may be used throughout the summer months by Mongolian pastoralists – accords with the kinds of relationships that take place inside it. The idea that a child as a self-realizing individual should properly have a room to itself may be unarguable from the point of view of a white, middle-class Manhattan apartment dweller; this is simply not an issue for people whose well-being is above all a matter of their ties with others they call kin and in a one-room Fijian house there can be no neutral position, for the space is valued and referred to in such a way that it demands respectful behavior and especially the recognition of fine distinctions of status.

In one way or another, everything the child is learning about the world in the course of daily life implicates its relationship to those other people who live alongside him or her, as well as those people's relationships with one another. This goes for what the child learns about clothes and food and drink, about keeping clean, about gods and/or ancestors, about plants and earth and animals, about pleasure and pain, about space and place, about cars, trains, and aeroplanes, about love and death, about houses and the objects they contain, about number, dreams, sun and stars, and weather, about bodies and sex, about the very rhythm of every day. Literally everything about people, everything they know and everything they do, has reference to particular forms of social relations. And because humans are biologically social animals, the very processes of learning are social too.

In earlier (but still prevailing) models of what it is to be human, "social cognition" is taken to be a particular form of learning, distinct from cognition proper or, in other words, from learning about number for example, or space, or the physical world. From an anthropological point of view, this distinction between social learning and other learning cannot make sense because, as comparative ethnography makes clear, humans are born into a set of social relations and the history of those social relations and we cannot ever step outside the ever-changing dynamic of their continuing significance for us. The challenge from an anthropological perspective is, therefore, to find out how, in any given case, these social relations inform the development of our ideas of the environing world.

As an anthropologist, I am interested in how we human beings come to be who we are and how it comes to be the case that the dynamic and transforming processes that form us are simultaneously conservative. So, for example, despite profound changes wrought by colonization, war, conversion to one world religion or another, the different peoples studied by anthropologists retain their historically differentiated collective uniqueness as Fijians, for example, or English, or Samburu, or Inuit, or Australian Aborigine, or French, and so on and so on. Even in the face of so-called globalization, anthropologists continue to find that relations between people within any given collectivity are characterized by particular forms of kinship, for example, and particular forms of political economy, and informed by particular ideas of self and person-hood, body–mind, gender, and sociality. These social relations and the ideas and practices that inform them are *at once* as subject to trans-formation *and* continuity (conservation) as any other aspect of human being. How can this be so?

My explanation turns on an idea that the conserving and transforming properties of what humans say and do are aspects of the self-same microhistorical process through which we become ourselves. The process is one in which mind is continuously brought into being as a function of the whole person in inter-subjective relations with others in the environing world. Inter-subjectivity is a necessary concept because it alerts us to the way that our understandings of ourselves and the world are founded in our recognition of one another as human and in our relations with one another.

Inter-subjectivity is shorthand for: I know that you are another human like me, and so I know that you know that because I am human, I know that you are too. It is this capacity for recursive thought, or "theory of mind" as psychologists term it, that makes human learning a micro-historical process. Our inter-subjective relationship to one another is always bound to be historically prior because, whenever we encounter one another, we do so as carriers of our own, always unique, history and whenever we speak to one another we speak out of the past that we have lived. I make sense of what you are doing and saying in terms of what I already know: any new information is assimilated to my existing struc-tures of knowing. This process at once transforms that information in the course of its assimilation (and to this extent *conserves* what I already know) and transforms my existing structures of knowing in the course of their inevitable accommodation to the new information (and to this extent *changes* what I know).

In other words, during the course of our early development as children and indeed throughout our lives, our active engagement in the world of people and things effects continuing differentiation of the mental pro-cesses through which we know what we know. Mental processes are subject as much to change as to continuity, but as we grow older the mental processes we bring to bear on the world become progressively less subject to radical change precisely *because* they are already highly developed. The longer they've been functioning to assimilate infor-mation, the more highly differentiated they already are, the less our mental processes can transform as a function of accommodation to new situations. The corollary of this is that young children who immigrate from one country to another rapidly learn a new language and accom-modate to new modes of relating to other people, while mature persons who encounter new ideas and practices willy nilly substantially transform those same ideas and practices in assimilating them to their own. It follows that the developmental process in which, from birth onwards, I constitute my ideas of self and other, of relationship, of the world, is one that in effect conserves (even while it transforms) the ideas and practices I encountered early on and made my own in the course of the day-to-day, many and manifold, inter-subjective relations in which I was nurtured, neglected, loved, rejected, made much of, instructed, played with, ignored, left to my own devices, and so on and so on. Our engagement in the peopled world is always an emotional one and so all our long-held ideas and practices are imbued with a feeling of rightness that goes well beyond any mere rationalization – an observation that holds as much for what we consider it proper to reject as for what we maintain. So, for all we have the world in common we "live the world" as if it conformed to our own ideas of it. Thus despite our thirty years in the same London street, my next-door neighbor and I inhabit different environing worlds: his history lies in Muslim Syria and mine in Irish Catholic Australia and we hold rather different ideas about all kinds of things – except that in our own distinctive ways, we're both Londoners.

Once we begin to understand development as a microhistorical process, we can realize that every human being embodies and manifests his or her own history. It follows that for each and every one of us, the lived present contains within it its own past and its potential future; it is our artifact, an emergent aspect of the way that, as living systems that are human, we function at once to constitute and incorporate our own history – that is, the history of our relations with others in the peopled world. And the lived present is always emergent because we cannot know what today will bring. Transformation, as is clear enough above, is an aspect of how living systems (including humans) function to develop and maintain themselves over time, but while this kind of change is continuous and inevitable, it is not radical in the sense of the kinds of historical changes precipitated, for example, among Pacific peoples by European expansion, colonization, and conversion to Christianity. To the extent that the conditions of our existence are radically changed by major historical events, so our ideas and practices change in accommodating to them.

An anthropology of human development thus enables us to understand how we humans come to differ so profoundly from one another in the ways we are the same, and to be so similar to one another in the ways we are different. Knowing that our development over time is a microhistorical process enables us to see how continuity and change are aspects of one another, rather than separate phenomena. It enables human scientists to analyze the processes through which we each arrive at our certainty that the peopled world conforms to our understanding of it. It enables us to understand better not only other peoples, but also ourselves and our own children. To take just one example, understanding development as a microhistorical process in which we each make sense of the world suggests that TV violence is bound to inform children's ideas of relationship and sociality, gender and personhood, just by virtue of the child's making sense of what he or she sees on the screen. Parents do not and cannot make their children into what they are or become; what parents and other adults do is structure the conditions in which the child comes to know itself and the world of people and things.

So what is to be learned from an anthropology of human development? First, that we humans are in every case remarkably different in the ways we're the same, and by the same token extraordinarily similar in the ways we're different; we're at once united and kept apart by whatever history we have in common. Second, that if an anthropologist, sociologist, or psychologist is to understand the particular humans who are the object of their studies it makes sense to begin with an awareness that every human being incorporates the history of his or her relations with others – a history that is at once social and personal, physical and psychological – and that to explain any aspect of what it is to be human demands an explanation of this microhistorical process or at least an acknowledgment of it. Third, that neither as academics nor as policy-makers should we presume to know what is good for others: where we do so it's almost bound to be the case that we're imposing on others conditions that may be good for us but probably not for them; and this is so even where (hand on heart) we have consulted with those we aim to help – the problem here being that even to ask the relevant questions requires real, in-depth, long-term knowledge about the people with whom we're speaking and the real respect in which such knowledge is founded. This observation holds as much for studies undertaken "at home" – in predominantly white, middle-class, suburban Sydney, for example – as it does for those carried out in Benin or Fiji or Madagascar.

The fundamental condition then, of finding out about others, lies in knowing that really and truly you know nothing about them, but that you can come to know something provided you grant to all those others the same humanity that you grant yourself: that is, that because *all* our ideas and practices are historical products, what others say and do is *as valid* in its humanity as what we say and do ourselves. Who knows but that by understanding how this can be, we may arrive at some deeper (more humble, more compassionate, more skeptical) insights into ourselves.

# 12   The social child

*Tim Ingold*

## The theory of socialization

In every society, in every generation, children grow up to become knowledgeable members of the communities in which they live. Sociologists and anthropologists have classically described this process as one of socialization. The new-born child, they say, comes into the world as an entirely *asocial* being – equipped, to be sure, with certain innate response mechanisms, but without any of the information that enables adults to function as persons in the social world. Socialization, then, is the process whereby this information is taken on board. Among other things, the child acquires rules for categorizing and positioning other people in the social environment, and guidelines for appropriate action towards them. Consider, for example, the way a child learns to behave towards kin. It is taught to recognize the people in its familiar surroundings as belonging to specific categories – such as (in our society) mother, father, uncle, aunt, brother, sister, cousin, etc. – and that for each category, certain kinds of behavior are appropriate or inappropriate. Furnished with the rudiments of the kinship system, the child can then begin to participate in social life. The originally asocial infant has become a social being, a *person*, equipped to play his or her part *vis-à-vis* other persons on the stage of society.

This view of socialization has to be understood in the context of general ideas about humanity and nature that are deeply embedded in our own, so-called "western" tradition of thought and science. Of course we recognize that non-human animals undergo processes of development, taking them from infancy to maturity. For animals of many species this process goes on in a thoroughly social milieu – think of elephants, for example, or wolves, or chimpanzees, all of which spend much time in the company of their own kind and relate to one another in manifold and complex ways, just as human beings do. Yet, whereas we are inclined to regard the growth of the animal as a purely biological process, wholly confined within the world of nature, we are equally convinced that there is *more* to humans than their biology – that although each of us may start out, at birth, as biological organisms, wholly ignorant of society and culture, we nevertheless end up as persons with specific social identities and cultural competencies. Somehow, it seems, humans are supposed to grow out of biology and into culture, or out of the world of nature and into the world of society. It is by the very measure that the human *transcends* nature that he or she is regarded not "merely" as an animal but as a social and moral being. Through their socialization, in short, human beings are said to be "raised up" from their natural state, in infancy, to a state of social completion.

## From learning as socialization to a socialized theory of learning

I want to stress three points about this classical account of learning as socialization. First, the notion that children are molded through the experience of socialization – as though they were but passive recipients of rules and representations that "descend" on them from above – is decidedly adult-centered. It reflects the failure of social scientists, until recently, to recognize that children are agents with purposes and perspectives of their own. In reality children are involved, as much as are their teachers, as active and creative participants in the learning process. They participate by making their own contribution to shaping the contexts in which learning occurs and knowledge is generated. Whether we are talking about an interaction at home between mother and infant, or in a western schoolroom between teacher and pupils, these contexts are *negotiated*. One way of putting this would be to say that socialization is a two-way process, in which children are agents in the socialization of their parents as much as are parents agents in the socialization of their children.

The second point follows. If socialization entails the active participation of both children and grown-ups, then it cannot be a *prelude* in the career of each individual for his or her entry into the world of society. Far from starting out on the margins of this world, children can learn only because they are fully involved in it to begin with. Indeed every infant embarks on life from the very center of the social world, and begins at once to interact with other people in his or her surroundings. Thus socialization is not preliminary to involvement in social life, as rehearsal is preliminary to performance. Rather, it is above all through the "hands on" experience of engaging with others in practical situations of everyday life that learning takes place. Children learn not to gain entry to the social world but to make their way within it.

Nor does learning end with childhood, and this brings me to my third point. Of course childhood experience may have a formative quality, underwriting all that occurs in later life. But adult experience too, especially that of raising children, can be transformative. As I have already mentioned, parents continue to be socialized by their children, and even grandparents by their grandchildren, as well as vice versa. When you look at it this way, it is clear that socialization – if we are to call it that – is a process that carries on over an individual's entire lifetime. There is no point in the life-cycle at which socialization could be said to be "complete," marking off the period of preparation from the attainment of full personhood.

In short, if we are to describe learning as socialization, then we must also acknowledge that this process is always two-way, that it continues from cradle to grave, and indeed that it is integral to the knowledge-generating practices of the lived-in world. For my part, however, socialization is a word I would rather not use. It is hard, with a word like this, to get away from the image of shaping up a biologically given raw material to a finished, socially prescribed state. I contend, to the contrary, that learning is never finished, any more than is social life itself, and that people do not, in the course of their lives, become any *less* biological, or any *more* social or cultural, since they are simultaneously biological, social, and cultural from beginning to end. Learning is a social process; it is not a process in which individual human beings are turned into social persons. To accommodate this view, we need to replace the theory of learning as socialization with a socialized theory of learning.

## Learning as enskillment

If socialization is not apt to describe what is going on when children learn, what word should we use instead? I prefer *enskillment*. By this I mean that learning is comparable to what goes on in situations of apprenticeship, in which the artisan learns the skills of a trade by hands-on experience, under the tutelage of an accomplished master. To establish this view of learning as enskillment, I want to isolate, and criticize, four assumptions that are built into conventional theories according to which learning involves the "internalization" of a ready-formed body of objective knowledge.

### Assumption 1: Knowledge is given in advance of its implementation in practical settings

This assumption follows directly from the conventional idea that culture consists of a body of information that is "passed along" like a relay baton from one generation to the next. In psychological literature, the distinction between the inter-generational transfer of information, and its application in practice, is made by means of a contrast between *social* and *individual* learning. Thus you might, for example, acquire a set of recipes for cookery by social learning, but making them work calls for practice in the kitchen – that would be individual learning. But this is not how I teach my daughter to break eggs in a mixing bowl. Rather, we are together in the kitchen; my hand holds hers, which holds the egg, and together we break it, so that she can get the feel of just how hard to knock the egg against the bowl. Every egg is different, but you learn from practice to judge from the sound of the first, tentative knock how hard to strike the second time. There are no rules for this, no instructions. There can be no program for cracking an egg. It is a knack that we have to discover for ourselves. But we do so under guidance from others already skilled in the art. This process of *guided rediscovery* is surely social, yet it takes place within the very context of our practical engagement in the kitchen.

*Assumption 2: Knowledge is located "inside" the individual rather than "out there" in the world*

Much work on social learning and socialization rests on the idea that, in some mysterious way, external knowledge is brought across a barrier into the mind of the child. Accordingly, learning is conceived as a process of *internalization*. I believe this idea has to be rejected. Even in the western schoolroom, where the explicit aim is to pass on authorized knowledge from teacher to pupil, what the pupil learns may not be quite the same as what he or she is taught. Whether in the kitchen or the classroom, knowledge is not simply "passed down" to the child from an authoritative source in society, but is continually generated in the inter-personal contexts of joint activity, in which more experienced hands lend guidance and support to novice participants. This is how, in the kitchen, novices learn to crack eggs. Likewise in the classroom, the information that children receive from their teachers or textbooks only becomes knowledge in so far as it is incorporated, in the course of their maturation and development, into their own patterns of awareness and response. Thus there is no question of knowledge crossing a barrier from the outside to the inside. Novices grow into knowledge rather than having it handed down to them. This knowledge is not an internal property of human minds, but is rather a property of the whole system of relations set up by the presence of the practitioner in a richly structured environment. We cannot, for example, say whether knowledge of cookery is on the side of the cook or the kitchen. For you only get an omelette from a cook-in-the-kitchen.

### Assumption 3: Each individual learns for him- or herself in isolation from contexts of participation in everyday social life

This assumption underlies the organizational structure, and even the physical layout, of many of the more traditional teaching institutions of the western world. Thus the classroom is marked out as a dedicated space for learning, insulated from the world outside its doors where the knowledge acquired therein is eventually to be applied. And however many pupils may be seated there, each is conceived in theory as an independent learning unit, equipped with desk and writing materials to work on their own. They are not supposed to communicate among themselves. In practice, the enforcement of such an arrangement is more likely to be detrimental than conducive to learning. For children do not learn in isolation, in settings removed from those of everyday life. Whether inside or outside the classroom, they learn with one another and with more experienced partners through guided participation in the tasks of everyday life. This view of learning, in which the role of teachers or mentors is not so much to pass on ready-made knowledge as to provide the scaffolding that enables novices to grow into it, was originally advocated by the Russian psychologist Lev Vygotsky. Influenced by Vygotsky's theory, many anthropologists have begun to approach learning as a matter of *understanding in practice*, by contrast to the idea of *acquiring culture* entailed in orthodox models of learning as the intergenerational transmission of information. The practitioner who understands is one whose action *on* things is grounded in an active, sensuous involvement *with* them, who watches, listens, and feels as he or she works, and responds with care, judgment, and dexterity.

### Assumption 4: The transmission of knowledge is separate from its generation

If learning were simply a matter of handing down the knowledge traditions of a culture, then we would have to look elsewhere to find the sites where knowledge is actually created. The assumption is that learners can contribute nothing to the knowledge base of a society. They can only receive what comes to them from those deemed to be more knowledgeable than themselves. Yet although the adult members of a society charged with the instruction of the young might imagine that education consists in the transmission of already established knowledge and values from those who know more to those who know less, the reality is that knowledge undergoes continual regeneration within the interactive contexts of learning. It is impossible, then, to separate knowledge transmission from knowledge generation. There is no difference, in practice, between learning culture and creating culture, since the contexts of learning are the very crucibles from which the cultural process unfolds. In this process, what each generation contributes to the next is not a body of representations or instructions – that is "information" in the strict sense – but rather the specific contexts of development in which novices, through practice and training, can acquire and fine-tune their own capacities of action and perception.

## Conclusion

The study of learning, up to now, has tended to be two-pronged. Anthropologists have concentrated on the cultural content of what is transmitted across generations, while psychologists have focused on the "mechanisms," allegedly universal, by which the human mind is able to take up the information presented to it. I believe this dual approach is unhelpful. For learning, as I have shown, is not really a process of transmission at all, nor is culture a body of information that is downloaded from one generation to the next. It is very misleading to think of the mind as a container whose ready-made and universal capacities are filled with all manner of specific cultural content. The minds of novices are not so much "filled up" with the stuff of culture, as "tuned up" to the particular circumstances of the environment. It is this tuning that enables them to make their way in the world. And wherever they are, there is always somewhere further they can go. Thus learning continually overshoots its destinations, and astonishes us with the discovery of capabilities and possibilities we had never dreamed of before. Astonishment is both the engine and the reward of learning. Nothing more stifles the spirit, or is more inimical to human development, than a system of education that insists on closure and that measures advance by the march, along a predetermined route, to a fixed and final target.

SUGGESTED READINGS

Bruner, J. S. (1986). *Actual minds, possible worlds*. Cambridge, MA: Harvard University Press.
Geertz, C. (1973). *The interpretation of cultures*. New York: Basic Books.
Goldschmidt, W. (1993). On the relationship between biology and anthropology. *Man* (n.s.), 28, 341–359.

Ingold, T. (2000). *The perception of the environment: essays on livelihood, dwelling and skill*. London: Routledge.

Lave, J. (1990). The culture of acquisition and the practice of understanding. In J. W. Stigler, R. A. Shweder, and G. Herdt (eds.), *Cultural psychology: essays on comparative human development*. Cambridge: Cambridge University Press.

Lave, J., and E. Wenger (1991). *Situated learning: legitimate peripheral participation*. Cambridge: Cambridge University Press.

Palsson, G. (1994). Enskilment at sea. *Man* (n.s.) 29, 901–927.

Poole, F. J. P. (1994). Socialization, enculturation and the development of personal identity. In T. Ingold (ed.), *Companion encyclopedia of anthropology: humanity, culture and social life*. London: Routledge.

Rogoff, B. (1990). *Apprenticeship in thinking: cognitive development in social context*. New York: Oxford University Press.

Schwartz, T. (1981). The acquisition of culture. *Ethos*, 9, 4–17.

Toren, C. (1993). Making history: the significance of childhood cognition for a comparative anthropology of mind. *Man* (n.s.), 28, 461–478.

Trevarthen, C., and K. Logotheti (1989). Child in society, society in children: the nature of basic trust. In S. Howell and R. Willis (eds.), *Societies at peace*. London: Routledge.

Vygotsky, L. (1978). *Mind in society: the development of higher psychological processes*. Cambridge, MA: Harvard University Press.

# 13 Learning about human development from a study of educational failure

*Gillian Evans*

In 1996, the then Chief Inspector of Schools in England referred to the problem of boys' increasing failure to match girls' achievements in school; particularly problematic, he suggested, was white working-class boys' failure to learn. By 2003 statistics revealed that only 18 percent of white working-class boys at school-leaving age (sixteen years old) achieved the minimum of five or more formal exam passes with grades between A and C. Marginally worse were Afro-Caribbean boys, of whom only 16 percent achieved a basic standard in secondary school qualifications, while boys from immigrant families of Indian, Pakistani, Bangladeshi, and Chinese origin were outstripping White and Afro-Caribbean boys' achievements.

Evident here is a classificatory confusion between race, class, nationality, and ethnicity, and it poses real problems for comparison. Leaving this aside, however, a focus on white working-class boys alone suggests that every year 30,000 boys in England are leaving secondary school with no formal qualifications. By school-leaving age their educational level is likely to be on par with boys just finishing their first year at secondary school at the age of eleven and, in any year, 10,000 white working-class boys are disappearing completely from the school system. Highlighting the failure of the majority of white working-class boys to do well at school allows us to reflect critically too on the educational failure of the majority of Afro-Caribbean boys, which is a problem that is usually characterized and analyzed in racial, and not class or cultural terms. Are these boys failing because they are working-class or because they are Afro-Caribbean? Why are white boys classified according to class and black boys according to an encompassing Afro-Caribbean identity? If white working-class boys and Afro-Caribbean boys are both failing because of issues to do with class, then why aren't they classified together? And what exactly is going wrong when a child's class position becomes an indicator of the likelihood of failing to do well at school?

The focus of educational research in the last twenty years has been on gender, race, and multiculturalism, with little or no attention being paid to the continuing relevance of class position to educational achievement and how it might be articulated with other social distinctions such as race, gender, and culture. It seems that educational sociologists and other social scientists don't know what to do about class anymore. Indeed, economic indicators might suggest that, as Prime Minister Tony Blair observed in 1998 "we're all middle class now" – a remark which, presaging as it did the death of the working-class in England, caused a furore in the tabloid press. Having lived for twelve years on a working-class council estate in Bermondsey, Southeast London, I was not surprised; so far as I could see the people I thought of as working-class people were alive and kicking. But I started to think about what it means to be working or middle class. I wasn't thinking in Marxist terms about people's differentiated relations to the means of production. Class for me was an ethnographic not an analytical category; it implied a value judgment and referred to everyday distinctions between kinds of persons in England.

Read any nineteenth-century novel and it is clear that social standing in England is about a complicated and emotive combination of two key variables: the amount of money a person has access to – which of course is to do with relationship to the means of production – and manners, which are to do with a way of being in the world and are what Bermondsey people refer to in contemporary times as their *culture*. Manners understood in this more general sense, as a way of being in the world, stand for upbringing, and point to the history of how one has come to take for granted the person one is. Taking a developmental perspective enables us to recover that history. We can then explain how, through a process of learning in childhood, people develop a particular set of manners or what might also be called a specific bodily or embodied disposition towards the world and other people in it.

What follows provides a brief ethnographic account of how a white working-class boy may develop into what people where I did my field research call *a Bermondsey bod* and, in the course of achieving his reputation, inevitably fail at school.

## Being a man in Bermondsey

Bermondsey in central southeast London is an area that occupies roughly a square mile south of the river Thames and between London Bridge in the West and Tower Bridge in the East. During the industrial revolution Bermondsey was known as the larder of London because of an industry focused around dockside factories processing foodstuffs imported from countries the world over. Nowadays, despite demographic disruption and profound economic transformations arising from the closure of the docks in the 1970s, a core of white working-class ex-dockers and factory workers, their families and descendants, continue to imagine the community in terms of closely knit ties of both residence and kinship criteria or what people refer to as being *born and bred Bermondsey*. The historical precedence of fierce territorial rivalry between Bermondsey people and Roaders, who are white working-class people living on the wrong side of the major through roads which form the south western and southern boundaries, undermines any idea of a homogenous white-working-class in London and emphasizes what anyone moving through London should know: white working-class London is divided into manors about which people continue to be fiercely proud.

Apart from these territorial distinctions there are several other relevant distinctions within Bermondsey itself. Firstly I discovered that social class distinctions are best understood in terms of the kinds of differences that people themselves find relevant. They distinguish between two kinds of persons in England: common and posh. Further distinctions are then drawn between kinds of common people in Bermondsey itself, but the differences between common people recede in the face of the perceived threat to the basis of community belonging that is posed by the increasing presence of non-white people, including first and second-generation immigrants of African, Asian, and African-Caribbean origin, who are thought of by so-called *real Bermondsey* people as outsiders who don't belong. This perception of threat, which takes the form of a death knell for Bermondsey, has led in contemporary times to a shift in the idea of group relatedness among real Bermondsey people away from kinship and residence criteria and towards an explicit discourse of ultra-conservative cultural nationalism, which is racially conceived of as a whiteness which has to be defended against the threat of blackness.

Apart from a reputation for "racism," Bermondsey men also have a notoriously violent and criminal reputation, especially for thieving; the status of gangsters is mythologized. The truth, however, is that the majority of men are trying to make an honest wage. Some have taken up employment in the new industries like newspaper publishing, but everyone knows someone who is making "a little something extra on the side" and there is a ready supply of stolen goods. The point to emphasize is that, in Bermondsey, boys are coming to terms with their developing masculinity in a place where what it means to be a man is far removed from the idea that teachers and other education professionals have about what it is legitimate for a boy to aspire to be. In Bermondsey it is important to understand that the development and reproduction of economic and political relations are inseparable from the specific means of getting prestige which, in school and on the street, means that boys, to be valued, must get respect by cultivating a reputation. This involves learning how to withstand violent intimidation and, in time, learning how to be intimidating as the best means of defense against the intimidation of others.

There, on the street, and eventually in school, as a result of belonging to a group of boys for whom being intimidating and learning to withstand intimidation is a social good, Bermondsey boys (*bods*) develop status and influence; they become Lords of what they call their own *manor*, which is the area of Bermondsey. But having a reputation on the street doesn't sit easily alongside the humility required for doing as one is told at school, or for initial success at the bottom of the employment ladder, which is the place where *bods* with no qualifications find themselves. Little by little, therefore, the door opens wider to educational failure and the world of illegitimate gains that *bods* are accustomed to through the criminal lives of one or more of their fathers, uncles, cousins, or older siblings.

My eighteen months of concentrated fieldwork – in school, on the street, in youth clubs, in pubs and clubs – provided me with an appreciation of the various means of gaining social status in Bermondsey. Without this, it would have been impossible for me to draw a more complex picture of the likely reasons for white working-class boys' educational failure. The question becomes not so much: why are white working-class boys failing at school? But rather: *which* white working-class boys are failing at school?

### Tom and Mary

At Tenter Ground Primary School in Bermondsey I meet ten-year-old Tom; he lives with his mum, step-dad, and younger sister in a two bedroom flat on an old housing association estate opposite the school. Tom's mother Anne is a *born and bred* Bermondsey woman; her husband and Tom's step-father, Pete, is a dustman; he is the father of her second child, Tom's little sister Mary, who is seven years old. At home, Tom is a complete Mummy's boy, often sitting on his mother's lap for a cuddle while she steals a reluctant kiss from him. They share a joking relationship in which he plays teasing games with her, cheeking her back when she tries to give him instructions and corrections. He knows how to go as far as he dares before she chases him, her hand raised in good humor, threatening to clout him. Laughing loudly, Tom often runs from the room to escape Anne's clutches and when her nagging gets him down he runs freely outside onto the street, which demands from him an entirely different disposition. Knowing that his parents are fiercely protective over him, a Bermondsey boy *bowls* (walks like a tough boy) because his parents and older siblings' or cousins' reputations are behind him. In general things couldn't be more different for Tom's sister Mary. She is not allowed to play out unless she is safe in the garden square at the back of the flats and she is quieter and more serious than Tom, spending more time at home playing close to her parents' company. Mary is extremely feminine, immaculately turned out with waist-length straight brown hair that is lovingly tended by Anne. She enjoys reading and writing and is at least three years in advance of Tom's reading ability even though she is three years younger than him. Commenting on the difference between her two children, Anne says, "Tom? Tom's common as muck, he's got a mouth on him, no doubt about that. He's like me really, not like Mary. She's gentle like her Dad and well spoken." Mary, who is her teacher's favorite at school, often teases Tom at home because she can read better than her older brother who is always in trouble at school.

### Learning and caring

The social organization of Tom's classroom, like all the others, is characterized by a distinctive spatio-temporal rhythm related to the teacher's attempts to manage the children's behavior. Stillness, quiet attention to what the teacher says, and concentration on working through designated tasks within a specific time, signify children's application to formal learning. The tranquility required of children involves the suppression of their desire to move about, engage with each other and objects around them as they please, and to make noise as they move from one space and activity to another.

As children's movement and language is constrained at school, so they learn in time what kind of participation is required of them at particular times in specific spaces. This requirement is first of all a bodily disposition, a restraint that embodies order and readiness for concentrated application to work that demands thinking – here to be understood as a conceptual mastery of abstract symbols. That this requirement is difficult for some children to achieve is clear to see in the frequent interventions of the teacher, who devotes a large measure of her energies to trying to manage their bodily comportment. The children who have most difficulty with this kind of restraint are boys and particular boys are the worst offenders. Their inability to participate appropriately in the classroom means that these boys are quickly labeled as badly behaved and said to have emotional and behavioral difficulties. It is the individual boy who has a problem; he is rendered pathological while the peer group as a social phenomenon and the problem it poses to teachers is never considered. Therefore the form that classroom participation takes and the discrepancy between this and the kinds of participation that boys require of each other is never considered to be problematic. The whole of the school day as it unfolds in the spaces of the building becomes a virtual battle ground in which the fight to inculcate in children a disposition towards formal learning is waged against their more fundamental desire to play, move, interact freely and competitively, and make noise. The extreme expression of this more general conflict is witnessed in the teacher's continuous focus on managing the comportment and misbehavior of the most disruptive boys. Tom is by no means the worst offender, but he struggles to get through a school day without getting into trouble and the amount of time he devotes to learning anything through schoolwork is minimal. As a result he is far behind the age-related expectations for academic ability in his class and finds himself in the lowest ability group for both numeracy and literacy.

The opposite of the learned disposition that teachers require of children in the classroom is the playful, rowdy, intimidating, sometimes violent, apparently frenetic movements of particular boys. They assert their presence to each other and to other children in ways that enable the reconstitution on a daily basis of the pecking order of their disruptive, as opposed to academic, dominance. The dynamic of this volatile process works alongside and periodically interferes with the pace of the teacher's rhythm for curriculum delivery. A large measure of the teacher's and children's emotional and physical resources are preoccupied by having to cope with the heightening tension and challenge to authority that disruptive boys' distraction from their own and other children's learning creates.

In *common* households like Anne's, for example, an appreciation of the value of formal learning rarely takes the form of shared activity during the early relationship of caring between mother/father/carer and child. Whereas at school learning and caring are considered to be synonymous, in common households they are not. This does not mean that the failure of individual children, like Tom, to learn well at school, means, as education professionals at school are apt to conclude, that common parents don't care for their children. Certainly it was true that there were serious troubles in Tom's home; the home and the stability of family life was disrupted by Tom's mother's problems, all of which would lead the educational professionals to believe that their interpretation of Tom's behavior at school was the correct one. They might conclude that boys who are disruptive at school have mothers, or other primary carers, whose abilities to care for their children have been disrupted. They wouldn't be entirely wrong. All of the six most disruptive boys in Tom's class, including Tom, were living in households in which, somehow or other, the mother's capacity to care for her children was disrupted. My research demonstrates, however, that the educational professionals' hypothesis is only partial and therefore not as helpful as it might be.

Take Tom's sister, Mary, for example. She is well suited to, enjoys and is doing well at formal learning in school. Mary throws a spanner in the education professionals' hypothesis. If disruptive boys come from disrupted homes with deficient caring relations that render the boys pathological, why isn't the same thing happening to their sisters? Tentatively I suggest that it is because they do not usually have the same degree of freedom to play on the streets, as their brothers are more likely to do. Girls are less likely, therefore, to participate in peer groups in which being tough, looking for trouble, and resisting authority are ways to gain prestige. These boys are not pathological and neither is their home life necessarily deficient. It is just that the form of participation these kinds of boys require of each other on the street is deemed to be an illegitimate form of development because it conflicts with, and disrupts, the forms of participation that are required and legitimated at school. Gender differences are, therefore, always going to be educationally significant in schools in areas where boys enjoy a large measure of freedom to compete violently for prestige on the streets. At the very least then, we need to understand how class and gender intersect in order to be able to explain the failure of certain kinds of white working-class boys to do well at school. With an adequate theory of the person and a commitment to building a systematic body of cross-cultural evidence we should also be able to explain so much more.

### Learning as social and situational process

My research is concerned to bring to an analysis of social class an ethnographic understanding of what it means to be white and working class in England today. This means that I want to understand it, as far as possible, in the way that the working-class people themselves live and understand the distinctions they are preoccupied with. I focus on how children come to embody a developing sense of their class disposition as a differentiated set of manners – that is, a specific way of being in the world – because I am interested in how this disposition affects their chances of success at school.

I take a developmental perspective because I am interested precisely in trying to recover, for purposes of analysis, the history of how we come to be who we are – uniquely particular and collectively distinctive kinds of persons. In order to understand this process of becoming a particular kind of person – whether Maori rugby player, Inuit fisherman, Yoruba drummer, Masai warrior, or white working-class English man – I need a theory of learning that can help me to explain (a) how each of these men becomes what they are because of similar processes of human development and (b) how they come to be so different as men. Understanding human development means making sense of the specificity of the history that one is living through and, in living through it, bringing history into being.

Clearly this theory of learning is not confined to, but can encompass, the specific form of classroom learning. I call it a theory of the person because it is concerned with the development of the whole person; it isn't just relevant to studies of education, social class, gender, race, or culture, because it is to do with human being and becoming in its broadest sense. Of course there is nothing new about turning to the study of children and childhood; social scientists have often utilized a developmental perspective in order to try and understand how things have come to be the way they are among adults. In anthropology, for example, this approach began in the 1930s with the American "culture and personality" theorists' concern to understand, through studying children, how a relationship arises between distinctive "cultures" and the "patterning" of "personality." Conventionally the emphasis was placed on culture or society and everything that stands outside the child as a conditioning force, but this approach ignored how the child actively brings itself into being – that is, how the child develops by making sense of who it can be in relation to the ideas that others have about what it is appropriate to be and become. What is required then is a theory of learning that explains development as an intrinsically social process without falling back on the assumption of socialization where the child can only be the more-or-less passive recipient of adult ideas. The challenge is to get a sense of the processes through which the child dynamically comes to know itself on an on-going, minute-by-minute basis, by making sense, in practice, of its social position *vis-à-vis* others.

At school, for example, children are trying to understand what adults expect of them and at the same time they are also making sense of their own and other children's ideas about what it means more generally to be a child. The discrepancies between adults' and children's ideas about what it means to be a child can be huge. For the researcher who is preoccupied with children's development and who does not take adult ideas about children to be necessarily representative of children's experiences, it is as if children inhabit parallel worlds in which they are preoccupied at one and the same time with each other and their own concerns, and with always having to make sense of and attempting to conform to or resist adult ideas about how children should behave. Furthermore, children at school are simultaneously learning about the difference between what is expected of them by the adults and children they encounter there, and what is required of them at home and in other more familiar places in the neighborhoods they live in.

Comparisons and contrasts between the ways that children learn in these different situations often reveal discrepancies in children's behavior. These discrepancies, when examined further, indicate that what children learn and indeed the way that they learn is specific to *the situation in which they are learning*. This has important implications for the way that we make studies of children and child development. We cannot assume, for example, that because we think we know how a particular child or even a group of children behaves in one situation – a school classroom for example – that we have understood that child or children and can predict how they will behave in another situation, such as at home, or on the street.

So, when trying to investigate what it means to be a child who is learning how to become a particular kind of person, it is important that research be conducted in as many situations as possible. And because ideas are always substantiated in social practice, social practice becomes the principal object of study. In particular, the recognition that learning is situationally specific should lead us always to seek to find out what are the various forms of participation that are required of children in the many and various social situations in which they are all the time learning what it means to become a particular kind of person.

# 14   Dynamic views of education

*Lynette Friedrich Cofer*

A Navajo medicine man of great age and wisdom was asked to relate the story of how children were taught in the old ways to find knowledge, purpose in life, and harmony with nature. He spoke of the teachings of the elders about daily running to the East to greet the dawn with prayers.

He runs races early in the mornings. He takes snow baths and ice water plunges in the winter. He is advised to run as far as he could and back and to yell at the top of his voice as he runs to develop strong lungs and a loud voice. He must blow all the evil things out of his system, like cheating, hate, stealing, jealousy, greed, and lying. He must inhale the good clean air that comes with the dawn in long deep breaths, which is like taking in good health, prosperous life, and harmony with beauty. These are the teachings of the elders and we did what they told us to do. When one sleeps until sunrise, his voice will not be heard. If he yells into the early dawn like the coyote, you will have a strong voice to sing loud and clear without getting out of breath. This is so true because I still have a strong voice at my age and can sing all night yet.

His account is a life story about connections among all levels of experience – physical, mental, and spiritual. He looks back on the joy he felt in running as a young child; the pride he took in being able to endure the icy water and follow the guidance of the elders. He speaks of the relations he experienced with nature as he ran to celebrate the dawn, drawing in pure air with alertness, resolve, and self-control, expelling those aspects of self that limit relations with others. His body led the way to knowledge from childhood to old age.

In the long history of education, many societies have sought to help children realize individual potential and achieve harmony with others and with nature. The desires of early US educators to foster personal and societal connections are clear in the appeals for the common school by Horace Mann as well as proposals by later reformers, notably John Dewey. For an individual to become an effective member of a demo-cratic community, Dewey believed the child must have "training in science, in art, in history; command of the fundamental methods of inquiry and the fundamental tools of intercourse and communication" as well as "a trained and sound body, skillful eye and hand; habits of industry, perseverance, and, above all, habits of serviceableness." Children had to be leaders as well as followers, with "powers of self-direction and power of directing others, powers of administration, ability to assume positions of responsibility" as citizens and workers. In a rapidly changing society, schools needed to provide children with training that would given them self-possession as well as adaptability, a sense of cultural ownership through participation, and the power to shape and direct social change.

Dewey's transactional views have much in common with current dynamic systems approaches. In dynamic systems views, development is about relationships, as organisms and human individuals grow in living systems. All traits, whether physical or behavioral, are the result of developmental processes both within the individual and between the individual and its surround. Educational plans, to be realistic, must view the child in school as an individual within a network of relationships that may or may not foster healthy patterns of development. Evaluation efforts, too, need to include careful examination of embodied individual children across time in classrooms within local schools. The child is not the blank recipient of a given practice, but the co-creator of new meanings with teachers and other students. Those meanings can be positive, leading to new alertness and involvement with school, excitement about learning, and feelings of connection with the wider culture. New meanings, however, can be negative, and lead to feelings of fatigue, isolation, failure, and decisions to drop out of school. The latest federally mandated educational reforms represent the most sweeping attempts to influence public education in US history. Those attempts have already yielded changes that reverberate through the system and can be examined in light of dynamic views of human development.

George Bush's plan to reform education (Bush, 2001) was given the label "No Child Left Behind" (NCLB) and enacted in 2002 after receiving approval from a huge majority of both parties. There were many proponents of the legislation who believed that the plight of children who were poor, from minority or immigrant families, or in special education needed to be addressed at the federal level. These children were not receiving the same quality of teaching or being held to the same standards and expectations as children from more affluent families. Schools were to be reformed to end educational inequalities that prevented these children from gaining access to the American dream. Now, more than two years later, educators, legislators, and entire states are in what educational reformer George Wood has called "open revolt" against NCLB. Tracing some of these developments provides a powerful example of the unintended consequences of applying a linear, single causal approach to complex social problems.

The nub of the NCLB proposition is "accountability," as measured by standardized test scores. The efficacy of all schools and districts is to be evaluated through federally approved tests. States are told when and how tests are to be administered and in which subjects. State implementation plans must be approved at the federal level. Each identified sub-group must show "Adequate Yearly Progress" (AYP) every year in order to achieve 100 percent proficiency in math and reading by 2014. On this single performance criterion, schools that raise their scores escape punishment and may qualify for professional development for teachers, funding of math and science partnerships with universities, and grants for technology. Failure to raise scores may result in the loss of federal monies and funds for Title I, the program that gives additional help and resources to low income children. Federal sanctions for schools include financial penalties such as state payment for children to transfer to "higher performing" schools of their choice and to obtain vouchers for supplemental service providers, such as the for-profit Sylvan Learning Centers. More dire consequences include loss of jobs for principals, pay and job loss for teachers, and school closures. The states are responsible, without additional remuneration, for record keeping, reporting, and conducting augmented levels of supervision over local schools and districts.

In the two years since the inception of NCLB widespread protests have taken place by state policymakers of both parties who decry drains on state budgets and intrusions into state autonomy. Nine states have taken steps to block the use of state or local funds to implement this legislation or to opt out of its requirements by refusing federal monies. They note that the government has failed to fund NCLB by some $17 billion to date and that the added costs of meeting sanctions go well beyond budget estimates. Although federal money accounts for only 10 percent of all education spending, the new federal regulations require 100 percent "accountability." Moreover, the gap between wealthy and poor schools has expanded. A new study by the Education Trust documents the effects of recession on state and local budgets. Wealthier districts compensated for much of the slowdown by raising property taxes, a response few high poverty districts could manage. States have no federal money to help as they have to try to meet the requirements of NCLB (*New York Times* 10/6/04).

Examples of negative, unintended consequences of the standardized test mandate abound, and researchers predict that nearly all schools in all states will fail under the law's criteria within a few years – including many that already score high and others that show improvement. Stanford Education Professor Linda Darling-Hammond cites states like Minnesota, where nearly 80 percent of the schools are "failing," because states with the highest standards will have the most schools found wanting, even if their students achieve at levels substantially above those in other states. So schools can be inadvertently rewarded for lowering standards, and many have done just that. There is no comparability among states on standards. Schools can also be deemed "failures" because one sub-group, e.g. Asian students, had one or two too few present on test day, or several new immigrant children who had not achieved language "proficiency" within months took the test.

But the ripples go beyond the issue of underfunded one-way mandates and application of labels. Holding schools to tough test standards was supposed to increase effectiveness. Initial reports from Texas indicated huge gains in scores and reduced gaps between the average scores of white students and students of color – the so-called "Texas Miracle" – the model for NCLB. But by 2000, analyses of test data and graduation rates by Walter Haney and other independent foundation analysts revealed that dropout rates for Black and Hispanic adolescents had risen markedly after ten years of testing. More than 50 percent of minority adolescents did not graduate from high school. The "improvement" was simply an artifact of the high dropout rate of the lowest-scoring students. The gap between minorities and Whites had widened.

Further doubt was cast on Texas test scores by the fact that national test scores had not increased over the period, and there was a large increase in the number of students failed who needed to repeat 9th grade, the year before the critical 10th grade test was required. So with all incentives tied to test scores, it became better for some children never to make it to 10th grade. Sadly, the "push-out/dropout" finding for minority group children has now been documented in a number of states. Linda Darling-Hammond notes growing evidence that policies that reward or sanction schools based on average student scores (rather than tracking individual scores over time) create incentives to retain low-scorers in grade and encourage them to leave school. Many of the steepest increases in test scores have occurred in schools with the highest retention and dropout rates.

The emphasis on test scores has already led to changes within class-rooms, often demoralizing teachers and discrediting their efforts to create knowledge with children. Rice University Professor Linda McNeil's ethnographic case studies of Texas schools identify the "mandating of noncurriculum." Teachers are forced to spend sub-stantial class time directing students to bubble in answers and learn to recognize "distractors." Scarce school funds are spent not only on tests but for test-prep materials and consultants from private test companies who "train" teachers to use the TAAS-prep kits. Teachers are forced to set aside their own best knowledge and drill students on information whose primary (often sole) usefulness is its likely inclusion on the test. "The testing, by having students select among provided responses, negated teachers' desires that their students construct meaning, that they come to understandings or that they connect course content with their prior knowledge." Rote test preparation takes time from class participatory in real curriculum. Of particular concern are her findings that the education of minority children is most compromised by content dominated by "basics" and test drill.

The dismal picture that is emerging is that those students most in need of help, the children policy-makers intended to help through NCLB, are being most harmed. Poor schools are poorer, and the law concentrates the costs and burdens of implementing its public school choice requirement on high-poverty urban districts. Only a tiny minority of children have been able to use the school transfer option and most went merely from one school with low-achieving levels to another school with similarly low-achieving levels. There are more serious teacher retention problems in these same schools, but more progress is asked from them than from less diverse, affluent schools. Schools are at once less welcoming of low-achieving children and less able to provide an engaging curriculum.

Yet there may be other serious consequences of these new educational reforms and the focus on testing of academic subjects. One measure of how far the embodied child has slipped from our views of education is not only the failure to include any mention of the physical needs of children in NCLB, but the failure of the many critics of the new law to note the oversight. There has been a steady erosion of physical education for all children at all grades in the last thirty years, with a particularly sharp drop in the last ten years. Only about 29 percent of students receive what is called "daily physical education" even when numbers are inflated by inclusion of students (far more males than females) who are elite athletic team participants. Nearly all states have abandoned tests of physical fitness. One of the few state reports available finds only about one in five students in grades 5–9 met standards for health-related fitness and more than 40 percent did not meet minimum standards for cardiorespiratory endurance. (It should also be noted that US physical education and fitness assessments are in marked contrast to increases in Western European countries, Australia, New Zealand, and Japan.)

The failures to note the deficits in physical education are particularly strange since child and youth health concerns make headlines in other parts of newspapers. The disconnection is striking. There has been a 100 percent increase in the prevalence of childhood obesity since 1980. Type 2 diabetes among adolescents, once so rare it was called "adult-onset diabetes," has risen dramatically. Serious attention and affective problems have also increased. An estimated 8 percent of children have a learning disability and an estimated 3.3 million children (6 percent) have Attention Deficit Disorder. In the self-reported Youth Risk Behavior Surveillance System (YRBS) data, which do not include youth dropouts, nearly one third reported feeling sad or hopeless almost every day for more than two weeks and had stopped doing usual activities. Prevalence rates for prescribing sedatives/hypnotics and antidepressants have grown substantially through the 1990s. Public health concerns are underscored by the fact that most pre-scriptions are not approved for use with children, and drugs are being prescribed at earlier ages of initiation and for longer duration of treatment without studies assessing treatment and clinical outcomes.

These appalling health statistics were included in the Presidential Report by the Secretary of Health and Human Services and the Sec-retary of Education in 2000 along with recommendations for wide-spread increases in physical education in school, and new community investments in safe recreational facilities close to home. The health statistics for minority children and youth were worse, often significantly more dangerous, than for others. But the Report did not elicit outcry from either political party or from the general public, nor did it affect the rhetoric of school reform to end the "achievement gap."

The question of how we conceptualize human development is central to the dilemma. In NCLB, the child is divorced from his or her body, family, and social context and assumed to absorb knowledge in the same way as every other child. "Molding" of minds in school appears as the sole determinant of behavior. However, the individual child is never seen because the significant "data" are normative test scores. Students are depersonalized, presented only as aggregate numbers. The dropouts and others disappear, particularly in urban schools with high numbers of minority children. Linda McNeil notes that no more than half of the same children may take tests in two successive years. There is no provision to look at individual improvements over time and no mention of what failure and retention in grade might mean to children (and teachers).

Systems approaches underscore the significance of much less publi-cized efforts to alter the course of US education. Like John Dewey, educational reformer Linda Meier argues that the central functions of education in a democracy are to "know how to exercise judgment on matters of considerable complexity and uncertainty." In several books, she documents success in creating schools in low-income neighborhoods – success measured by high graduation rates and high college attendance rates. She founded with Ted Sizer the Coalition of Essential Schools (CES). The CES common principles emphasize small schools and classrooms, where teachers and students know each other well and work in an atmosphere of trust and high expectations, personalized instruction to address individual needs and interests, and multiple assessments based on performance of authentic tasks. School reform is seen as an inescapably local phenomenon, the outcome of groups of people working together, building a shared vision, and drawing on the community's strengths, history, and local flavor. How do CES advocates define educational standards? "We need standards held by real people who matter in the lives of our young. School, family, and community must forge their own, in dialogue with and in response to the larger world of which they are a part. There will always be tensions, but if the decisive, authoritative voice always comes from anonymous outsiders, then kids cannot learn what it takes to develop their own voice."

In scientific debate, the nature–nurture controversy has waxed and waned. Dynamic systems perspectives enter the debate with powerful interdisciplinary findings and insights of relevance for educational policy. The specific physical, biological, and social environments within which the individual organism develops are seen as inseparable parts of a developmental system. Organisms and environments are bi-directional and co-define development. Our focus turns to the ways in which individuals come to recognize their connections with self and others and learn to communicate effectively about matters large and small. Authentic accountability, then, must be seen in terms of connections between individuals and their abilities to contribute to and participate within a democratic community. The well-intentioned but misguided edicts of NCLB can serve to illuminate long-standing inequities. Unless we repeal the legislation and its course of unintended consequences, public schools may be irreparably damaged. If we wish to address, rather than measure and punish, the very real problems of children and schools within our society we need to begin afresh with new assumptions and new and inclusive public discourse and debate.

This chapter comes full circle if we return to the story of the Navajo elder and the cultural model he was given to find balance between body and mind, between self and others. He was taught means to achieve physical and emotional harmony, to use and hear his own voice as he grew in wisdom. He was taught to see and understand the ways in which individual and societal well-being are linked in living systems. The example has much to offer us as we reconsider our efforts at educational reform.

SUGGESTED READINGS

Bush, G. W. (2001, January 29). *No child left behind*. US Department of Education. www.ed.gov/inits/nclb.

Darling-Hammond, L. (2004). From "separate but equal" to "no child left behind"; "the collision of new standards and old inequalities." In D. Meier, and G. Wood (eds.), *Many children left behind* (pp. 3–32). Boston: Beacon Press.

Dewey, J. (1902). School as a social centre. *Middle Works*, 2, 93.

Friedrich-Cofer, L. (1986). Body, mind, and morals in the framing of social policy. In L. Friedrich-Cofer (ed.), *Human nature and public policy: scientific views of women, children, and families* (pp. 97–174). New York: Praeger.

Haney, W. (2000). The myth of the Texas miracle in education. *Educational Policy Archives*, 8(41).htpp://epaa.asu.edu/epaa/v8n41.

McNeil, L. (2000). *Contradictions of school reform: educational costs of standardized testing*. New York: Routledge.

Meier, D. (2002). *In schools we trust: creating communities of learning in an era of testing and standardization*. Boston: Beacon Press.

Meier, D. and Wood, G. (2004). *Many children left behind*. Boston: Beacon Press.

*Promoting better health for young people through physical activity and sports* (Fall, 2000). Report to the President from the Secretary of Health and Human Services and the Secretary of Education. www.cdc.gov/nccdphp/dash/presphysactrpt

Wood, G. (2004). Introduction. In D. Meier and G. Wood (eds.), *Many children left behind* (pp. vii–xv). Boston: Beacon Press.

# 15 Embodied communication in non-human animals

*Barbara Smuts*

I'm reading in my favorite chair, which rests on the floor at dog level. For the last twenty minutes my dog Bahati ("Ba" for short) has been resting out of sight contentedly gnawing a bone. But when I open my laptop with a click, she instantaneously materializes before me, like a character beamed from the Starship Enterprise. "Hey, Bahati," I say, glancing at her briefly, and then resume typing. Without moving or making a sound, she compels my attention through the sheer intensity of her presence. I look up again and, for a few heartbeats, meet the steady gaze of her topaz eyes. Then, before she can distract me further, I say forcefully "You had a long walk. Now I need to work." While I'm speaking, she flies through the air past me. As she whooshes by, she turns her head toward me so that her muzzle brushes my face just as I finish speaking. She twists in mid-air and lands facing me, sitting, about three feet away. Adopting an appealing expression, she lifts a paw and waves it up and down in front of me (not a trick she's been taught). Again I tell her that I need to work. Undaunted, she raises both paws at once, shifting her torso upright into full entreaty position. The thick mane of gold fur around her face and neck fluffs out as she rises, adding to her appeal. I lose my composure and start to laugh. This elicits a rabbit-like hop and she is in my face, licking. I simultaneously stroke the soft fur on the side of her neck, murmuring endearments. After a few seconds, I shift away and say in my deepest, most serious voice, "Ba, I'm going to work now. Go take a nap!" She looks at me hard, wagging her tail. I succeed in keeping a straight face for several seconds. She leans forward and so do I; the tips of our noses touch briefly. Then, with an elegant leap, she flings herself onto the sofa behind me. Uttering a deep sigh, she falls instantly to sleep.

I start with this episode, which occurred just as I was beginning to write, because it is a good example of *embodied communication*, the focus of this chapter. I have participated in hundreds, perhaps thousands, of instances of embodied communication with Bahati and my other dogs; it is a critical part of our inter-species language. (Although speech sometimes plays a role in these informal interactions, my own experience, as well as recent research, suggests that dogs often respond more to human body language and tone of voice than to the words themselves.) All large-brained social animals, including humans, possess the cognitive and emotional capacities needed to communicate in this way. Interpreting my interaction with Bahati will help to clarify what I mean by embodied communication and why I think it is important.

Bahati wanted my attention and I wanted to work. Our interaction negotiated these conflicting desires. Ba used gaze, motion, gesture, and touch to draw me into active participation, and we shared a brief interlude of mutual gazing. But Ba wanted more, and she employed appealing antics to lure me into further contact. After some mutual touching (her licking, me stroking), she wanted to continue engaging; by keeping a straight face, I resisted. Our noses coming together indicated mutual satisfaction with the negotiated outcome. Finally, Bahati acknowledged the end of the encounter with the emphatic nature of her departure and by choosing a location behind me, which precluded further eye contact.

But what did it all mean? There is no one answer. Our interaction communicated desires, expressed emotion, invoked a playful mood, and accomplished a mutually satisfying goal: afterwards, we could each settle comfortably into our respective modes, separate but still very much connected. If you ask what our interaction was about, the best answer is that it was about *us*.

If you could *see* the episode between me and Bahati rather than just read about it, you would notice each of us fine tuning our actions (including my voice) to the nuances of the other's behaviors, so that, over the course of the interaction, our behaviors increasingly overlapped in time, culminating in mutual nose-touching. This pattern characterizes a frequent kind of interaction between my dogs and myself. The dogs tend to initiate these interactions when we are *metaphorically* "out of sync" due to a difference in our desires, moods, or intentions. As the interaction proceeds, the extent to which we are *literally* "in sync" increases, and this experience somehow resolves the dissonance between us, perhaps by providing reassurance that our bond remains intact despite my preoccupation with other matters.

Meaning in interactions like these does not reside in the specific behaviors shown, nor does the interaction refer to something "out there" in the world. Rather, meaning is mutually constituted, literally embodied as two individuals' behaviors ("the parts") combine to create something new ("the whole"). I use the term *embodied communication* to refer to interactions whose meaning lies more in such *emergent properties* than in the lower-level, individual actions of the participants.

Below, I draw on my fieldwork with baboons to illustrate some of the emergent properties that embodied communication produces, and what these properties might mean in the context of a relationship.

I first became aware of the importance of embodied communication (hereafter referred to as EC) while studying wild savanna baboons. These large, ground-dwelling monkeys live throughout East Africa in cohesive troops of 30–150 animals. Females stay in their natal troops and are related by kinship, while males move between troops. The baboons I studied were at first afraid of me, but after a period of acclimatization, they allowed me to observe them from the inside, revealing the most subtle details of their behavior. While collecting data, I followed an individual baboon for thirty minutes at a time, recording every social interaction he or she participated in. More recently, I videotaped interactions so that I could review them later in great detail.

Based on the published studies of baboons at the time I began my research (mid-1970s), I expected that the majority of their interactions would involve fights, chases, threats, or "approach–retreat" interactions, in which a higher-ranking individual supplants a lower-ranking one, usually to take over a feeding site. I also expected to see friendly behavior, especially grooming, among close kin and between temporary sexual partners. However, to my surprise, when two baboons came near each other, usually none of these things happened. Instead, they were much more likely to enact a brief greeting ritual. I call these "rituals" because they followed a characteristic format in which one baboon would approach and present his or her hindquarters to the other (a polite gesture in baboon society). What happened next, however, varied considerably, as the baboons drew upon a rich repertoire of behaviors, including looking back at the other over the shoulder, reaching with a hand or foot to touch the other's body, making eye contact, making friendly faces, emitting soft grunts, lip-smacking, hugging, and standing bipedal and leaning in, so that the other baboon's nose touched one's chest. They also showed more assertive behaviors, such as mounting from behind (which occurs between members of the same sex as well as between males and females).

Anthropologist John Watanabe and I studied greetings between adult male baboons. Adult males constantly compete for mating opportunities and thus tend to have hostile relationships with one another. A male baboon in his prime uses stares, stalks, and threats to provoke his rivals into showing defensive, conciliatory, or avoidant responses, which raise his status and lower theirs. A male can try to avoid engaging in such psychological warfare, but if he consistently walks away from greeting attempts by other males, he loses face. Male–male greetings are thus generally rather tense.

Our study identified three main patterns in male–male greetings. When two prime males in roughly similar physical condition greeted, each had the goal of mounting the other, because being on top expressed higher status. Since neither male wanted to be mounted, such greetings frequently involved extensive circling as each jockeyed for an advantageous position from which to mount while trying to avoid being mounted. Often, one male abruptly turned and walked away before a solution occurred, and the greeting remained incomplete. A second pattern characterized greetings between a male past his prime and a younger, more physically fit male. Typically, the young male approached, and the older male presented and allowed himself to be mounted.

Contrast these two types of greetings with a third, much rarer kind. Occasionally, two older males will form an enduring partnership in which they take turns helping each other to defeat younger, stronger males, which often results in one of them winning an opportunity to consort with a fertile female. Sometimes one member of the team will end up with the female, and at other times, the other will. We observed one pair of such partners, Alex and Boz, greeting over and over (more often than any other pair of males in the troop). During a given greeting, one would usually present and the other would mount, or they would adopt some other asymmetric roles. However, across the several dozen greetings we observed between them, each male played the superior role half the time. This precise equality came about because whichever male was on top in a given greeting initiated the next greeting by presenting his hindquarters, thereby offering to even the score.

Through each of these patterns, the two males enacted their relative status. In the first example, both males did roughly the same thing, consonant with their similar status, and they could not find a way to come together, revealing their ongoing rivalry. In the second example, the asymmetry of the behaviors and the willingness of the older male to be mounted reflected the large difference in status between them and the older male's acknowledgment of his inferior rank. Greetings between Alex and Boz precisely mirrored their cooperative partnership during competition against other males. In this case, however, the symmetric pattern was not detectable within their greetings; it emerged only when we searched for a pattern across multiple greetings.

Male–female greetings in baboons also show different patterns, depending on the nature of the relationship. Baboon males weigh twice as much as females and sometimes attack them, so females tend to be nervous around males. However, most females have one or two male friends whom they groom and hang out with. A female's male friends protect herself and her infant against other males (non-friends). Both friends and non-friends often greet. Analysis of videotaped interactions of baboons interacting with friends and non-friends showed, not surprisingly, that greetings between friends more often involved especially intimate behaviors, like hugging and prolonged mutual eye contact. In addition, for a given action by either sex (such as reaching to touch the other or moving toward or away from the other), when non-friends greeted the behavior was performed significantly more quickly than when friends greeted. These faster actions afforded fewer opportunities for overlapping behaviors and for smooth coordination of responses, so that greetings between non-friends appeared jerky and awkward compared to the smoother, more coordinated greetings between friends.

Baboon greetings illustrate some key features of EC that apply to many other species as well. First, as mentioned above, in EC, meaning arises from the pattern of interaction rather than the behaviors shown by each individual.

Second, EC is dynamic, so greeting patterns change over time. For example, an incipient friendship between a male and female baboon is often first detectable through changes in their greeting pattern. The greetings of non-friends and the greetings of friends both show a symmetric pattern; in the former instance both individuals perform quick motions, while in the latter, both perform slower motions. In contrast, when a male is interested in developing a friendship with a female, their greetings initially become more asymmetric as the male shifts his style to slow, careful approaches and gestures, while the female continues to show the quick, guarded responses typical with non-friends. But eventually, in some cases, a female will begin to accept more touching, move more slowly, maintain eye gazing for longer, and in general behave more like a friend. This shift (which, if it occurs, usually takes weeks or months) indicates that she shares his interest in developing a friendship. Thus, as a male and female move from non-friend status to friend status, their greetings at first show a symmetric pattern, then change to an asymmetric pattern, and eventually resume a symmetric pattern but of a different kind. The opposite also obtains: increasingly curt greetings can be a female's way of telling a friend that she is no longer interested.

Third, EC involves creativity. Although the participants share a repertoire of behaviors, no two interactions are the same, since the behaviors can be expressed and combined in a virtually infinite variety of ways. Also, pairs sometimes develop new forms of EC unique to them. For example, one pair of long-standing baboon friends consistently eliminated the usual hindquarter presentation and instead approached face-to-face, drew their heads together, and touched each other's faces gently while gazing into each other's eyes. My dog Safi and I co-created a morning ritual in which we performed the "downward dog" yoga pose in synchrony, with her front paws and my hands on the floor facing each other a few cm apart. Such novel creations are perhaps a way of saying, "Our relationship is special." Pairs can also co-create novel forms of EC that become conventionalized "shorthands." For example, Bahati sometimes looks at me expectantly and I raise my hands with my palms facing her. This brief interaction is Ba's way of requesting a treat and my way of saying, "Not now."

Fourth, EC rarely involves an ordered back-and-forth exchange of discrete signals (e.g. one stands still while the other moves, followed by the reverse). Instead, mutually overlapping gestures, facial expressions, sounds, and postures occur. The degree of such overlap and the manner in which it occurs produce patterns that can vary from uncoordinated/dissonant/awkward to coordinated/harmonious/graceful. Dynamic systems researchers sometimes describe such interactions as dances. "Dancing" patterns are often discernible to the naked eye. However, analyses to determine what underlies these patterns are still important, since, for example, a non-graceful "dance" could emerge in many different ways. As described above, the awkward impression given by non-friend greetings is due, at least in part, to their relatively abbreviated gestures and movements. In another instance of EC, however, awkwardness could arise because two individuals failed to synchronize their behaviors.

Fifth, EC often provides a context in which individuals can negotiate relationships without, at least in the short term, incurring material consequences. For example, two prime male baboons vying for status could simply fight until one of them gave up and accepted an inferior position. However, male baboons possess formidable canines and even winners of fights can sustain serious injuries. Thus, if two males can work out their status relationship without fighting, it may be advantageous for both to do so. Similarly, a male could try to develop a new friendship with a female by trying to remain near her much of the time. However, a female baboon usually moves away from any non-friend male within a few seconds of his approach, presumably because such a male can prove dangerous to her or her offspring. Through brief greetings, a male can communicate his desire to form a friendship and a female can learn about and respond to that desire without having to risk being close to the male for long periods of time. Thus, EC can be viewed as a relatively inexpensive, efficient, and safe way for non-linguistic animals to express *how they feel* and *what they want* (or do not want) in relation to others.

Sixth, EC is part of a complex and dynamic relationship system and must be studied using concepts and methods appropriate to the study of such systems. From the standpoint of traditional behavioral science, one might ask: does EC simply express the current state of a relationship, or does it function to create, maintain, and change relationships? In other words, what is cause and what is effect? From a systems perspective this question does not arise, because any given instance of EC can be both. For example, when two adult male baboons greet and one mounts the other, the interaction expresses the status difference currently existing between them, and it also helps to maintain that difference. Even in instances in which a change in greeting patterns seems to precede a change in other aspects of a relationship (for example, the different greeting pattern characteristic of an incipient male–female friendship described above), changes in greetings do not necessarily *cause* a change in the relationship. Rather, changes in greetings *are* a change in the relationship, and this particular manifestation of change is just one component in a system of interactions in which every aspect of a relationship is tied to every other aspect through bi-directional feedback loops (sometimes called "systems causality"). In other words, through EC, relationships are simultaneously enacted and negotiated.

Clearly, EC helps build, negotiate, and change relationships, but why might this form of communication be especially appropriate in the relationship context? We do not know the answer to this question because it has rarely been asked. But, using the framework of evolutionary theory, we can speculate about potential answers.

Evolutionary biologists have emphasized that natural selection is about competition for limited resources, which, they argue, favors communication that manipulates and deceives others. Abundant research shows that manipulation and deceit (not necessarily involving conscious motivation) do occur among nonhuman animals and, of course, among humans. This, however, is just one side of the picture. We also know that cooperation is critical to survival and reproduction in complex social animals. When individuals share overlapping interests (such as in rearing offspring or forming a fair coalitionary partnership, like Alex and Boz), they need to communicate in ways that build trust and facilitate an effective partnership. Even competitors can benefit from honest communication, as described above for male baboons who both gain by using EC, rather than risky fighting, to negotiate relative status. The value of honest communication in contexts like these presents an evolutionary dilemma: given that natural selection sometimes favors deceit, how can animals tell when someone is communicating honestly?

The examples cited in this chapter suggest that EC may be particularly well-suited as a channel for authentic communication, for two reasons. First of all, the ability, through EC, to produce graceful, dance-like patterns may accurately reflect the actors' motivations to cooperate and/or their capacities to function well together as partners. Discrete signals, like a particular call or gesture, could allow individuals to communicate *about* cooperation – but they might not be truthful. Embodied communication that produces dance-like patterns *is* cooperation, an unfakeable demonstration that in this context, at least, two individuals are sufficiently mutually attuned and well-matched that they can co-create an entity – the dance – that transcends their individuality.

An example from bottlenose dolphins illustrates this idea. In the wild, males of this species form long-term coalitions in pairs or trios. Coalition members ("partners") cooperate to court estrous females and to guard them against "thefts" by competing coalitions. These behaviors require precise coordination of actions among partners. When partners are engaged in routine traveling and foraging together, they tend to surface synchronously. They maintain synchrony even when they are scattered among other dolphins surfacing at various times. Suppose that, under routine conditions, the degree of synchronous surfacing between potential male partners helps them communicate whom they are interested in, determine who is interested in them, and estimate how easily they can develop precise coordination with particular partners. Such communication could save males a lot of time and effort compared to the process of using trial and error to find the best partners.

A second way embodied communication can enhance honesty involves the costs or risks that such communication sometimes entails. How does a female baboon know that a male attempting to cultivate a friendship will actually provide protection for her and her infant? As described above, to develop a friendship with a female, a male baboon must invest weeks or months finely tuning his actions to her moods and rhythms. Given the female's option of abandoning a friend who doesn't help her out, it would be pointless to incur such costs unless he really did intend to follow through.

These examples suggest that, when it comes to EC, the medium really is the message. A male dolphin interested in forming a partnership with another male cannot fake his ability to surface synchronously with him: either he can do it well or he can't. And a male baboon incurs costs when courting a female that make little sense unless he is interested in genuine negotiation.

With language, it is possible to lie and say we like someone when we don't. However, if the above speculations are correct, closely interacting bodies tend to tell the truth.

Dogs and other social animals are supremely skilled at EC. Not only do they communicate authentically, but they often seem to know exactly how to say something so that we understand what they mean. The authenticity and sensitivity of their communication is one reason we develop profound attachments to our animal companions.

These traits can also explain why contact with friendly nonhuman animals is so often therapeutic. I know several people who take their dogs to hospitals and nursing homes to spend time with patients. Each tells a moving story about someone who withdrew so deeply that no one could reach them. Then one day a dog walked into the room, approached the unhappy person and contacted him or her in some way – and the person smiled or spoke for the first time in weeks. In each instance, the dog was described as approaching the person in an atypical, special way, as if sensing exactly what was needed.

Many people who associate with companion animals have had similar experiences. My dog Safi consistently responded to my sadness or discomfort by placing her head gently on my lap (if I was sitting) or chest (if I was prone) and gazing deeply into my eyes. She was so sensitive that she often noticed a shift in my mood before I did! Another dog friend, Kobi, offered solace right after I learned of the unexpected death of someone I cared about. I was sitting on the floor. She sat in front of me and then wrapped her front paws around my neck, literally pulling me into a close embrace that lasted for several seconds.

In addition to comforting us in our sadness, other animals also help us to be happy. They remind us that we, like them, can communicate playfully and creatively with our bodies, and when we do, they meet us more than halfway. As experts in EC, they have much to teach us. I am reminded of something an artist once told me. For many years, he had painted the same canvas side by side with another artist. One day, he heard about a zoo elephant who loved to paint. She held the brush in her trunk, and zoo staff provided paints and canvases for her. Zoo authorities agreed to let the artist try painting with the elephant. Together, they created a number of abstract paintings that were displayed at my university's art museum. No one could tell which strokes were hers and which were his. Deeply curious, I asked him what it was like to paint with the elephant. He replied that he had always hoped to relinquish his individual agency when painting with his friend but had never quite succeeded. With the elephant, he said, his sense of himself as a separate being completely disappeared, and he felt as if they were painting from a single, shared consciousness. The elephant, he said, had no investment in the outcome of their activity and so was completely present to the experience. Painting with her allowed him to achieve a similar state of total presence.

These and many other stories like them suggest that relationships with other animals can help put us in touch with capacities in ourselves that can be hard to reach, caught up as we are in thinking, planning, judging, and communicating through language. A more intuitive, immediate, and open way of being is our evolutionary heritage. I hope that in the future, happy animals will play a much larger role in clinical practice and other helping contexts, and that their inclusion will foster greater respect and caring for all creatures.

Understanding and participating in EC is important not only in our relations with non-human animals but also in our relations with other humans. In recent years, scientists studying animal behavior and those studying human development have increasingly used videotaping to examine social interactions in fine detail. As these two groups of researchers share their findings, it becomes increasingly evident that they are studying the same phenomena: ways of communicating that can be described as embodied, creative, co-regulated, mutually contingent, and so on. As indicated in several chapters in this volume, this convergence is particularly apparent when we compare nonhuman animal communication and human infant–caregiver interactions. This shouldn't be too surprising. Infants, after all, are baby animals, whose only entry into the world of relationships is through the interaction of their bodies with other bodies who know how to play creatively, animal to animal.

SUGGESTED READINGS

Clothier, S. (2002). *Bones would rain from the sky: deepening our relationships with dogs*. New York: Warner Books.
Connor, R. C., R. A. Smolker, and A. F. Richards (1992). Dolphin alliances and coalitions. In A. H. Harcourt and F. B. M. de Waal (eds.), *Coalitions and alliances in humans and other animals* (pp. 415–443). Oxford: Oxford University Press.
Csyáni, V. (2005). *If dogs could talk: exploring the canine mind*. New York: North Point Press.
Odendaal, J. S. J., and R. A. Meintjes (2003). Neurophysiological correlates of affiliative behaviour between humans and dogs. *The Veterinary Journal*, 165, 296–301.

Raina, P., D. Waltner-Toews, B. Bonnett, C. Woodward, and T. Abernathy (1999). Influence of companion animals on the physical and psychological health of older people: an analysis of a one-year longitudinal study. *Journal of the American Geriatrics Society*, 47(3), 323–329.

Serpell, J. A. (1991). Beneficial effects of pet ownership on some aspects of human health and behavior. *Journal of the Royal Society of Medicine*, 84(12), 717–772.

   (1996). *In the company of animals: a study of human–animal relationships*. New York: Cambridge University Press.

Smuts, B. B. (1999). *Sex and friendship in baboons* (2nd ed.). Cambridge, MA: Harvard University Press.

   (2001). Encounters with animal minds. *Journal of Consciousness Studies*, 8(5–7), 293–309.

Watanabe, J. M., and B. B. Smuts (2004). Cooperation, commitment, and communication in the evolution of human sociality. In R. W. Sussman and A. R. Chapman (eds.), *The origins and nature of sociality* (pp. 288–309). New York: DeGruyter.

# 16    Children in the living world: why animals matter for children's development

*Gail F. Melson*

On a fine spring day, a happy blur of waving arms and jumping feet greets me as I arrive to observe outdoor playtime at the preschool. A half dozen three and four-year-olds are playing "chase" with Lucy. The children become more excited, shrieking and whooping, as Lucy whizzes with whirlwind speed around them. At this point, the teacher, Meridyth, intervenes, reminding the children how small Lucy is, and how they must be careful not to get too rough with her. An internal struggle between heightened arousal and "chilling out" seems to play across the children's faces. I see one little boy, who has skidded to a halt in mid-chase after Lucy, unconsciously clench and unclench his fists as he listens to the teacher's admonitions.

Blake, eight years old, is sprawled on the couch, lazing away another Saturday morning in front of the TV. When Scot appears, Blake slides over, patting the couch seat next to him with an encouraging, "Come here." After a few moments on the couch, Scot jumps down, goes to the door, and casts a fixed look back at Blake, who keeps staring at the screen. Scot comes back to Blake, nudges him for attention, and as soon as he looks up, Scot bounds back to the door. He stands in front of it, seeming to stare right through the door to the snowy outside. After a few seconds, Blake lets out a long sigh, mumbles, "Oh, Ok, I hear you," hunts for his shoes and coat, and shuffles off.

Jesse stomps into the house, marches up to her room and slams the door behind her as she flings herself on the bed. Another hard day is winding down for the thirteen-year-old. She barely hears Misty, who has padded up the stairs to the bedroom door and waits silently behind it. Jesse jumps up, scoops up Misty and retreats once more, jangling the "That means you!" sign on the door. As Jesse curls up in fetal misery on the bed, Misty gazes into her face, and slowly licks her hand. Jesse's body relaxes, a smile escapes her, and she murmurs, "good Misty."

These three scenes capture moments in significant relationships in children's lives. Like other important ties, these relationships – the preschoolers with Lucy, Blake with Scot, and Jesse with Misty – involve every facet of the child's being – emotions, learning, moral reasoning, communication, and more. The children will tell you they are attached to Lucy, Scot, and Misty. But what do these relationships mean, what is the nature of this attachment, when we consider that Lucy is a Beagle puppy, Scot is a ten-year-old black Labrador, and Misty, a seven-year-old calico cat?

The idea that pets matter to children seems almost a truism, so obvious it is unworthy of close attention. Surveys tell us that most parents who have animals in their household – and over 70 percent of US households with children do – acquired pets "for the children." For many parents (and teachers who have classroom animals), pets seem a ready vehicle to teach responsibility, provide comfort, nurture consideration for others, and generally "enrich" a child's experience. Popular culture joins the images of the tow-headed tyke and the puppy, the pert little princess and her fluffy Angora, bathing children and pets in each other's aura. Both are cute, dependent, and decorative, a "natural" duo.

At the same time, scientific study of child development has been stubbornly "humanocentric," narrowly focused on human–human relationships, and ignoring children's many connections with non-human life forms, particularly other animals. Whether scholars are assessing attachment bonds, the learning opportunities found in play, the seeds of moral reasoning, or the promotion of kindness – all on display in child–animal relationships – it is only in ties with other people that developmental significance is thought to reside.

By looking more closely at what Lucy, Scot, and Misty are doing with, and for the children in their lives, we can see past both popular culture imagery and scholarly blinders to the complex, dynamic relationships that children have with the animals sharing their lives. Like human relationships, these cross-species ties are co-created, as child and animal participate together in evolving routines, modes of communication, and exchanges of stimulation and affection. After all, the most common household pets – dogs and cats – evolved as species in the company of humans, so that for these animals, their natural ecology is the human home. As in other relationships, children hone their sense of self *through* contact with animals. This "development through relationships" applies to children in the animal world no less than in the world of other humans.

For the preschoolers in the first scene, Lucy is a familiar fixture of their classroom, a beloved playmate. She loves high intensity "chase" and "catch" games. As the children pour out for outdoor play, they can tell by Lucy's play poses and expectant body language that she's ready for the games to begin. The dog's ability to build with the child reciprocal exchanges and play routines means that Lucy, within her canine repertoire, is a full participant in this relationship. Playing with Lucy, some of the children get especially excited, shrieking and jumping up and down, carried along in the boisterousness of rough-and-tumble play. The teachers become more vigilant then, reminding the children how small Lucy is and that they must be careful not to get too rough with her. In this mix of excitement and adult-supported restraint, young children rehearse the rhythms of urgency and control. In this way, animals' combination of arousing appeal and dependence may help young children as they struggle to command their emotional swings, a process developmentalists call "emotional self-regulation."

A few of the preschoolers in this classroom have language delays or other disabilities. Monica, slow in language development, had been taught sign language and, as a result, had started the school year with a vocabulary of about 300 signs. Gradually though, over the next six months, her hands had fallen silent. The special education teacher assisting her explained: "About age three, children get more sophisticated, and they do not see other people in their environment signing. They don't want to stick out." However, Lucy had an interesting effect. "When Monica saw the dog, running on the playground, darting in and out of view, that was such a novel, exciting event, that this propelled her. She very excitedly signed and tried to say: 'puppy.' When the puppy would disappear, Monica would come up to me with 'Where is puppy?' using her signs and speech approximations."

As with Monica, children find the behavior of other species attention grabbing, emotion-engaging, and motivating. Therapists working with children who have attention deficits, learning disabilities, or emotional problems are increasingly harnessing this observation to focus and engage these children. In particular, clinicians are discovering that supervised caring for animals often produces calm, focus, and greater openness to treatment.

For example, a psychiatrist, Dr. Aaron Katcher, developed the "Companionable Zoo," an array of "pocket pets" like gerbils, hamsters, and rabbits, for boys at a Philadelphia area residential treatment center for severe conduct disorder, an emotional illness involving poor impulse control combined with out of control aggression. After six months of careful monitoring, the boys caring for animals in the "zoo" showed remarkable improvement. Although previously these boys often had required physical restraint, while caring for the animals not a single instance of behavior requiring such restraint was recorded. In contrast, boys at the same facility, with equally severe illness, who participated in a hiking and outdoors program (Outward Bound) showed no improvement. At Green Chimneys Children's Services, another residential treatment center for children with severe emotional illness, the therapeutic milieu is infused with nature and animals, from therapeutic horseback riding, to caring for animals at the "farm," to dogs in the dormitory residences and in the classrooms. A therapist at Green Chimneys explained to me how she starts a therapy session by placing a small soft creature, like a hamster or gerbil, on the chest of a child who has suffered from sexual and physical abuse: "Our children haven't been touched enough in healthy ways, and they need that clean, good physical touch that we all need as human beings. Animals can provide that kind of second chance to be held and nurtured in that way."

What do we see with Blake and Scot? First, Blake invites Scot to join him on the sofa with a pat and a verbal invitation, "Come here." As any pet-owning reader will attest, humans talk to their animals, not only issuing familiar commands, but murmuring endearments – "Good boy" – reporting the day's events, confiding secrets, and venting anger. Over 90 percent of adult pet owners talk regularly to their animals, and this seems true of children as well. What's been called *doggerel* or *petese* has some features in common with *motherese*, the conversational form that mothers (and other humans) use with babies. Children speak to their own and others' pets in a higher-pitched, soft singsong, often ending an utterance with a rising inflection, as if posing a question, and inserting pauses for imaginary replies. In these "dialogues," children fill in the "take" of a verbal "give and take" on the part of the non-verbal pet. Of course, pets, especially dogs and cats, are responding; their body language and nonverbal sounds are highly communicative. Scot clearly and urgently made his needs known.

While *motherese* highlights the distinctive aspects of language and calls the baby's attention to them, *petese* crooners, even preschoolers, fully realize that their pets are not candidates for future membership in the human linguistic community. Instead, *petese* promotes and affirms intimacy. We see this in the features of *petese* that are distinct from *motherese*. As Jesse shows us, when children or adults have been observed talking to their dogs and birds, they place their heads close to the animal's head and invariably stroke, nuzzle, and pet the animal, seemingly compelled to combine touch and talk. Voices lower to a confidential murmur and facial muscles relax. By contrast, when adults or children speak *motherese*, they have animated, wide-eyed expressions, with tenser facial muscles. Babytalk is less fused with close physical contact than is *petese*, an affirmation of the bond between animal and human.

What can we learn from listening to *petese*? Although we are just beginning to study how children communicate with animals, there are some intriguing possibilities. One theory, called the *biophilia hypothesis*, considers human beings as innately primed to be attuned to life. In particular, humans are interested in animals, since the human species evolved along with other animals on whom humans depended for survival. Although cultures shape this predisposition toward other forms of life, we would expect children the world over to approach other animals, particularly those within their families, as other beings who share their world. This means that children's relationships with animals are likely to be important cross-culturally, but the particular form that importance takes is likely to vary. In contemporary North America and other economically developed societies, children tend to experience animals primarily as "sentimental" others. That is, the decline of animal husbandry, rural ecologies, and wildlife in general means that companion animals become relatively more important as the economic and utilitarian functions of animals fall away, or become distant from children's everyday experience. Animals kept in households are most likely to address solely social–emotional needs. Thus, the cultural–historical view considers *petese* a reflection of the way beloved animals convey to children a sense of availability, acceptance, and affirmation, inducing communication fused with aspects of the relaxation response.

The biophilia hypothesis and the cultural–historical view are not contradictory, but rather complementary. The former recognizes how culture and history shape an innate predisposition of attentiveness toward life forms. The latter is congruent with assumptions of evolutionarily based tendencies.

Although Blake, Jesse, and other petese-speaking children treat their companion animals *as if* they were linguistic partners, much of children's (and adults') intimate dialogue with pets uses the language of body, gesture, and tone, as the interchange between Scot and Blake showed. The multi-channel, verbal and non-verbal, communication inherent in child–pet dialogues may help children hone their skills in picking up cues to internal states of other beings from body movements, facial expressions, and voice tone or pitch, all important components of emotional intelligence. How might children do this? Consider eleven-year-old Kate's explanation of how her cat Gina "talks" to her: "You can sort of tell what she's saying, cause she'll jump up, try to push against the porch door and meow until you open it and she'll rub against one of our cabinets until we give her a treat, and in the middle of the night, she'll make these sounds, because she doesn't know where anybody is, or she wants someone to come pet her."

Empathy develops as a child learns to put herself into the shoes of others. Although dozens of studies examine how children develop empathic skills and put them to use toward other people, only a handful consider what's involved in putting oneself into the "paws" or "hoofs" of others. This requires a greater imaginative leap, a bigger stretch, to decode the sounds and movements of another species.

A conventional view of these dialogues might use ideas like projection, generalization, and association. In this view, children learn the building blocks of relationships with human caregivers and then, if there are animals around, children simply repeat these patterns with them as well. A dynamic systems approach, by contrast, recognizes the distinctive, irreducible features of child–animal interaction and sees these features as emerging out of both the child's and animal's behavior with each other.

This view opens us to ways in which inter-species relationships are different from human–human relationships and helps us consider implications for development. For example, as children deal with the stresses of growing up, the continuing availability of intimate dialogues with pets may provide a non-judgmental outlet for the uncensored expression of feelings. Children feel a sense of unconditional love from their pets. Indeed, the most interactive and common species – dogs, cats, horses – do bond with their owners, often in as deep and fundamental a way as do the humans with them. But, even when the huge brown eyes only *seem* to be gazing in adoration, but in reality are just waiting for a "treat," children often feel understood, accepted, and loved.

As Jesse shows us, an angry or depressed teen can always hug a favorite stuffed animal, squeeze a pillow, or complain to the bedroom walls, but only a pet provides a sentient, feeling presence, the helpful illusion of an audience that does not demand clear, articulate expression. The niceties of turn-taking, reciprocity, and mutual acknowledgment that make up conversational competence (and undergird our reliance on human social support) don't apply. Dialogues with pets offer a time-out from the anxieties of human interchange. This may be why one pioneering study found that children's blood pressure decreased when reading aloud to a dog, but increased when reading to a friend. (More recent studies find that the dog's blood pressure also goes down in this situation.)

When we turn our attention to the full panoply of children's relationships, including those across as well as within species, what I have called a *biocentric* view of development, we are able to ask new and interesting questions about development. How do infants and young children come to understand different modes of being? Infants make a core distinction early, although precisely when is debated: the movement of living things contrasts with the movement of inanimate objects. Consider the cognitively enriching qualities of animals to young children. Here are living beings packed densely with interesting (and distinct from human) movements, sounds, smells, and opportunities to touch. Observations of infants and toddlers with their dogs and cats (and with lifelike toy dogs and cats) show babies smiling, following, and making sounds to the living animals much more than to the toys. The living animals, in turn, respond to the children – nuzzling the babies, rolling over for a tummy rub, or licking the babies' faces. Here we see reciprocal interaction of living animal with child, the give-and-take of two beings aware of and in tune to each other. In dynamic systems terms, child and animal are creating routines that are emerging out of their relationship.

Does animal imagery in children's dreams, art, and play fuel creativity, order chaotic emotions, rehearse and thus tame preoccupations and fears? It is remarkable that animals loom as such important characters, not only in the literature and art produced *for* children by adults, but also by children in their play, dreams, and stories. From Aesop's fables to animal totems, to the Brothers Grimm and Charles Perrault, humans have always invested animals with moral urgency and emotional power. While Freud believed that animal figures derived their power as "stand-ins" for loved but feared parents, a dynamic systems view encourages us to reach for a broader, more compelling account. The animal kingdom of the imagination does more than screen unacceptable or conflicted childhood passions. Animals also are a first vocabulary for many other aspects of onself. Rather than standing in for an already fully realized self, animal characters may be the raw material out of which children construct a sense of self. In this view, animal stories and symbols guide children into deeper understanding of what it means to have a *human* self.

What are the implications of children's acceptance of pets as relationship partners for the development of both empathy and cruelty in the face of difference? What are the childhood roots of adult debates over the moral standing of animals? Precisely because children accept animals as other living beings, they raise issues of just, fair, right, and kind conduct. Children are awash in contradictory cultural messages about the moral implications of human treatment of animals – some petted and indulged, others chopped up for burgers – and this is likely to make children's thinking about moral questions with respect to animals particularly complex. At the same time, animal family members, like the human ones, inadvertently provide many "teachable moments" to build moral intelligence. Robert Coles, that keen observer of children, recounted how he intervened to prevent his young son from playing too roughly with their dog: "The dog in his own way was a teacher, one who had helped all of us come to terms with the meaning of understanding: to put oneself in another's shoes, to see and feel things as he, she, or it does" (Coles, 1997, p. 84). Again, it was through the relationship that father, son, and dog built together that these lessons were learned.

The answers to these questions may pay off in better understanding of children in their human contexts. From a biocentric perspective, however, there is an imperative to grasp the significance of child–animal relationships on their own terms, not simply because of possible implications for human relationships. We are becoming more aware of our inter-connections with other species and natural settings, even as these links are becoming more fragile in a globally warmed, ecologically threatened world. Efforts to reconnect are proliferating: therapeutic horseback riding, animal visitations to nursing homes, fish tanks in doctors' waiting-rooms, and plant-"greened" senior centers are among the many. Our focus on enhancing human experience through connection with animals and nature must not blind us to human responsibility for the animals and environments under our opposable thumb. All too many family, classroom, and recreational environments that are enriched with animals for the benefit of children fail to take full responsibility for animal welfare. The dynamic system of child, animal, and environment means that all elements must be nurtured for their optimal development. Children's attunement to animals warns us to ensure that children not lose their sense of connection to other species as they grow to adulthood. In children's intimacy with other species lie the seeds of their future stewardship of the planet.

SUGGESTED READINGS

Beck, A. and A. H. Katcher (1996). *Between pets and people: the importance of animal companionship*. West Lafayette, IN: Purdue University Press.
Coles, R. (1997). *The moral intelligence of children*. New York: Random House.
Kahn, P. H. Jr. (1999). *The human relationship with nature: development and culture*. Cambridge, MA: MIT Press.
Melson, G. F. (2001). *Why the wild things are: animals in the lives of children*. Cambridge, MA: Harvard University Press.
Myers, E. O. (1998). *Children and animals: social development and our connection to other species*. Boulder, CO: Westview Press.

*Part IV*

Dynamic systems approaches to mental health

# 17 A dynamic developmental model of mental health and mental illness

*Stanley I. Greenspan*

Sally, an eight-year-old girl, was put on Zoloft, a selective serotonin uptake inhibitor (SSRI) because she was becoming more "compulsive" and fretful, according to her mother. She was washing her hands twenty times a day, refusing to let her mother leave her "alone" at school, and would only play with children at her house. She and her mother were seeing a child psychologist employing "behavioral strategies" involving rewarding "appropriate behavior," but when the symptoms got worse, Sally was put on medication. The medication, however, made the symptoms even more severe. That's when mother came in for a second opinion and I had an opportunity to conduct a comprehensive evaluation.

I learned that Sally was very sensory and affectively over-reactive, ever since she was an infant. While she had precocious language skills, her ability to sequence actions and engage in "big picture thinking" (i.e. see the forest for the trees) was limited. Mother was very anxious and tended to intrude and overload Sally by yelling a great deal, always demanding Sally do this or that and offering almost no soothing inter-actions. Father was a workaholic and didn't get home until Sally was asleep and on weekends was either short-tempered or into his work.

Sally was attentive and verbal, but very reactive to sensations, including loud voices or even rapid gestures. She did some pretend play, but it focused mostly on fears, such as dolls running from witches or "perfect worlds" where "everyone is nice." She reacted to any hint of anger or assertiveness by creating these perfect worlds. Anger also tended to make her think in a fragmented manner (jumping from one subject to another) and talk of "being a bad person." Peer play occurred, but was limited to creating "nice scenes" in drawing or pretending, and avoided competition. At school, she was doing well with verbal skills and less well in math, but was beginning to miss more and more of school.

When I reviewed the reports of the therapists who were working with Sally and her family, little of this dynamic, developmental picture was

157

presented. Only her symptoms and "maladaptive behaviors" were described.

When this fuller dynamic understanding was constructed, I was able to recommend an intervention plan that addressed Sally's full range of strengths and challenges. While the details of this case would take too much space to describe, the following highlights may be informative.

We were able to wean Sally off the medication, which was leading to more sensory and affective hypersensitivity. We were able to learn how increasing stress at home and school contributed to her symptoms becoming worse. Her family and school were helped to provide soothing interactions. Mother and father were helped to change the family dynamics and support Sally's experience and expression of a wide range of feelings, including assertiveness and anger. The home program included lots of reciprocal emotional exchanges characterized by back-and-forth co-regulation and gradual broadening of the range of affects exchanged. It also included opportunities for imaginative play (e.g. Floor Time) and problem-solving conversations. Sally's individual therapy also focused on broadening her ability to experience the full range of age-appropriate feelings, including assertiveness and competition, and to engage in "big picture thinking" and self-soothe.

Over a period of six months, Sally made significant improvements in not only her symptoms, but in all the more fundamental areas, such as her ability to engage in regulated exchanges of affective communication, express and understand a wide range of feelings, organize her thinking, cope with anger, play with peers, and separate from her mother. Importantly, the family dynamics changed so that Sally's growth will probably be supported in the future.

Children like Sally (as well as adults with mental illness), however, are unlikely to receive the type of developmentally guided comprehensive approach just described. In most cities of the United States and the world, she is much more likely only to have the initial approach, which was not helpful.

What does this case tell us about different ways of thinking about mental health and illness?

Mental health has always been an elusive concept. What does it mean to be mentally healthy? Does it only mean to be free of symptoms of maladaptive behavior? Unfortunately, there has been a trend to such a narrow view, which is what was initially guiding Sally's therapy and presently guides most therapeutic programs.

Or does mental health mean to have warm, satisfying relationships, being able to cope with expected stresses, and being successful in school and later in one's career? Does it mean to be joyful and happy and yet also tolerate and experience deep levels of loss and sorrow when life's circumstances are challenging? Does it also mean carrying a high moral and ethical standard that can survive group pressure?

I believe it means all of the above. As such, being mentally healthy is neither simple nor easy to conceptualize or measure. The key is to avoid overly narrow definitions, which, tempting as they are, provide easy, but false, solutions.

The most useful way to approach understanding mental health is to look at the developmental capacities that need to be mastered to achieve it.

We have developed a framework to understand the most essential developmental capacities of a growing person. These include the person's emotional, social, and cognitive or intellectual capacities. We call these functional emotional milestones because they stem from emotional interactions.[1] These start with *regulation and interest in the world*, the child's ability to remain calm and attentive while processing and responding to a variety of sensations in an organized way. Next is the way in which the child *engages in relationships*, how he interacts and relates to the caregiver playing with him or her, the child's ability to engage warmly and intimately. Then comes the *intentional use of affects, gestures, and behavior*, the child's ability to enter into back-and-forth affective gesturing, using a broad range of emotional interests. Next is the child's ability to use *interactive affect signaling to problem-solve, form a presymbolic sense of self*, and regulate mood and behavior, his or her ability to organize behaviors and affects into purposeful patterns in the context of the expectations of the environment. Then comes the ability to *transform behaviors and actions into symbols or ideas*, which represent wishes, desires, and affects. Can the child use symbols and ideas imaginatively and creatively with a wide range of themes and thoughts? Then comes the child's ability to *create logical bridges or connections between his own ideas and the ideas of another person*.

If the child has mastered these fundamental functional emotional developmental levels, advanced levels are possible. These later levels build on the basic ones and include *multi-cause and triangular thinking* (e.g. a child can figure out several reasons why a thing might be happening, instead of only one, and can hold in mind at least two other possible views of a thing); *gray-area, reflective thinking* (a child can weigh and judge the relative causes of events); and thinking from a sense of self and internal *standard of thinking* (i.e. the child now has

---

[1] Greenspan (1997b); Greenspan (1997a); Greenspan and Wieder (1998).

a sense of self that is relatively stable and the child can use this to form an opinion about experiences, i.e. make judgments, and reflect on what he's learning). Once these advanced stages are in place, they enable an individual to increase his or her range and depth of experience and negotiate a series of additional stages during adolescence and adulthood (see table 17.1 at the end of the chapter).

Within each of these functional emotional developmental capacities resides certain critical abilities. For example, the ability to relate warmly and intimately with others is part of *forming relationships*. The ability to read and respond to social and emotional signals and "read people" as well as to express a range of feelings resides in the capacity for *intentional, two-way emotional signaling* and using *affective signaling to solve problems, construct a preverbal sense of self, and regulate mood and behavior*. Once embarked on, a particular stage doesn't stop as the next stage comes in. Rather, the prior stage continues growing. Relationships continue to become more subtle and reciprocal. Emotional signaling becomes richer, deeper, and broader.

As can be seen, we have identified fifteen levels of functional emotional development that build the capacities and competencies that we ordinarily associate with mental health, ranging from the capacities for intimate relationships all the way to the capacity for judgment and reflecting on one's own feelings.

A mentally healthy adult has relative mastery of all these essential capacities. Interestingly, they are often all used in most daily interactions. Even the simplest communication often involves paying attention, engaging, reading and responding to affective gestures, and problem-solving, as well as using ideas creatively, logically, and reflectively.

Of particular importance are the four levels of development and related competencies that precede and build our capacity to symbolize our world and engage in higher-level thinking and social skills. In these four basic levels, there are embedded many of the most critical building blocks of mental health and also the seeds of mental illness (if they are not mastered). For example, our ability to test reality, interact socially with others, form relationships, control our behavior, regulate our moods, integrate love and anger (and other polarities of emotions), and form a sense of self that's cohesive rather than fragmented, are all part of these early stages.

When a caregiver engages with her infant in a nurturing relationship and reads and responds to that infant's capacity for emotional signaling, and thereby fosters long chains of back-and-forth emotional gesturing and problem-solving, the wondrous abilities just described begin to be learned. The baby gets a sense of what intimacy is all about.

The baby practices and finds pleasure and satisfaction in being purposeful and taking initiative (because their signals are being responded to). As the baby's interactions become part of an elaborate pattern of reciprocal interactions, the baby learns not only to problem-solve, but to control his behavior (appropriate behavior gets one response and inappropriate behavior gets a different response). The baby feels as well as observes the difference between his parent's big smiles, nodding approval, and eyes lighting up and frowns, annoyed, or disgusted looks. The baby's interest in the parent's responses and his ability to use them to regulate behavior, however, only occurs as part of these long chains of back-and-forth, affective interaction. In contrast to regulation through back-and-forth emotional signaling, frightening punishments are often responded to with resentment and fear, rather than the desire to please and the internalization of a sense of right and wrong.

The caregiver's capacity to "up-regulate" or "down-regulate" the baby's moods through these sensitive emotional interactions helps the baby maintain a more even mood, rather than fall prey to the extremes. In addition, the ability of the caregiver to hang in there with these long, pleasurable interactions through thick and thin, through the angry times and the happy times, teaches the child that love and hate and other emotional polarities are part of the same relationships (i.e. part of the same "me" and part of the same "you"). And from these integrating experiences, a sense of "self" that unites the different parts into a larger whole is formed. Most importantly, if the caregiver is comfortable with all the feelings that constitute a baby's humanity, including not only pleasure and curiosity, but also anger, disgust, sense of loss, and even fear, then the caregiver helps the baby use interactions to modulate these feelings and eventually make them all part of a regulated "self."

We then see a child who can express and experience inside himself, and eventually label, the full range of human feelings. If the parent is uncomfortable with some of these feelings and becomes withdrawn or unavailable in the face of anger or overly reactive and punitive in the face of assertive defiance (rather than being modulating and interactive), the baby begins having constrictions in the feelings he can experience, express, and eventually label and reflect on. These, as well as biological differences that make these early interactions more difficult, can seed later problems rather than healthy development.

## Mental illness

Mental illness, like mental health, is a complex concept. It is also tempting to over-simplify our approaches to mental illness. Among the over-simplifications has been a tendency to focus only on symptoms without adequate understanding of underlying mechanisms. For example, one might focus on a person feeling bad about themselves or not sleeping well or sleeping too much as symptoms of depression without focusing on the underlying mechanisms, which might involve turning anger inward, a series of underlying biochemical or physiological differences, or both. Similarly, there's a tendency to focus on the genetics or genetic susceptibility to different mental illnesses without adequate understanding of the experiential and environmental factors or even metabolic factors that influence genetic expression. There are developmental pathways that lie between genes and behavior.

Many years ago American psychiatry attempted to focus on observable phenomena, such as symptoms, with the understandable goal of making psychiatry more objective and scientific. However, we may have shifted too far away from the search for understanding underlying dynamics. The field may have literally "thrown out the baby with the bath water," as Sally's case illustrates. While many clinicians use a broad biopsychosocial model, which includes psychodynamic understanding, symptoms, and biological patterns, treatment approaches have tended to be more "reductionistic." They have focused on biological treatments for symptom change and/or short-term therapy, rather than prevention or reworking underlying patterns.

We have constructed a dynamic, developmental approach that offers the promise of understanding underlying dynamics and developmental pathways, and, at the same time, dealing with observable and verifiable behaviors and symptoms. This approach focuses on understanding the developmental steps or organizations leading to mental health and mental illness. It takes into account both the biology and experiences of the individual. We conceptualize this as a *developmental bio-psycho-social approach*.

In this approach, we recognize that development is a very complex process involving not only interactions between biology and experience, but that at each stage of development biology and experience come together in different ways to create competencies or difficulties, including disorders.

In other words, between the biological factors a baby might inherit and his behavior as an adult lie many intermediary or developmental levels of organization. Each one of these builds competencies or vulnerabilities, difficulties, and disorders.

This process is especially complex because of the bi-directional nature of the forces that affect these intermediary developmental organizations. At each of the stages (see table 17.1), experience cannot only alter behavior, but can also change the underlying biology of the organism. For example, learning experiences can change the physical structure of synapses in neurons involved in the brain when it converts experiences into long-term memories. Extra experience with one or another sensory pathway can increase the neuronal connections in that pathway.

On the other hand, certain physical differences in a baby may invite the caregiver to provide or not provide certain types of experiences. A baby with low muscle tone who is under-reactive to sound and touch will often be somewhat unresponsive. Many parents will respond to the baby's unresponsiveness with a lack of involvement. This usually makes the baby even more unresponsive and withdrawn. However, if we can change the direction of this process and help the caregiver to woo the low-tone, under-reactive baby into pleasurable nurturing interactions (e.g. by being highly energetic and persistent and finding sources of pleasure), this same baby can become outgoing, assertive, curious, and delightful. Clinically, we've observed differences in social, language, and cognitive outcomes in such children, depending on how the caregiving environment responds to their biological differences.

It's a two-way street! In other words, neither biology nor experience alone is destiny. Not only do the two interact together, they interact in a multi-directional way.

Furthermore, as biology and experience interact, they create a series of developmental organizations, each one of which can build competencies or disorders. The baby with low muscle tone can successfully or unsuccessfully negotiate his early capacity for forming relationships. This then serves as a foundation for intimacy and trust or self-absorption and, perhaps, suspiciousness. At the next level, learning to use emotional signaling to regulate mood and problem-solve, the emotionally labile toddler can experience more dramatic mood swings with caregiver patterns that are too intrusive or withdrawn or become a better mood regulator with caregiver patterns that sensitively up-regulate and down-regulate according to the baby's mood.

In order to operationalize the notion of intermediary developmental organizations, we have found it helpful to characterize the child's biology, environment, functional emotional developmental stages, and interactions. We call the model, which looks at the child's individual differences, their emerging developmental organizations and capacities, and the interactive relationship patterns leading to competency or challenges, the Developmental, Individual-Difference, Relationship-based model (DIR).[2] It is a developmental bio-psycho-social model in

---

[2] Greenspan and Weider (1998); Greenspan (1997a).

which three dynamically related influences work together to direct human development.

The first influence is what the child brings into the world by way of his biological and genetic makeup. The child's biology, however, does not express itself directly. It expresses itself in the way the child "processes" experience. The child processes what he hears (auditory processing), sees (visual–spatial processing), touches (tactile processing), and smells, as well as how he plans and carries out actions and moves in space. As part of this processing, the child shows different ways of not only comprehending sensations, but reacting to them. He can be under- or overreactive (or sometimes both) in each sensory modality. To the degree that caregivers can work with the child's processing differences, often they can facilitate competencies. To the degree they can't, either due to family patterns or the nature of the processing difficulties themselves, they may facilitate challenges or problems.

These early formed, biologically based, hardwired structures can create a readiness to learn. They do not by themselves, however, determine the content of learning. Nor do they, by themselves, create advanced tools for learning, such as symbol formation and abstract and reflective thinking. These require learning interactions with caregivers and others.

A second influence, the environment, which includes cultural and family factors, as well as the physical environment, creates a unique amalgam of thoughts, behaviors, and ideas that the child's caregivers or others in his environment bring to the interactions with him. We can characterize these environmental and family patterns in terms of the degree to which interactions and family patterns support or undermine the mastery of the functional emotional capacities (see tables 17.1 and 17.2 at the end of the chapter).

The third influence involves the child/caregiver interaction patterns. The child brings his or her biological differences into these interactions. The caregiver brings the family and cultural patterns, including his or her own history, into the interaction pattern. These interaction patterns then determine the child's capacity for relative mastery (or non-mastery) of the functional emotional developmental capacities (i.e. the ability to be attentive, calm, and regulated; engage with intimacy with others; and communicate, think, and reflect).

The DIR biopsychosocial model creates a detailed picture of a person's unique developmental profile. It describes the earliest presymbolic and symbolic levels as well as later ones. Generally, we tend to focus on higher levels of functioning, which are explored through verbal descriptions of the content of the patient's mental life. In this model, however, it is also possible to look at presymbolic, foundation-building, emotional interactions.

It is often compelling to look at the symptoms and dramas of the moment when considering different types of problems and personalities. To understand symptoms and personalities more fully, we need to also delve into an individual's early presymbolic structures or organizations. In this way we can understand the "stage" on which the current drama of life takes place. This perspective is essential for understanding pre-senting problems and symptoms.

In creating a functional emotional developmental profile, it is important to look for both competencies and achievements, as well as deficits and constrictions. A deficit means a stage of functional emo-tional development has not been mastered and, therefore, a core ability such as the capacity for relating has not been mastered. A constriction means that the stage and its corresponding ability has been partially mastered, but without the full range, depth, or stability that would be optimal. For example, a child learns to relate to others, but not deeply and with great warmth, or he tends to withdraw when he's angry (see table17.2).

The DIR model has enabled us to characterize different mental health disorders, as well as healthy development. We've been able, for example, to characterize the developmental organizations that tend to precede the formation of full-blown disorders in a variety of conditions. This enables early identification as well as the formulation of preventive strategies. The characterization of these developmental organizations, in fact, leads to the formulation of very specific prevention and early intervention approaches. Consider the following very brief examples of insights into early developmental patterns and intervening organizations of a few disorders.

### Depression

We've observed specific early interaction patterns that contribute to a vulnerability towards depression. These involve the stage of co-regulated, reciprocal, affective, problem-solving, and mood-regulating interactions. When the toddler or preschooler evidences strong affects, the reciprocal partner, instead of modulating up or down to help keep the child regulated and in an even mood instead tends to either with-draw (even temporarily), slow down significantly in their own responses so that it's experienced as a withdrawal, or overreact and intrude in a somewhat hostile way, disrupting a calm sense of relating. In all of these instances, instead of a pattern of modulation where the caregiver up or down-regulates to help the child's moods stay even, there is a temporary rupture in the co-regulated pattern of interaction. This results in dysphoric affects, often a sense of loss, and sometimes humiliation or anger. We see, sometimes only temporarily, a child experiencing some of these catastrophic affects rather than the modulating ones that are more adaptive.

As the child moves into the symbolic realm (assuming these patterns have not been overwhelmingly disruptive), these more dysregulated patterns make it difficult for the child to construct a nurturing image of a caregiver that can be symbolized in times of loss, stress, or anger. The child also comes to expect strong affects will lead to loss of soothing and nurturing interactions. We see both these patterns frequently occurring in adults with depression. Their loss is two-fold. Often an event in their lives may involve loss, which routinely would precipitate some sadness in anyone. But, they can't call on a nurturing internal image to help them feel better and don't have the co-regulated patterns of interaction in their basic character structure, making it hard for them to engage in their current relationships in a soothing and modulating manner.

In addition, individuals with this pattern tend to be sensory hypersensitive and, therefore, affectively reactive, making their need for modulating, soothing, co-regulating interactions greater than would otherwise be the case. We have been able to develop preventive intervention approaches and treatment programs based on these insights.[3]

### Anxiety

Children vulnerable to anxiety, in contrast to depression, have a different type of co-regulated interactive pattern. What we tend to see with individuals vulnerable to anxiety is a pattern whereby the parent overreacts to the child's communications (i.e. emotional gestures) so that the child is frequently feeling dysregulated and overwhelmed. The child vulnerable to anxiety tends to be sensory hypersensitive, just like the individual vulnerable to depression. The difference is that here, instead of experiencing a loss or rupture in the relationship, the child is constantly feeling overwhelmed and experiences dysphoric affects associated with overload and being overwhelmed. This child especially requires long chains of soothing, reciprocal interactions.

As this child progresses into the symbolic realm, constantly experiencing affects in an overwhelming manner, she is unable to use affects as a symbolic signal for various coping strategies. Instead of serving as a signal, such as "I better do something about this aggressive partner I

---

[3] Greenspan (1997a, 1989); Greenspan et al. (1998).

have," the individual feels overwhelmed and what for another person is a signal, is the first step in an escalating feeling of anxiety, sometimes leading to panic. Later relationships also tend to be more difficult as the individual expects, based on the earlier reciprocal affective patterns, to be intruded on or overwhelmed. Preventive intervention and treatment strategies that work with the patient's early organizations and expectations are looking clinically promising.[4]

## Conclusion

A dynamic developmental model of mental health and illness offers promise for the future. It can integrate the historical insights on human functioning with new biological and developmental findings. In this way we can move away from current trends toward overly simplistic, reductionistic models of human functioning toward innovative, dynamic prevention and treatment approaches.

Table 17.1 *Stages of functional emotional development*

| Functional emotional developmental level | Emotional, social, and intellectual capacities |
| --- | --- |
| Shared attention and regulation | Affective interest in sights, sound, touch, movement, and other sensory experiences. Also, initial experiences of modulating affects (i.e. calming down). |
| Engagement and relating | Pleasurable affects characterize relationships. Growing feelings of intimacy. |
| Two-way intentional, affective signaling and communication | A range of affects becomes used in back-and-forth affective signaling to convey intentions (e.g. reading and responding to affective signals). |
| Long chains of co-regulated emotional signaling and the formation of a presymbolic self | Affective interactions organized into action or behavioral patterns to express wishes and needs and solve problems (showing someone what you want with a pattern of actions rather than words or pictures). |
| | a. Fragmented level (little islands of intentional problem-solving behavior). |
| | b. Polarized level (organized patterns of behavior expressing only one or another feeling states, e.g. organized aggression and impulsivity or organized clinging, needy, dependent behavior, or organized fearful patterns). |

---

[4] Greenspan (1997a).

Table 17.1 (*cont.*)

| Functional emotional developmental level | Emotional, social, and intellectual capacities |
|---|---|
| | c. Integrated level (different emotional patterns – dependency, assertiveness, pleasure, etc. – organized into integrated, problem-solving affective interactions such as flirting, seeking closeness, and then getting help to find a needed object). |
| Creating representations (or ideas) | 1. Words and actions used together (ideas are acted out in action, but words are also used to signify the action). |
| | 2. Somatic or physical words to convey feeling state ("My muscles are exploding," "Head is aching"). |
| | 3. Using action words instead of actions to convey intent ("Hit you!"). |
| | 4. Conveying feelings as real rather than as signals ("I'm mad" or "Hungry" or "Need a hug" as compared with "I feel mad" or "I feel hungry" or "I feel like I need a hug"). In the first instance, the feeling state demands action and is very close to action and, in the second one, it's more a signal for something going on inside that leads to a consideration of many possible thoughts and/or actions. |
| | 5. Global feeling states ("I feel awful," "I feel OK," etc.). |
| | 6. Polarized feeling states (feelings tend to be characterized as all good or all bad). |
| Building bridges between ideas: logical thinking | 1. Differentiated feelings (gradually there are more and more subtle descriptions of feeling states – loneliness, sadness, annoyance, anger, delight, happiness, etc.). |
| | 2. Creating connections between differentiated feeling states ("I feel angry when you are mad at me"). |
| Multi-cause, comparative, and triangular thinking | Exploring multiple reasons for a feeling, comparing feelings, and understanding triadic interactions among feeling states ("I feel left out when Susie likes Janet better than me"). |
| Emotionally differentiated gray-area thinking | Shades and gradations among differentiated feeling states (ability to describe degrees of feelings around anger, love, excitement, love, disappointment – "I feel a little annoyed"). |
| Intermittent reflective thinking, a stable sense of self, and an internal standard | Reflecting on feelings in relationship to an internalized sense of self ("It's not like me to feel so angry," or "I shouldn't feel this jealous"). |
| Reflective thinking with an expanded self; the adolescent themes | Expanding reflective feeling descriptors into new realms, including sexuality, romance, closer and more intimate peer relationships, school, community, and culture, and emerging sense of identity ("I have such an intense crush on that new boy that I know it's silly. I don't even know him"). |

Table 17.1 (*cont.*)

| | |
|---|---|
| Reflective thinking with an expanded self; into the future | Using feelings to anticipate and judge (including probabilizing) future possibilities in light of current and past experience ("I don't think I would be able to really fall in love with him because he likes to flirt with everyone and that has always made me feel neglected and sad"). |
| Reflective thinking with an expanded self; the adult years | Expanding feeling states to include reflections and anticipatory judgment with regard to new levels and types of feelings associated with the stages of adulthood, including: |
| Reflective thinking and the separation, internalization, and stabilization of the self | The ability to separate from, function independently of, and yet remain close to and internalize many of the positive features of one's nuclear family and stabilize a sense of self and internal standard. |
| Reflective thinking and commitment, intimacy, and choice | Intimacy (serious long-term relationships). |
| Extending the self to incorporate family and children | The ability to nurture and empathize with one's children without over-identifying with them. |
| Middle age | The ability to broaden one's nurturing and empathetic capacities beyond one's family and into the larger community. |
| | The ability to experience and reflect on changing perspectives of time and space and the new feelings of intimacy, mastery, pride, competition, disappointment, and loss associated with the family, career, and intra-personal changes of mid-life. |
| The aging process | The ability for true reflective thinking of an unparalleled scope or a retreat and narrowing of similar proportions. There is the possibility of true wisdom free from the self-centered and practical worries of earlier stages. It also, however, can lead to retreat into one's changing physical states, a narrowing of interests, and concrete thinking. |

Table 17.2 *Overview of the levels of emotional transformation and thinking and the different degrees of mastery possible at each level for the first nine stages*

**Self-regulation and interest in the world (homeostasis)**
**(first learned at 0–3 months)**

| 1 – Maladaptive | 3 | 5 | 7 – Adaptive |
|---|---|---|---|
| Attention is fleeting (a few seconds here or there) and/or very active or agitated or mostly self-absorbed and/or lethargic or passive. | When very interested or motivated or captivated can attend and be calm for short periods (e.g. 30 to 60 seconds). | Focused, organized, and calm except when overstimulated or understimulated (e.g. noisy, active, or very dull setting); challenged to use a vulnerable skill (e.g. a child with weak fine motor skills asked to write rapidly), or ill, anxious, or under stress. | Focused, organized, and calm most of the time, even under stress. |

**Forming relationships, attachment, and engagement**
**(first learned at 2–7 months)**

| 1 | 3 | 5 | 7 |
|---|---|---|---|
| Aloof, withdrawn, and/or indifferent to others. | Superficial and need-oriented, lacking intimacy. | Intimacy and caring is present but disrupted by strong emotions, like anger or separation (e.g. person withdraws or acts out). | Deep, emotionally rich capacity for intimacy, caring, and empathy, even when feelings are strong or under stress. |

**Two-way purposeful communication (somatopsychological differentiation) (first learned at 3–10 months)**

| 1 | 3 | 5 | 7 |
|---|---|---|---|
| Mostly aimless, fragmented, unpurposeful behavior and emotional expressions (e.g. no purposeful grins or smiles or reaching out with body posture for warmth or closeness). | Some need-oriented, purposeful islands of behavior and emotional expressions. No cohesive larger social goals. | Often purposeful and organized, but not with a full range of emotional expressions (e.g. seeks out others for closeness and warmth with appropriate flirtatious glances, body posture, and the like, but becomes chaotic, fragmented, or aimless when very angry). | Most of the time purposeful and organized behavior and a wide range of subtle emotions, even when there are strong feelings and stress. |

**Behavioral organization, problem-solving, and internalization (complex sense of self) (first learned at 9–18 months)**

| 1 | 3 | 5 | 7 |
|---|---|---|---|
| Distorts the intents of others (e.g. misreads cues and, therefore, feels suspicious, mistreated, unloved, angry, etc.). | In selected relationships can read basic intentions of others (such as acceptance or rejection) but unable to read subtle cues (like respect or pride or partial anger). | Often accurately reads and responds to a range of emotional signals, except in certain circumstances involving selected emotions, very strong emotions, or stress or due to a difficulty with processing sensations, such as sights or sounds (e.g. certain signals are confusing). | Reads and responds to most emotional signals flexibly and accurately even when under stress (e.g. comprehends safety vs. danger, approval vs. disapproval, acceptance vs. rejection, respect vs. humiliation, partial anger, etc.). |

Table 17.2 (*cont.*)

## Representational elaboration and differentiation (first learned at 18–48 months)

| 1 | 3 | 5 | 7 |
|---|---|---|---|
| Puts wishes and feelings into action or into somatic states ("my tummy hurts"). Unable to use ideas to elaborate wishes and feelings (e.g. hits when mad, hugs or demands physical intimacy when needy, rather than experiencing idea of anger or expressing wish for closeness). | Uses ideas in a concrete way to convey desire for action or to get basic needs met. Does not elaborate idea of feeling in its own right (e.g. "I want to hit but can't because someone is watching" rather than "I feel mad"). | Often uses ideas to be imaginative and creative and express range of emotions, except when experiencing selected conflicted or difficult emotions or when under stress (e.g. cannot put anger into words or pretend). | Uses ideas to express full range of emotions. Is imaginative and creative most of the time, even under stress. |

## Emotional thinking

| 1 | 3 | 5 | 7 |
|---|---|---|---|
| Ideas are experienced in a piecemeal or fragmented manner (e.g. one phrase is followed by another with no logical bridges). | Thinking is polarized, ideas are used in an all-or-nothing manner (e.g. things are all good or all bad. There are no shades of gray). | Thinking is constricted (i.e. tends to focus mostly on certain themes like anger and competition). Often thinking is logical, but strong emotions, selected emotions, or stress can lead to polarized or fragmented thinking. | Thinking is logical, abstract, and flexible across the full range of age-expected emotions and interactions. Thinking is also relatively reflective at age-expected levels and in relationship to age-expected endeavors (e.g. peer, spouse, or family relationship). Thinking supports movement into the next stages in the course of life. |

## Triangular and multi-cause thinking (reflective)

| 1 | 3 | 5 | 7 |
|---|---|---|---|
| Unable to be logical. Tends to get fragmented or piecemeal where logical bridges between ideas are lost. | Can be logical, but only in a concrete manner, and is unable to reflect on multiple reasons and indirect influences for age-expected experience. | Can reflect on multiple reasons and feelings and consider indirect influences for some age-expected experiences, but not others (e.g. for competition, but not closeness and intimacy). Cannot be reflective in this way when feelings are strong. | Can think about and reflect on multiple reasons for feelings for age-expected experiences. Can look at indirect influences (e.g. "She is upset because he is mad at her parents, not me"). Age-expected experiences would include experience with parents, siblings, peers, and school, and a full range of feelings from dependency to curiosity and anger and loss. |

## Affectively differentiated (gray area) reflective thinking

| 1 | 3 | 5 | 7 |
|---|---|---|---|
| Unable to be logical. Tends to get fragmented or piecemeal or very polarized in thinking. | Can be logical, but only in a concrete manner, and cannot reflect on multiple reasons and indirect influences for age-expected experience. | Can reflect on multiple reasons and feelings and consider indirect influences for only some age-expected experiences and events and not when feelings are very strong. | Can reflect on varying degrees of different feelings for a range of age-expected experiences or events (e.g. "I feel a little angry, but mostly disappointed that Dad forgot his promise"). Age-expected experiences would include experience with parents, siblings, peers, and school, and a full range of feelings from dependency to curiosity and anger and loss. |

Table 17.2 (cont.)

## Reflective thinking based on internal sense of self and standards

| 1 | 3 | 5 | 7 |
|---|---|---|---|
| Unable to reflect on multiple causes or engage in gray-area thinking, is sometimes logical in only a concrete manner or becomes polarized or fragmented in thinking. | Can be reflective and consider multiple causes and engage in gray-area thinking, but is unable to simultaneously reflect on moment-to-moment experiences and an inner standard or sense of self. | Can reflect on feelings or experiences of the moment and, at the same time, compare them to a longer-term view of themselves and their experiences, values, and/or goals or ideals for some age-expected experiences, but not others (i.e. with peers, but not with parents, or with closeness, but not with anger). Cannot be reflective in this way when feelings are strong. | Can reflect on feelings or experiences of the moment and, at the same time, compare them to a longer-term view of themselves and their experiences, values, and/or goals or ideals. Can be reflective in this way across the full range of age-expected experiences, and in the context of new cognitive capacities (i.e. for probabilistic, future oriented thinking).[*] |

SUGGESTED READINGS

Greenspan, S. I. (1989). *The development of the ego: implications for personality theory, psychopathology, and the psychotherapeutic process.* New York: International Universities Press.

(1997a). *Developmentally based psychotherapy.* Madison, CT: International Universities Press.

(1997b). *The growth of the mind and the endangered origins of intelligence.* Reading, MA: Addison Wesley Longman.

Greenspan, S. I., and S. Wieder (1998). *The child with special needs: encouraging intellectual and emotional growth.* Reading, MA: Perseus Books.

# 18 Dyadic microanalysis of mother–infant communication informs clinical practice

*Beatrice Beebe and Joseph Jaffe*

Our research began in the 1960s with the study of adult dialogue by Joseph Jaffe and Stanley Feldstein. Our interest was in features of speech rhythms relevant to the communication of mood, the phenomenon of empathy, and the breakdown of effective dialogue. Speech rhythms include turn-taking, pausing, and interrupting. By the late 1960s, when Daniel Stern and Beatrice Beebe joined the team, our interests widened to the study of mother–infant dialogues. Since then, the analysis of speech rhythms has been expanded to analogous rhythms of many modalities (gaze, vocal quality, facial expression, touching, head movement, and posture).

This dyadic "microanalysis" research looks at the joint behaviors of two people. It operates like a microscope, identifying in detail the instant-by-instant interactive events which are so fast and subtle that they are usually lost to the naked eye (ear), and operate largely out of awareness. The analysis of different modalities of communication operates like the stains lighting up different coexisting structures under the microscope. Using this approach we discovered that maternal depression affected facial expression and gaze direction in opposite ways: mothers and infants were vigilant to each other's facial shifts, but withdrawn from monitoring each other's visual availability, as we describe in detail below.

The discoveries made with this research have tremendous implications for early intervention in mother–infant communication disturbances. Both embodying the unusual combination of researcher and psychoanalyst, Beebe and Jaffe are intensely concerned with translating research findings into clinical interventions. Beebe offers a video-assisted therapeutic consultation to mother–infant pairs presenting for treatment, observing them in the same split-screen, videotaping format used for research pairs, and using research findings to guide treatment interventions. A therapeutic viewing of the videotape with the parent is the springboard for the treatment. We will illustrate this approach with two mother–infant treatment cases. In addition, we use this approach in an ongoing project to treat mothers who were pregnant and widowed in the World Trade Center disaster of September 11, 2001, and their infants and young children.

## History of our research program

The history of our research program shows how an increasingly detailed picture of the interactive system emerged. In the 1960s, when Jaffe and Feldstein set out to study communication in adult psychotherapy, voice recording of therapy sessions was becoming popular. Psychotherapy was still defined as a "talking cure," so words and sentences sufficed for raw data. We rendered these words *computer readable*, and the very first digital computer at the New York State Psychiatric Institute soon followed. Process research in all therapies that utilized interviews seemed within reach.

But we knew that words were not enough. The "music" needed to be brought to life. Our problem was that there was no easy way to record or measure the non-verbal communication that accompanied the words. We studied movie film frame by frame, by numbering the frames sequentially, but videotape and computers were still uncommon. Gaze coding was done by hand, in real time, on running paper tape. And once videotape was available, we had no automated system to quantify movements of interest, such as face and gaze. Thus, the field of non-verbal behavior research was both theoretically and technologically years behind the automated linguistic analysis of speaking and listening.

### Dyadic systems view of communication

Our approach to non-verbal face-to-face exchange was based on a "dyadic systems" view of communication in which any action in a dyadic relationship is jointly defined by the behavior of both partners. The power of this definition is particularly evident when social roles cannot be actualized in the absence of the other, such as in predator–prey, or approach–avoid patterns such as "maternal chase – infant dodge."

The coding of *dyadic states* was our concrete contribution to the systems notion, as we describe shortly. The concept of dyadic states was developed at a time when the reigning psychological model was stimulus-response theory, a one-way process, in which the passive receiver could not influence the sender during message transmission. This model was inadequate for face-to-face communication, a simultaneous, bidirectional exchange, in which sending and receiving are concurrent and reciprocally evoked.

## Dyadic microanalysis of vocal rhythms

In the 1960s, dialogue was conceptualized simply as two alternating monologues, such as "question–answer" interviewing, without any consideration of a dyadic process, generating phenomena such as interruptions, or the exchange of turns.

To study dialogue, two-channel voice recordings could easily be produced via microphones attached to therapist and patient. But we wanted an automated way of obtaining data that would obviate long hours of transcription. An analogue-to-digital (A to D) converter, the *A*utomated *V*ocal *T*ransaction *A*nalyzer (AVTA), coded the parallel speech streams into sequences of sound and silence, that is, "speech rhythms." Dispensing with the words, and substituting the ongoing vocal rhythms, enabled us to *automate* our analysis of the communication process. This breakthrough played a central role in our research for the next forty years.

The AVTA system samples a conversation between partners A and B at regular "split-second" (0.25 sec) intervals. As we will see below, analyzing interactions in such fine detail yielded a goldmine of important information about infant development. We used the AVTA system to generate dyadic states. At each instant of sampling we code one of four dyadic states: 0 = both silent; 1 = A speaks and B is silent; 2 = B speaks and A is silent; and, 3 = both speak. Each state is a slice of a dyadic relationship, but the *individual* gets lost in two of them. Note that when partners A and B are doing the same thing, *i.e.*, state 0 (both silent) and state 3 (both speaking), the distinction between speaker and listener is momentarily lost. If both are silent, who is the speaker, and if both are talking, who interrupted whom? Only a *sequence of states* solves this ambiguity and preserves the continuity of roles. By preserving sequence, the data become analogous to a movie film, rather than a still photo.

First, we imagined that at each instant the partners make simultaneous, but independent "decisions" to vocalize or not. But in our model, each pair of decisions is contingent upon their joint "dyadic state" at the previous instant. Next, a "turn rule" was introduced that acted like a parliamentarian, assigning the turn as a "right of way" to the alternating speakers. A partner gained the turn at a moment of unilateral speech, and kept it (despite any sounds of the listener) until the listener vocalized unilaterally, defining a *turn switch*.

Within the turn, the ambiguous "joint silence" was then assigned to the person who holds the turn. The ambiguous "joint speaking" was termed an interruption, assigned to the listener unless it resulted in a turn switch, in which case the interruptor becomes the speaker.

Together, these tactics "rescued the individuals" who had been homogenized in the four dyadic states. Thus, we could define a separate turn for each individual; within each turn, states were defined dyadically. This approach allows study of both the *dyad and the individual* in a dyadic context. Our sound–silence model of communication was later applied to other kinds of nonverbal interactions, such as "gaze-on, gaze-off" and "approach–avoid."

What was by then dubbed the "Jaffe–Feldstein conversational model" grew from six to ten states to further subdivide states of joint silence and joint speaking. This enabled measurement of those brief silences between speaker and listener as they exchange turns. First considered a "reaction time," it was soon renamed a "switching pause" that was terminated by a "turn switch." *The matching of switching pause durations between partners* was a crucial early discovery: each partner tends to wait a similar amount of time before taking a turn, facilitating a smooth exchange of turns. This discovery led directly to the establishment of Jaffe's Department of Communication Sciences at NYSPI in 1964. The descriptive papers of Jaffe and Feldstein of that era were published in *Science* (1964) for monologue, in *Nature* (1967) for dialogue, and led to a book, *Rhythms of dialogue*, in 1970.

The switching pause became the most powerful predictor of outcomes in our research and in that of other investigators as well. In our later work it predicted infant attachment and cognitive outcomes. The switching pause is uniquely dyadic, in the sense that it does not exist in a monologue. It begins as the turnholder stops speaking, and it ends as the listener begins to speak. The switching pause is related to the turn rhythm and is interpreted as a complex regulation moment, composed of reciprocal speaker-listener role-exchange involving synchronized disengagement and re-engagement. In this sense it is a fundamental aspect of the structure of dialogue. That may account for its clinical usefulness, as we illustrate below, in the mother–infant treatment of "Roberta."

### Preverbal conversations

In the 1970s, our basic research on dyadic vocal timing changed its focus from adult–adult to adult–infant vocal and movement (gaze, face, touch) interactions. At that time, a long-term project of split-screen, video-recording of mother–infant interaction was begun by Dan Stern (a postdoctoral fellow) and his graduate student, Beatrice Beebe. The adult work on dialogic timing influenced our infancy work through our focus on (a) the dyadic systems approach which studies both the dyad and the individual in a dyadic context, (b) the temporal structure of dialogue, (c) the bidirectional coordination of rhythms in which each partner's behavior is coordinated with that of the other, (d) the relation of dialogic timing coordination to affect and bonding, and (e) the impact of a novel partner, the stranger, on dialogic timing.

We sensed that the dyadic timing system is a fundamental under-pinning of both adult and child conversations. From this perspective, both vocalization and movement (gaze, facial expression, etc.) are parts of a larger communicative "package" that may be organized by a common rhythmic time base. For example, mother–infant vocal rhythms are correlated with those of looking, head movement, and gesture. As such, vocal rhythm is one easily quantified index of the rich communicative "package" that mothers and infants display and coordinate in face-to-face interaction. That makes it an ideal candidate for use in research.

Our team found startling similarities between the temporal patterns of adult conversation and the time patterns of mother and infant vocal and movement behaviors (such as gaze, head orientation shifts, facial changes). Mother–infant gaze interactions, for example, followed the same contingency structure as adult–adult verbal interactions, in the sense that much of what is happening any moment can be accounted for by the most recent event (within a second). We speculated that this form of contingency may be a universal formal property of dyadic commu-nication, detectable in gaze patterns long before the onset of speech. Moreover, in both adult conversations and mother–infant vocal exchanges, the duration of the switching pause is matched (correlated). Because switching pauses regulate the turn exchange, aspects of a dia-logic structure are thus already in evidence prior to speech onset, and are regulated in a manner similar to adult conversation.

We also documented approach–avoid patterns, dubbed "chase and dodge," in which maternal head approach (looming) predicted infant avoidance movements (head back, down, and away), and infant avoidance movements predicted maternal "chase" (head and body movements following the infant's direction of withdrawal). This pattern turned out to have great clinical usefulness, illustrated in the mother–infant treatment case of Linda and Dan, below.

### Current research: adult–infant vocal rhythms

Although key infant researchers in the 1970s and 1980s appreciated the critical importance of the coordination of mother–infant rhythms, and considered it central to mother–infant bonding, our study of four-month vocal rhythm coordination (of vocalizations, pauses, and switching pauses) and twelve-month attachment and cognition outcomes is one of the few empirical demonstrations of this idea. Four-month vocal timing taps a system in which the infant is highly competent. By four to five months, infants discriminate duration, rate, and rhythm. Furthermore, sensitivity to timing necessarily involves sensitivity to affective and cognitive information.

Our highly detailed analysis of vocal timing paid off. *High* degrees of coordination between four-month infants and strangers in the lab was associated with optimal infant *cognitive* scores at twelve months. In contrast, *midrange* degrees of coordination between mother and infant, and stranger and infant, in home or lab, was associated with secure infant *attachment* at twelve months; high and low degrees predicted insecure attachment. High response to novelty is thus favorable for cognition, whereas midrange degree of coordination may allow more flexibility in a secure attachment climate. Very high coordination (associated with disorganized and anxious-resistant attachment) may index vigilance under conditions of uncertainty, challenge, or threat; very low coordination (associated with avoidant attachment) may index withdrawal.

We construed our patterns of dialogic vocal timing as procedures for managing aspects of the "pragmatics" of social interactions: the "how" of communication, rather than the "what." Infant and adult are organizing procedures for when to vocalize, when to pause, and for how long; procedures for managing attention, activity level, turn taking, joining and being joined, tracking and being tracked. Because these dialogic timing procedures predicted social/cognitive outcomes, we argued that through these procedures, infants and adults come to expect and procedurally represent the timing of ongoing vocal interactions, out of focal awareness. If so, these procedures may bias the trajectory of developing personality styles (such as joining, interrupting, management of turn taking, vigilant or withdrawn tracking) and may be spontaneously retrieved when similar contexts occur. This concept is illustrated in the treatment case of Roberta and her mother, described below. Roberta's mother tended to interrupt Roberta, finishing Roberta's sentences for her. Roberta's mother had had similar experiences with her own mother interrupting her.

*Clinical implications of vocal rhythms.* These dialogic vocal timing procedures provide a unique entry into clinical intervention in mother–infant treatment. Infants presenting with the symptom of avoiding gazing at the mother's face can often be lured back into visual contact when the mother is taught to match the tempo of the infant's vocalization-pause rhythm. Frequently the switching pause is mis-regulated in dyads presenting for treatment, as we see in the case of Roberta, below. Mothers can be taught to wait slightly longer after they vocalize, to see if the infant will "take a turn;" and to "get into synch" with the infant after the infant vocalizes, by matching his switching pause before resuming her turn.

*The case of Roberta.* Roberta and her mother were referred for treatment by the mother's therapist when Roberta was sixteen months. Although a full-term infant, Roberta had suffered multiple invasive medical procedures in the first month of life because of acute asthma. She had thus experienced pain, over-arousal, and helplessness. Roberta now bit herself whenever severely frustrated, and this symptom did not yield despite numerous consultations with the pediatrician, who now gave Roberta a clean bill of health. Roberta and her mother were invited to "play as they would at home," as they were videotaped in our split-screen filming lab. They played face-to-face, both sitting on chairs at a low table.

Mother sat with shoulders tensed, leaning forward, smiling, but with a quizzical raised-eyebrows look. Roberta was delighted with the toys, exclaiming "bird, mommy!" Mother rapidly asked many questions, directing Roberta's attention. There was little time for Roberta to develop her own play themes. Mother was so coordinated that she often finished Roberta's sentences for her.

Roberta then became alert to a slight sound of the camera moving, and mother herself alerted to Roberta's attention shift. As Roberta carefully watched the camera, mother was highly coordinated with Roberta's rhythms of vocalization and gesture, "joining" Roberta. But immediately mother tried to shift her to something else, pointing to another toy, as if to try to control her interest. Roberta frequently altered her own focus to follow that of mother. But eventually, as mother continued to redirect her, Roberta heightened her intense attention to the camera, avoiding the mother.

After many repetitions of this pattern we began to see that mother's joining through rapid, contingent high coordination was in the service of shifting Roberta, as if to ward off where Roberta might go, namely into over-arousal and self-biting. We also saw that the turn-switching between mother and Roberta was extremely rapid. The switching pause was often truncated as mother rushed in, highly coordinated, but leaving little room for Roberta. Frequently mother actually interrupted Roberta. We speculated that mother's worry about Roberta had made her hypervigilant to the slightest shifts in Roberta, even though mother was affectionate and warm. For her part, Roberta's biting herself may have been a solution to her hyper-arousal, first caused by a medical condition, but now also precipitated by mother's own anxiety and fear for Roberta.

Following the videotaping, in a series of sessions utilizing therapeutic viewing of the videotape, mother was helped to see her own hyper-sensitivity to Roberta and how it might escalate Roberta. When we pointed out how she tended to finish Roberta's sentences for her, she remembered that her own mother had been that way with her. Mother was helped to slow down, to pause more, and make more room for Roberta. In follow-up videotaping sessions three and six months later, Roberta's self-biting was much less frequent. At follow-up a year later, it was very rare.

## Current research: the effects of maternal depression on multiple mother–infant communication modalities

Under the leadership of Beatrice Beebe, with the collaboration of Jaffe, Feldstein, and Patricia Cohen and her statistical team of Karen Buck and Henian Chen, the design of the vocal timing study was repeated and expanded in a major NIMH-funded study of self-report depression (CES-D) at six weeks postpartum. Both video (completed) and audio recording (in progress) were performed. The video study demonstrated that six-week maternal depression had strikingly different effects on the different communication modalities of gaze, face, vocal quality, and touch during mother–infant four-month face-to-face play.

Depressed mothers and their infants showed a "split" in attention (gaze) vs. affect (facial/vocal quality) coordination. In depressed mothers and their infants, neither partner was as coordinated with the other's shifts of gaze on and off the partner's face as controls were. But depressed mothers heightened their facial coordination with infant facial and vocal shifts, as if becoming "overly thrilled" as infants became facially or vocally more positive, and "overly disappointed" as infants became facially or vocally more distressed. Similarly, infants of depressed mothers reciprocally heightened their vocal quality coordin-ation with maternal facial shifts, overly sensitive to maternal facial fluctuations. Compared to controls, these infants were more likely to become vocally positive as maternal facial expressions were positive; and more likely to fuss or whimper as mothers sobered, frowned, or grim-aced. Thus, compared to controls both depressed mothers and their infants were "vigilant" to each other's moment-by-moment affective shifts, while at the same time paying less attention to whether the partner was visually available for engagement.

In the modality of touch, depressed mothers and their infants showed a form of dyadic conflict: an "infant approach – mother withdraw" pattern. Infants heightened their self-touch coordination with shifts in maternal touch patterns, but mothers lowered their touch coordination with infant self-touch shifts. Maternal lowered touch coordination may disturb infants' ability to anticipate the effects of their own behavior on maternal behavior. As we will see below, this pattern was evident in the mother–infant treatment of Linda and Dan, where Linda's high-intensity touch patterns were not sensitive to Dan's self-touch, self-soothe efforts.

Although the second-by-second video coding of separate modalities in this study took the labor of twenty PhD students across ten years, it yielded a goldmine of data which defines early communication disorders with remarkable multi-modal complexity and nuance. This identification of different kinds of communication difficulties in different communication modalities can teach clinicians to observe modality by modality for various kinds of dyadic patterns (such as mutual vigilance, mutual withdrawal, approach–withdrawal), rather than looking for more global patterns such as maternal "sensitivity" and "intrusion," or infant "withdrawal."

### Clinical implications of maternal depression: the case of Linda and Dan

Dr. Phyllis Cohen brought her patient Linda, in individual psychotherapy following a severe postpartum depression, and her five-month-old son Dan, to Beebe and Jaffe's filming lab in the Department of Communication Sciences, NYSPI. The pediatrician had noted the lack of a social smile and a "peculiar" quality; neurological testing (and early intervention testing) turned up no findings. Linda said that Dan is not interested in her, he does not love her, and she had an easier time with her first child.

Instructed to play with her baby as she would at home, Linda played with Dan face-to-face in our split-screen filming chamber. Linda was no longer severely depressed but nevertheless there was a residual interaction disturbance. As Linda leaned in toward Dan with a high intensity touch pattern, her hands on his belly, Dan looked away instead of orienting to his mother, making eye-contact, perhaps vocalizing or smiling. He moved his head down and away, looked down, sobered with a serious face, then frowned. He made no sounds.

Dan began to self-soothe by delicately rubbing his finger tips on Mom's hands; Mom pulled her hands away, disturbing his touch pattern, and moved her hands again into his belly, leaning in quite close. This pattern is very similar to that described above in the research on the effects of maternal depression: Linda's touch pattern was not sensitive to Dan's self-touch behavior. As she leaned in, Dan's head moved further away, and his foot pumped with an agitated quality, a "maternal chase – infant dodge" pattern. Each time Dan moved away, Mom called his name, asking him to look at her, and then plaintively asked if he did not like this game.

Following the filming, Dr. Beebe offered initial impressions. Dan was very aware of his mother, responsive to every move of her hands and head, but he was responding with withdrawal. He seemed to find Mom's play over-stimulating. By looking away so much he was able to reduce his arousal. This kind of play might be fine for another baby, but seemed to be too much for Dan. The first recommendation to Linda was to see if she could wait until Dan looked at her before trying to play, and see if Dan could respond if she kept her level of stimulation very low.

With ongoing individual sessions with Dr. Cohen, including therapeutic viewing of the videotapes with Dr. Cohen, and periodic visits to Dr. Beebe's filming lab every few months, Linda and Dan gradually began to find each other. Linda was gradually able to learn to wait until Dan returned her gaze and was visually available for engagement. This difficulty monitoring Dan's gaze is strikingly similar to that described above in the research on the effects of maternal depression. Linda was able to modulate her high-intensity, often rough touch games, so that Dan did not become as easily overwhelmed, perhaps a constitutional proclivity. Linda was taught how to match Dan's vocal rhythms, which often evoked Dan's visual interest, and he would then look at his mother. Treated over a three-year period, a follow-up when Dan was four years old showed a vital, enthusiastic child and a well-related pair.

This case illustrates how our dyadic microanalysis of the details of communication in the various modalities of vocal rhythm, as well as gaze, face, vocal quality, and touch, can inform clinical practice with mothers and infants. The details of the interaction patterns are used both for assessment of the difficulties as well as for the treatment itself. Therapeutic viewing of the videotapes, identifying the specific modalities through which the disturbances were communicated, was invaluable in helping the mother have "new eyes," new ways of seeing her child and her own responses, and new ways of behaving.

*World Trade Center disaster and pregnant widows*

When the disaster of September 11, 2001 struck, the infants and young children of the adult victims were in danger of being forgotten. We therefore began a treatment program for mothers who were pregnant and widowed, and their infants and young children, using therapeutic viewing of videotaped play interactions between mother and child. Dr. Beebe directs this program with Dr. Phyllis Cohen.

## Policy implications: basic research informs clinical practice

Even the best clinical eye must observe so many different things in an interaction that only global gestalts are registered. In contrast, micro-analysis uncovers aspects of non-verbal communication that the unaided human brain cannot report. For example, our finding that maternal depression affected gaze and facial patterns in opposite directions could not have been discovered with more global forms of coding. Further-more, this micro level is indispensable for formulating treatment inter-ventions. It is at this micro level that interactions are organized, and it is at this micro level that interactions go astray.

Continued basic dyadic microanalysis research on the effects of par-ental distress on parent–child communication and infant development is essential and should be a top funding priority. Although a great deal is now known about the effects of maternal depression on mother–infant communication and infant development, surprisingly little is known about the effects of other forms of distress, such as anxiety. This research is a critical source of information in designing early interven-tions and in teaching parent–infant clinicians, as well as other health providers such as pediatricians, how to evaluate early interactions.

A brief screening, based on split-screen video microanalysis of face-to-face interaction, together with a brief intervention, a therapeutic viewing of the videotape with a skilled parent–infant clinician, is an inexpensive and powerful tool that should be available to any concerned parent of an infant. Parent–infant clinicians should be recognized as members of a new clinical specialty and a priority for future training opportunities. Video-assisted mother–infant treatment interventions are based on infant research evidence of the nature of early interactions, but research that demonstrates the efficacy of this approach in double-blind studies is scarce and should be a funding priority.

SUGGESTED READINGS

Beebe, B. (2003). Brief mother–infant treatment using psychoanalytically informed video microanalysis. *Infant Mental Health Journal*, 24(1), 24–52.
    (2005). Mother–infant research informs mother–infant treatment. *Psychoanalytic Study of the Child*, 6.
Beebe, B., and F. Lachmann (2002). *Infant research and adult treatment: co-constructing interactions*. Hillsdale, NJ: The Analytic Press.

Beebe, B., J. Jaffe, and P. Cohen (2002). Support groups and video-bonding consultations for mothers and infants of 9–11. Manuscript, NYSPI, April. FEMA Liberty Fund; Robin Hood Foundation.

Beebe, B., S. Knoblauch, J. Rustin, and D. Sorter (2005). *Forms of intersubjectivity in infant research and adult treatment.* New York: Other Press.

Cohen, P., and B. Beebe (2002). Video feedback with a depressed mother and her infant: a collaborative individual psychoanalytic and mother–infant treatment. *Journal of Infant, Child, and Adolescent Psychotherapy*, 2(3), 1–55.

Jaffe, J., and S. Feldstein (1970). *Rhythms of dialogue.* New York: Academic Press.

Jaffe, J., B. Beebe, S. Feldstein, C. L. Crown, and M. Jasnow (2001). Rhythms of dialogue in infancy. *Monographs of the Society for Research in Child Development*, 66 (serial no. 265).

# 19 Current problems of Japanese youth: some possible pathways for alleviating these problems from the perspective of dynamic systems theory

*Alan Fogel and Masatoshi Kawai*

Yoshiko wouldn't reveal her son's name, because of fears that her neighbors in a suburb of Tokyo might find out. Three years ago, a classmate taunted her seventeen-year-old son with anonymous hate letters and abusive graffiti about him in the schoolyard. After that, he went into the family's kitchen, shut the door, and refused to leave and he hasn't left the room since then or allowed anyone in. The family eventually decided to build a new kitchen and Yoshiko takes meals to her son's door three times a day. There is a toilet next to the kitchen, but the boy has bathed only twice each year (adapted from a story by Phil Rees, BBC News, Sunday, October 20, 2002).

In this chapter, we will discuss the problem of Japanese adolescents and young adults called *hikikomori*, in which the teenager remains isolated in one room at home with limited contact with the outside world, perhaps via the internet, and with little or no communication with family members. They may make late-night shopping expeditions, leaving the home after parents are sleeping and avoiding any face-to-face contact with others, or they may not leave at all. The condition can last for many months or even years. There are believed to be over one million cases of *hikikomori* currently in Japan, which results in huge economic and social losses. In some cases, if parents seek to end the situation or force the child out, there can be violent attacks against the parents. Many parents are fearful of confronting their children, and the children themselves are fearful of other people and the outside world. So the problem remains without solution.

The conventional way of understanding this problem is to assume that it resides within the child, and that to alleviate the problem we need to find a way to change the child to fit in more with social expectations. From a dynamic systems point of view, however, the child is embedded

188

in a network of social relationships in the family and school, and those institutions are embedded in the history and current conditions of Japanese society and culture.

According to the dynamic systems perspective, stable patterns of social behavior (called *consensual frames*) emerge from the mutual relationship between constituents. In this case, the constituents are the child, the family, and the society. This means that the problems of young boys in Japan reflect an implicit consensual relationship between the child, family, and society that permits the problem to be maintained as a stable frame in the society (see chapter by Kerr, this book).

In the case of *hikikomori*, for example, the child can only remain in his bedroom because the parents are a consistent and reliable source of money, food, and an internet connection. Therefore, both parent and family play a role in supporting and maintaining the problem. In some way, although it is not beneficial, this frame may remain stable for long periods because it is safe and familiar. Can these problematic consensual frames be changed? Yes, but there must be a corresponding change in the family and society: the system of relationships must change. This means that the parents will need to change their behavior in order for the child to change his behavior. And that means stepping outside the familiar frame.

### Principles of systems change

In order to understand how to alleviate this problem in Japanese society, it is helpful to examine the process of change over time in social systems. Recent research has shown that as the existing consensual frames in a relationship begin to change, a variety of additional frames are spontaneously generated in order to assist the relationship through potentially difficult and chaotic times of change. These are listed in table 19.1.

Bridging frames are useful to help make a developmental transition between existing and emerging frames. Typically, bridging frames contain elements of both the existing and emerging frames (see table 19.2). In the case of romantic relationships, for example, there is typically a betrothal or engagement period in between courtship and marriage. The bridging frame of engagement contains some elements or components of the courtship frame; for example, the couple goes out together for enjoyment, play, and without family responsibilities. On the other hand, the bridging frame of engagement contains some components of the marriage frame because the couple begins talking about their future family life, and the in-laws and other family members become more

Table 19.1 *Frames that are created during a dynamic systems change process*

| | |
|---|---|
| Bridging frames | Link existing and emerging frames |
| Breakdown of existing frames | Disruption of existing patterns, unstable and chaotic |
| Recapitulation frames | Return of historical frames that were dormant |
| Re-organized emergent frames | New relationship patterns emerge and grow |

Table 19.2 *Bridging frames in a developmental sequence of dynamic systems change*

| EXISTING FRAME | $\rightarrow$ | BRIDGING FRAME | $\rightarrow$ | EMERGING FRAME |
|---|---|---|---|---|
| Courtship | $\rightarrow$ | Engagement | $\rightarrow$ | Marriage |
| Married couple | $\rightarrow$ | Pregnancy | $\rightarrow$ | Parenting |

involved in the couple's life. Thus engagement is a bridge between courtship and marriage by combining components of both together.

Bridging frames have the purpose of allowing people in a relationship to "try out" new ways of relating before committing themselves to embark on a newly emergent frame. Engaged couples, for example, can "try out" what it feels like to be married before the wedding. Bridging is a way of making developmental transitions more smoothly and with less fear or trauma resulting from the change.

## Breakdown of existing frames

In the example of romantic relationships, as the engagement period draws to a close and marriage is ready to begin, the courtship frame is reaching a state of breakdown. In this case, that existing frame has reached the end of its useful life and will cease to exist, except in memory. In the case of the end of the courtship period, the idea of breakdown need not have a negative significance if the couple truly wants to get married. The couple and family may greet the end of courtship and the beginning of marriage with a celebration.

In other cases, however, the breakdown of the existing system may be unwanted and undesired. Often, when dynamic systems change, there is a period of instability or chaos at the time of the developmental transition. This is the case with *hikikomori*, which may be seen by some people in Japanese society as a loss of the existing frame and a threat to the cultural fabric of Japanese society. It may be seen as chaotic and threatening.

### Recapitulation frames

Once the change process has begun, in addition to bridging frames, there may occur a brief return (recapitulation) of historical frames in the relationship. These are frames that had been well established for some period of time and then went through a process of breakdown and loss. Often these recapitulated frames seem to have been "forgotten" by the system. Yet somehow, the system retains a memory of its past and may bring back this older way of relating for a short period of time to help in the current developmental change process.

The recapitulated historical frame is "safe" and "familiar" even though it is not a long-term solution. It is brought back because the participants feel the need for some security in the face of the uncertainty of the impending change. For example, young children under stress will "regress" to become more "dependent." A child of six years may seem rather happy and independently self-regulated. When that child begins elementary school, however, there must be a developmental change from relating primarily to the family to expanding into a much larger frame of peer and teacher relationships. The child may suddenly and unexpectedly show more infant-like behavior such as clinging, having sleep problems, crying, or not eating. These behaviors which constitute a recapitulated frame will typically disappear once the child has made a successful adaptation to school and the newly emerging school frame is well established. Like bridging frames, recapitulated frames are temporary, constructed in the service of facilitating change.

### The problems of Japanese youth: previously existing consensual frame since the Second World War

An outline of the existing frame for family communication in Japanese society since the end of the Second World War is shown in table 19.3. In this frame, parents, especially mothers, were expected to be responsible for nurturing children and children were responsible for respecting parents. The first-born son and his wife had the further responsibility of taking care of his parents as they became older.

Embedded in all these family relationships was a sense of reciprocal *amae*. *Amae* is a Japanese word for a type of social relationship in which

Table 19.3 *Existing consensual frames in Japan since the Second World War*

*Family factors:*
  Nurture of children
  Filial piety by children and responsibility to parents of first-born sons
  Reciprocal *amae* relationships and non-verbal emotional communication
*School factors:*
  Conformity pressure, rejection if different
  Fear of failure

a person can expect care and indulgence from another. The person who wants or expects to receive some care or indulgence acts in a dependent fashion, soliciting protection and love from the other. Often, this pattern is such a familiar part of Japanese interpersonal relationships that the person seeking care is acting without consciously being aware of it. From the perspective of a person in western cultures, in which such dependency is seen as a sign of weakness, the person seeking *amae* may seem childish and spoiled.

*Amae*, as well as other patterns of emotional communication in the family, is primarily non-verbal, shown in body postures and facial expression, and without the need for verbal requests or explanations. In order to avoid conflict in the family, negative feelings are typically not directly expressed. People are admonished to "be happy" with the result that negative feelings become further suppressed.

Unlike the home, in which children could expect to be taken care of within the *amae* relationship, in the school setting expectations became imposed on the child. These expectations included conformity and encouragement of academic success. Children were expected to follow the group in which everyone was expected to be at the same level of achievement. Over- or under-achievers were taught to stay with the group and not stand apart from it. Children and their parents were also under intense stress during times of entrance examinations, in which a child's identity depended upon passing or failing.

## Societal changes in the previous ten to fifteen years: breakdown

Up until about ten years ago, this existing frame was relatively stable. Even though the expectations and responsibilities caused stress for young people in school and beginning their families, the level of stress was somehow manageable. This network of mutual expectations, the consensual frame, was dynamically maintained in Japanese society for many years. During the past ten years, however, Japan has seen major changes, the result of which is to raise the level of emotional stress and personal threat to intolerable levels for some individuals. When this happens in any social system, it can lead to the breakdown of existing frames.

Many factors have contributed to this change. Perhaps the main factor is the collapse of the so-called "bubble economy." Manufacturing and technology faced increased world competition and personal prosperity declined. Individuals lost their jobs and the promise of lifetime employment vanished in many sectors of the economy. Now the developed nations are in a post-industrial era in which personal creativity is more valued than uniformity of standards. This demand puts pressure on Japanese people who are used to not being different from others.

Another major change is the rapid increase in the use of the internet and cellular telephones, especially for young people. Those of us who did not grow up with these technologies have learned to use them as tools to get our work done and to stay in touch with the world. For children, however, the internet takes up a much bigger place in their minds and imaginations. It is not just a tool but a whole world in which one can get lost. Some children may take the internet world of chat rooms, blogging, and video games as more real than the interactive world of living human beings. On the internet, companions can be found day and night, more available than any real person in their lives. In addition, the internet takes time away from face-to-face interaction, physical play and exercise, reading books, and thinking for oneself.

A final change in the past ten years is a decline in the Japanese birth rate to the current one-child family. This no doubt is due to a combination of the other factors. Both husbands and wives may be forced to work outside the home in order to earn an acceptable family income. There is more focus on the self and more fear for the future that may keep people from wanting to bring children into these uncertain times. The result, however, is an only child who is highly indulged. If that child is male, there are conflicts between this indulgence at home and high expectations for academic performance and for taking care of the parents in their old age.

## Breakdown of consensual frames in family and school: threat and conflict

During times of system breakdown, the psychological experience can shift from normal to extreme. Research on trauma shows that during times of relatively rapid change, there is an increase in a sense of personal threat that can persist for long periods of time. Under the extreme sense of threat that comes with system breakdown, the traditional Japanese system of emotional communication that is not verbally expressed may block chances for mutual understanding and lead to extreme forms of withdrawal from society.

*Hikikomori*, primarily in males, is one symptom of this breakdown. In the absence of reliable systems of verbally communicating wants and needs, the adolescent's only perceived option is nearly total withdrawal from school and family. Why should Japanese males withdraw under stress while females of the same age seek to engage in society in new ways with the goal of self-actualization? The explanation for this difference may have to do with the relationship between male children and their mothers in the previously existing consensual frame. Male children, especially the first-borns, have a special responsibility to parents and mothers may seek to support their sons for success and not engage in any open conflict.

The mother–son relationship has been traditionally governed by non-verbal expression of *amae*: when the child acts needy, the mother automatically responds with what the child wants. From a western perspective, there is a co-dependency in this relationship. When the child is under stress and feels threatened, however, *amae* can take increasingly extreme forms as shown in table 19.4. Acceptable forms of *amae* reflect a desire for closeness, for needs to be met, and a wish to be protected. As the child's unexpressed needs become more extreme, however, *amae* behavior becomes increasingly disruptive. In the most extreme cases, it is possible to understand the sometimes violent behavior of *hikikomori* toward their parents or teachers as a desperate attempt to achieve emotional closure and relieve a perhaps intolerable sense of personal threat.

### Recapitulation of historical frames: *hikikomori* as a uniquely Japanese response to threat

Even if we agree that male *hikikomori* can be explained in part by extremes of mother–son *amae* in the face of a perceived threat, there is still a missing part of the picture. School refusal in the US affects both boys and girls equally, occurs at all ages, and in all social classes. In Japan, school refusal affects primarily males from relatively affluent families who are liberal and overprotective so that children can expect parental indulgence and financial support. Japanese *hikikomori* are typically adolescents who are shy, sensitive, and intelligent. In both Japan

Table 19.4 *Four levels of amae (adapted from Behrens, 2004)*

| |
|---|
| *Emotional* (Acceptable) |
|   1. Desire for closeness, intimacy, "childish" behavior |
| *Instrumental* (Disruptive) |
|   2. selfish, clingy, helpless |
|   3. acting desperate, making deals |
|   4. violent, abusive, unreasonable demands |

and the US, the child may withdraw from school because of being teased or bullied about being different from the norm but unlike Japan where the child becomes isolated from family as well as school, in the US the family is seen as a source of support and helps to actively encourage school return.

Perhaps one way to understand why *hikikomori* is uniquely Japanese is to see it as a recapitulation of a "forgotten" historical frame. During the period between 1636 and 1854, the so-called Edo period, almost the entire island nation of Japan was sealed off from foreign influence and foreign travel. It was the period of Shoguns and Samurais. Japanese people were forbidden to leave the country and foreigners were violently rejected or killed. There was, however, only one place of transaction with the outside world at the port of Nagasaki. This point of transaction can be considered a bridging frame. In the same way, *hikikomori* is a closing of the border of the child's world to outsiders with a small bridge to that outside world via the internet. In other words, from a dynamic systems perspective, the behavior of *hikikomori* – including extreme withdrawal and violent behavior – is a possible recapitulation of the existing social and cultural history of Japanese society.

### Possible solutions for *hikikomori*: Japanese bridging frames

In contemporary Japanese society, however, *hikikomori* is not welcomed, and parents and teachers would like to find ways to draw young people out of their isolation. In this section, we present some possible bridging frames that are based in Japanese forms of emotional communication. This means that communication need not verbally name and discuss directly the child's fears or concerns. Traditional Japanese forms of communication avoid conflict, support nurture and good feelings, and are based in appropriate forms of *amae*. Because the child does in fact feel threatened, it is essential in all the suggested forms of bridging listed below, to make the child feel safe and protected even if the sense of threat is not directly discussed.

At the *first level of Japanese bridging*, communication via the internet can be used but in this case with parents, teachers, or peer counselors (children from school who are especially trained to reach out to the withdrawn children). The internet can be used as a bridge to re-establish safe and enjoyable forms of communication with people close to the child. Parents and teachers can send messages of greeting or news, without talking about the "problem." They can also engage in playing video games with the child via the internet. Although this is not typical adult behavior, we are arguing that the "problem" is not "in" the child but rather "in" the system of communication and relationships which has broken down for the reasons given above. Thus, in order for the child to change, in a dynamic systems perspective, the adults must also change.

At the *second level of Japanese bridging*, parents, teachers, or peers can seek to engage in face-to-face communication with the child. We suggest that this communication take place in a safe area within the child's home which can be negotiated via the internet at first. This can be a particular room of the house, or there can be a temporary shelter built with fabric or the use of a camping tent. The child should be allowed freedom to choose when to enter and leave, and the communication in the safe space should be for play and enjoyment. Mediators from outside the family may be useful in facilitating parent–child contact in this safe environment.

Assuming these two levels are successful, a *third level of Japanese bridging* can occur outside the home. This again must involve safe and protected forms of playful or soothing communication. Among other things, this can include:

- Relationships with nature, together with other people
- Relationships with animals (such as pets at home or equine therapy, see chapter by Melson, this book)
- Relationships using Buddhist or Shinto practices (prayer, meditation, pilgrimage), two forms of indigenous Japanese religions

As one example, 20 *hikikomori* were brought together to take part in "Slow Walk Shikoku 88," organized by New Start, a non-profit organization from Urayasu, Chiba Prefecture. This was a long-distance pilgrimage between eighty-eight different Buddhist temples which brings together *hikikomori* for the purpose of sharing a common experience and re-engaging with the world via traditional Japanese practices. These young people are given gifts, *osettai*, from people in the communities along the way. According to the organizers, "Walking among the rich nature of Shikoku will revive their bodies, and the *osettai* will revive their spirits. The pilgrimage is a kind of hospital that offers the best kind of counseling."

The *fourth level of Japanese bridging frames*, the final level, is the return to school. This can occur in different ways. If the child returns to the school that he left, there should be safe areas for relative withdrawal or play within the school. This could include internet game rooms, or "safe" peer counselors who are trained in emotional communication. The school also needs to establish and enforce anti-bullying measures. Another possibility is for the child to attend special "free" schools in which a safe and accepting environment for learning has been established. There are a growing number of free schools in Japan. Finally, the child can be encouraged to join with face-to-face communities outside the family and school for safe and shared identities of common problems. These could be *hikikomori* support groups, or they could be groups especially for playful and enjoyable activities such as music, art, dance, or athletics.

## Possible solutions for *hikikomori*: western bridging frames

Western bridging approaches involve more direct and explicit communication with the child. This is done while still preserving a sense of safety and protection. The goal is for the child to talk about his feelings and eventually to play an active role in solving the problem of withdrawal. In the Japanese solutions proposed in the previous section, it is the family and school that sets the agenda and establishes the bridging frames. In the western approach, there is more input from the child and more room for the child's autonomy and creativity.

At the *first level of western bridging frames*, some type of challenge is presented to the child who is withdrawn. Many kinds of challenges may be possible but one is a partial denial by the parents of supplies of the child's favorite foods, money, or internet links until the child recognizes that he must play an active role to re-establish communication with the parents. At this level, the child may be acting out of self-interest, that is, talking to parents as a way to get the money, food, and internet. This is sometimes called "tough love," because the parent assumes that the child is not able to understand his own emotions and needs the challenge to "wake up" and notice that he is part of a family that loves him. Care must be taken to avoid challenges that may incite a violent reaction, and outside mediators may again be useful here.

At the *second level of western bridging frames*, the parents, teachers, or social workers can encourage explicit emotional communication. The child is asked to articulate his fears, concerns, and anxieties as well as his desires and hopes. Although the challenge to the child may produce some resentment or even anger, what is important is the arousal and mobilization of the child's emotions. While this may seem counter-intuitive within Japanese culture, within western society we find that only when the emotions are engaged and made explicit can the child take the next developmental step toward open and reciprocal emotional communication (see chapters by Fogel and by Greenspan, this book). This open and reciprocal communication is mutually respectful, accepting, and produces a sense of relief in the child because of being understood at a deep emotional level.

At the *third level of western bridging frames*, once the child's emotions are mobilized and the child is engaging with others at a developmentally appropriate level of shared understanding, children can then engage in cooperative negotiations with parents about ideas for returning to school. In the western culture, if the child is allowed to play a role in developing solutions to such problems, the child is more likely to make a commitment to participate in the eventual resolution.

This sense of personal autonomy, which is one of the traditional distinctions between Japanese and western cultures, fosters a growing sense of personal responsibility and respect for others in the process of decision making. Again, this may be counter-intuitive from a Japanese perspective in which one might think that too much personal autonomy causes further isolation and separation from the group. In fact, in healthy western families, autonomy is part of the process of forming mature and mutually respectful relationships with others. Only imma-ture forms of autonomy, such as might be seen in young children or people with developmental delays in self- and other-awareness, are primarily self-centered.

## Conclusion: a re-organized system of mutual relationship changes

According to our dynamic systems perspective, the problems of Japanese youth are not the problems of the children alone but rather reflect difficulties in the social systems of family and society. In order to achieve change, both the child and the adults must cooperate and invest in efforts to improve the situation.

We have presented possible Japanese and western solutions to the current crisis in Japan. Japanese solutions preserve existing forms of emotional communication and *amae* relationships while encouraging a return to more traditional roles. Western solutions rely on explicit emotional communication and leave open the pathway to the future as a result of cooperative negotiation of solutions between parents and children. The goal of both Japanese and western approaches, however, is exactly the same: to find ways of creating supportive, developmentally appropriate relationships that allow for personal and societal growth and development.

Although the path to the future may be uncertain, the principles of systems change may bring some source of comfort. Recall that historical recapitulation is always part of changes in social systems. Thus, no matter what will happen in Japanese society five or fifty or 500 years from now, it will always be Japanese. Japan will never lose its long history, and parts of that history will come back (recapitulate) to support the people when those parts are most needed. No matter which approach is chosen in Japan, it is clear that everyone needs to be involved – parents, children, and the community – in order to lead the way to create supportive family and school environments for the next generation of Japanese children.

SUGGESTED READINGS

Doi, T. (2004). *Understanding amae*. Dorset, UK: Global Oriental Publishers.

Fogel, A., A. Garvey, H. Hsu, and D. West-Stroming (2006). *Change processes in relationships: relational–historical research on a dynamic system of communication*. Cambridge, UK: Cambridge University Press.

Hamada, T. (2005). Absent fathers, feminized sons, selfish mothers and disobedient daughters: revisiting the Japanese "ie" household. *Japan Policy Research Institute.* Working paper no. 33 (www.jpri.org/publications/workingpapers/wp33.html).

Rothbaum, F. (2002). Family systems theory, attachment, and culture. *Family Process*, 41, 328–350.

# 20    A different way to help

*George Downing*

It is difficult to watch. On a videotape is a mother and a baby. Something is off. The infant, reclining in a plastic seat, looks ill at ease. He makes small fussing sounds. The mother, facing him, has a broad smile, and says, "What is going on? Are we a little annoyed? A little annoyed?" Her voice is rapid, high-pitched, friendly rather than aggressive. But the more they trade these signals back and forth, the more upset the child becomes.

This mother has been sent for therapy. She has mixed feelings about coming. Legally the court has required her to seek help at our unit. It is a mandated case of a rather typical kind. She is a single mother, somewhat isolated, in difficult economic straits, trying to make do with a four-month-old baby. The baby is not easy to handle, and on her side she feels inexperienced as a parent, and frightfully unsure of herself.

She is also a person prone to rage attacks. This goes on all too often between her and David, the infant. Recently in the night she lost it. David was crying intensely. She had already been up with him several times that night; nothing she had tried seemed to help. She grabbed him and started screaming. She shook him so violently he had to be brought later to a hospital emergency room. In that moment she lost control, it was all she could do to keep from throwing him against the wall.

The reason I am looking at a videotape has to do with a special type of professional intervention. It is called, in the form I practice and teach, "video intervention therapy." It is a rapid, effective way to change what is happening between parents and infants, or parents and children. This mother, Sue, was cooperative enough to let herself be filmed while interacting with her baby. Although wary, at the same time she was desperate for help. I assured her that what was seen would be kept confidential, and that it would be used only to help her find out, with my assistance, what could work better with David.

I also stressed that every baby is different. The idea would be that we would film a short video, that I would analyze its details, and then that she and I would look at parts of it together. This would provide important new information. She and I could then think about what we had discovered, and plan how she might use it at home.

Sue was skeptical but willing to go along. Our goals, we agreed, would be three: that David begin to sleep more restfully, that he calm himself more easily, and that he more often interact with her in pleasurable ways. Separate from this, I would help her handle her angry feelings more effectively.

It is easy to make a video of this kind. Five or ten minutes in length is enough. The video can be made in a services-delivery institution (in our case, a psychiatric hospital). Or in a therapist's or counselor's office. Or a parent or family can themselves make the video in their home, with a little prior guidance. Most parents choose the "home" version. Sue preferred to be filmed in our unit. We made the video right after the initial session. We planned a new session for looking at it together in three days.

Alone with the video, briefly preparing for this next session, I am struck by a number of things. In the interaction which has been filmed Sue of course wants to make a good impression, and is trying to do things right. But she can't really, not on a "micro" level. This means on the level of the quick, constant exchange of signals which is always in flow between two people relating to each other.

We aren't very conscious of this flow, normally. Yet in interaction with a baby it is the main thing, the most shaping basic reality. Superb research in the last three decades (e.g., by Beatrice Beebe, Elisabeth Fivaz-Depeursinge, Alan Fogel, Kavlen Lyons-Ruth, Mechthild Papousek, Philippe Rochat, Howard and Miriam Steele, Daniel Stern, Ed Tronick) has taught us an enormous amount about it. When I analyze a clinical video, I don't use fine-grained research coding. That would take a long time, and in clinical or counseling institutions time is in short supply. So I use a fast method of analysis I have developed. It usually takes a therapist or counselor fifteen to twenty minutes. The factors one observes are derived from research findings, however.[1] This approach to deciphering an interactional video can easily be taught, as can the skills for how the video is subsequently used in a meeting with the parent or parents.

---

[1] Invaluable in this regard have been years of personal exchange with Beatrice Beebe, Mechthild Papousek, and Ed Tronick. Both Beebe and Papousek, incidentally, have developed clinical video intervention procedures similar to my own. Of interest as well are methods created by Susan McDonough and Maria Aarts.

One thing I see right away, looking at Sue and David, is how their timing doesn't work. Sue is speedy and brusque. For an infant his age David is on the slow side. He needs time to take in what he is perceiving, and time also to form an adequate response with his own small body. In the drum-beat of her signals he is caught up short. As well, her face and her sounds of forced cheerfulness are too discrepant with David's affect state. They give no mirroring of his expressions.

Sue also has little feeling for when he is ready to receive stimulation, and when not. During more than thirty seconds he holds his head turned to one side, watching her from an angle. As she smiles and touches and vocalizes, he maintains this position, as if frozen. Sue then ups the stimulation, trying to reach him. He appears increasingly distressed. He twists more to the side, breaking off all eye contact. Her voice gets a slight growl in it. "You don't go for this, do you," she complains. Brief expressions of disappointment and then of irritation, flash across her face, to be replaced at once by the smile. With one finger she pokes at his face, trying to persuade him to turn back. His fussy sounds escalate into a tense, loud crying.

Three days later Sue is leaning forward intently, watching this same sequence. She remarks at once that it seems to her highly typical, an example of what occurs frequently at home, an example too of what "drives her up the wall." As for the details of what is going awry, she doesn't spontaneously make sense of that. (Sometimes parents can see these things right away, sometimes not.) So I will show her.

First, though, I point out some things she is doing right: her face is positioned where David can easily see it, she is indeed vocalizing as opposed to remaining silent, and generally she is seriously engaged in the interaction. She is pleased to hear that, and a little surprised. Then I suggest we look a couple of times more at the escalation sequence, and reflect about what, given that David is hard to calm, might function better with him here. As we watch, I now and then show a few seconds of exchange in slow motion, or frame by frame. Gradually she starts seeing David's side from a more sympathetic perspective. She comments, "He just doesn't understand that I am trying to help."

I realize we can use that idea. I suggest that she is in some way probably right, and that we ought therefore to think about what she might do to help him get more aware that she "wants to help." I explain too about "vocal matching," a phenomenon much studied in the research. If she were to continue to vocalize, but to let at least some of her sounds echo the same quality as his sounds, then this might well convey to him that she understands his state and wants to help with it. She could also sometimes make a "woe" sound like his and then modulate it downwards, showing him even more clearly how his state could move towards a calmer one.[2]

For the rest of the session we talk more about this. Partly we speak about how, at home, she can implement this alternative way with David. We even discuss a bit what she needs to do differently with her body, in order better to feel a "resonance" with what David is feeling, and then to use that resonance to send him back a good echo. Imagining that she is at home, interacting with David, she explores what might help here. What she first comes to, is a different way to hold her shoulders. Next she plays with making her breathing slower, and then finds several ways better consciously to sense the flux of emotion in her body.

Partly too we talk about her own childhood. It becomes apparent that the notion that parents can "tune into" what a child is sensing, and can help the child with that, was not operative in the quite brutal realities of her early family life.

Although when analyzing the video I had seen a number of negative interactional patterns, in this session I focused upon just one of them, the lack of affect matching. That works better. You show a parent some of the positive patterns, and then go into a thorough, concrete work with one of the negative patterns, and one only. This way, a lot is likely to get integrated. Things get extremely clear for the parent, thanks to the images seen, and thanks to the small "how could it be done differently with your body" explorations. The parent goes home with a coherent, understandable package, as well as, usually, with a new optimism.

Sue put to work what she had explored with me right away. Her style of interaction with David evolved nicely, and this made a critical difference for the two of them. She was able not only to keep her child, but also to begin finding many more moments of satisfaction in their exchanges. We did three additional video sessions, each based on a newly made video, and each targeting a different negative interactional pattern. We also had several sessions of a more traditional nature, without video, where I helped her develop more productive ways to deal with the excessive anger she carried inside her.

As Sue found out and put into practice new behaviors in the interaction, the circular effects were evident. David began to build up a wider range of positive affect expression, and showed this more frequently. Sue on her side started responding more creatively to his positive

---

[2] This is one of the many forms of what I call a "demonstrative twist." With regard to infant distress states, Beatrice Beebe has documented the effectiveness of parental tones which first match and then modulate downwards.

expressions, which was both gratifying for her as well as helpful for him. They learned about a new area of playfulness together. Sue was able to tone down her speedy tempo. David also became easier to calm, as well as better at calming himself if a distress state was not too intense.

The advantages of such work with video microanalysis are many. It costs little to deliver. It is tailored and specific. And it is versatile concerning who it can assist. For example, it can effect fast change with many parents whose motivation is low, and/or who suffer from concurrent problems, such as substance abuse or a psychiatric disorder. And as for the age of the child, this can be anything from a just-born infant to an adolescent. Especially concerning infants and small children, video microanalysis gives an access to the nitty-gritty of what is going on which is difficult to achieve by other means.

It can also easily be combined with other forms of social assistance or therapeutic intervention. Usually there is no difficulty adding it to an already existing delivery system, e.g. treatment for drugs or alcohol, outpatient psychiatry, social work intervention programs, counseling for families with children with special needs, or counseling for families who adopt.

Or it can be made the kernel of something new. For example, at the University of Heidelberg in Germany, a special unit has been created, with my collaboration, inside the medical school psychiatric hospital. Here mothers with more extreme symptomology (e.g. borderline disorder, depression with suicidal risk) can be hospitalized together with their infants. In addition to medication and some individual sessions they receive a concentrated dose of video microanalysis therapy. Also at Nordbaden Psychiatric Center, a large public hospital in Wiesloch just nearby, a similar unit, also with my collaboration, has been created, this unit specializing in video microanalysis treatment of schizophrenic mothers together with their infants. At both sites we are conducting outcome research, with quite favorable results emerging to date.

It can be useful to give advice to troubled parents. It can be useful to confront them legally, if a child is in danger. In some instances it can be useful to provide individual adult psychotherapy. But advice and legal pressure and traditional psychotherapy only go so far. A rich supplement to any or all of these can be the medium of videotape. Given the right expertise on the part of the therapist or counselor, a parent can discover the universe of human "micro-exchange." To her or him this will seem new, and likely will seem fascinating, even though it is a universe where she or he has been living all the time. It will also demystify how parenting can change.

SUGGESTED READINGS

Beebe, B. (2003). Brief mother–infant treatment: psychoanalytically informed video feedback. *Infant Mental Health Journal*, 24(1), 24–52.

Downing, G. (2004). Emotion, body, and parent–infant interaction. In J. Nadel and D. Muir (eds.), *Emotional development: recent research advances*. Oxford: Oxford University Press.

Fivaz-Depeursinge, E., and A. Corboz-Warnery (1999). *The primary triangle: a developmental systems view of mothers, fathers, and infants*. New York: Basic.

Fogel, Alan (1993). Two principles of communication: co-regulation and framing. In J. Nadel and L. Camaioni (eds.), *New perspectives in early communicative development*. London: Routledge.

Lyons-Ruth, K., S. Melnick, E. Bronfman, S. Sherry, and L. Lianas (2004). Hostile-helpless relational models and disorganized attachment patterns between parents and their young children: review of research and implications for clinical work. In L. Atkinson and S. Goldberg (eds.), *Attachment issues in psychopathology and intervention*. Mahwah, NJ: Lawrence Erlbaum.

McDonough, Susan (2004). Interaction guidance: promoting and nurturing the caregiving relationship. In A. Sameroff, S. McDonough, and K. Rosenblum (eds.), *Treating parent–infant relationship problems: strategies for intervention* (pp. 79–95). New York: Guilford.

Papousek, M. (2000). Einsatz von Video in der Eltern-Säuglings-Beratung und -Psychotherapie. *Praxis der Kinderpsychologie und Kinderspychiatrie*, 49, 611–627.

Rochat, P. (2001). *The infant's world*. Cambridge, Massachusetts: Harvard University Press.

Steele, M., J. Hodges, J. Kaniuk, H. Steele, D. D'Agostino, I. Blom, S. Hillman, and K. Henderson (2007). Intervening with maltreated children and their adoptive families: identifying attachment-facilitative behaviors. In D. Oppenheim and D. Goldsmith (eds.), *Attachment theory in clinical work with children: bridging the gap between research and practice*. New York: Guilford.

Stern, D. (2004). *The present moment in psychotherapy and everyday life*. New York: Norton.

Tronick, E. (2003). Thoughts on the still-face: disconnection and dyadic expansion of consciousness. *Infancy*, 4 (4), 475–481.

# 21    Why do siblings often turn out very differently?

*Michael E. Kerr*

No one has a definitive answer as to why the same parents often raise children that turn out very differently, but it happens time and again. I grew up in such a family. One of my brothers never "lifted off" to function independently of my parents. Occasional forays towards independence invariably ended in some type of crash and burn. He would lose a job, get sick, or be terribly lonely. My parents would again take care of him. He was a source of great anguish for my family. My other two brothers and I coped and assumed adult responsibility more easily. How to understand this? My parents were good, hard-working people and dearly loved all of their children.

In my practice as a psychiatrist specializing in treating families, I routinely consult with parents who are having more difficulty raising one child than the others. The child is usually having some mixture of academic, behavioral, or health problems. Whether he is the oldest or the youngest child, the parents often say that he or she seems less mature, more insecure, more intense, more sensitive, or more dependent than their other children. They are worried and usually at their wits' end about how to help their son or daughter.

The differences between siblings are not always marked, but statistical studies show that significant disparities in the overall life adjustment of siblings are more the rule than the exception. Common explanations for these differences include genes, peer influences, life traumas, bad parenting, and even bad luck. Some parents fear that the child is inheriting their emotional difficulties, despite concerted efforts to prevent it; other parents feel that the problem has little to do with them. One thing most parents of a child having significant problems do agree on is that they have invested more time, energy, and worry in that child than they have in his or her siblings. Parents say this despite sometimes feeling that they are not doing enough for the child.

In recent years, in an effort to understand human development more completely and to shed new light on questions such as sibling variation, a growing number of behavioral scientists have moved beyond a genes versus environment debate to study the complex interplay between nature and nurture. The thinking is that a child's development is governed by the interaction of many factors, such as his genetic make-up, intrauterine experiences, family relationships, and experiences outside the family.

Social scientists from many disciplines have been studying the impact of the family on development for a long time and have provided valuable insights. However, some unique family research began within psychiatry and the allied mental health disciplines during the 1950s that has greatly expanded our knowledge. Among the areas that these family studies have helped us better understand is this question of why siblings often turn out differently. One of these pioneering researchers was a psychiatrist named Murray Bowen. His studies spanned five decades.

Bowen and his group at the National Institute of Mental Health were the first to study whole families living on a research ward for long periods. Their early study was of families that had both a severely mentally ill adult child and a fairly normal child. Following the NIMH project, Bowen continued his work at the Georgetown University School of Medicine until his death in 1990. The studies at Georgetown expanded to include families with milder psychiatric problems, those with mainly behavioral difficulties, and those with chronic physical illnesses. His group also studied fairly well-adjusted families. A surprising revelation of these studies was that families differ in degree, not kind. The basic ways that family interactions can create problems that were discovered in the NIMH families are also present in families with milder problems. The interactions are simply less intense in better functioning families.

A core discovery from family research is that the family must be considered as an entity or "organism" in its own right. It is not a collection of psychologically autonomous individuals, but a highly interdependent relationship system. This discovery meant that theories of human behavior that were derived largely from studying individuals, such as psychoanalytic theory, were inadequate for explaining the phenomena that were being observed in families. A theory was needed that could address the whole as well as its parts. The new theory, *Bowen family systems theory*, emerged in the mid-1960s. Bowen developed it based on his group's research and on the work of others. The ideas and their applications have undergone continued development since that time.

An understanding of the new theory begins with an evolutionary perspective. Human beings have evolved to be profoundly social mammals.

The strong disposition to live in groups, the ability to work together to accomplish complex tasks, and a remarkable intelligence have enabled our species to adapt to a wide range of habitats. The building blocks of human social groups are tightly knit multigenerational family units. The powerful ties that exist between family members are assumed to reflect instinctually rooted forces for emotional attachment that are part of humankind's mammalian ancestry. Cultures enact laws to discourage people from abandoning a spouse or children, but it is unnecessary to legislate attachment. Unless bad experiences have made a person wary of relationships, if he leaves or loses one set of attachments, he will seek new ones.

Comfortably close connections activate brain chemicals that instill calmness and a strong sense of emotional well being. Relationships could be the best tranquilizers yet devised! A sobering counterpoint to the well-being that relationships can provide is captured by the familiar expression, "I can't live with him and I can't live without him!" It is not easy to be in an intimate relationship or to live in a group. Tensions inevitably arise. People can gain in myriad ways from living in a group, *but the dependency inherent in close ties and the pressure to make accommodations to preserve and manage the ties can push people to the edge – and over.* Problematic interactions leave some group members feeling isolated, overwhelmed, excluded, or out of control. Research shows that people experiencing such feelings over a long period are at risk of illness or other impairments in functioning.

Instability in important relationships threatens people in two fundamental ways: (1) it jeopardizes the security of attachments on which their well-being depends, and (2) it overloads their ability to cope with adverse social stimuli. Given the impact of unstable relationships, it is not surprising that human beings have evolved finely tuned sensitivities to social cues that alert them to threats to important relationships. We watch others for signs of attention and approval, we assess their expectations and whether we are meeting them, and we sense their distress.

Social cues that indicate a threat trigger anxiety. Anxiety triggers emotional reactivity and behavior that are designed to reduce the threat. For example, a man interprets his wife's facial expression and tone of voice as disappointment in him. Consequently, he says and does more things to please her. She brightens up and he feels less threatened. It would be difficult to be in relationships or to live in a group if people did not react to such cues and adjust accordingly. The responses temper urges to do what we want to do when we want to do it.

The innate urge to form relationships, reactivity to social cues, and ease with which relationships generate tension are the core elements in

Bowen theory that help explain why siblings turn out differently. The description of how these elements translate into the different developmental outcomes will begin at the point of a couple's courtship. I will simplify the description by using a family with only two children. I will accent the differences between the parents' interactions with each child by drawing starker contrasts than what occurs in real life.

Most couples have a fairly comfortable courtship, but most find it difficult to sustain that level of comfort and closeness over time. The early romantic attraction smoothes and soothes a relationship, but it also helps that couples typically face fewer responsibilities and conflicting demands during that time. It makes it easier to respond to each other's desires for attention, affection, and communication. Each person's willingness to invest sufficient energy in the relationship to keep the other happy is one reason that people pick each other.

Often, the first serious strain on a marriage is when the children come along. It is a strain no matter how much people want children. It raises the bar in terms of the spouses' expectations of themselves and of each other. Given the reality demands inherent in rearing children, it is reasonable for parents to depend more on each other during that time and not surprising that tensions arise. However, most families experience levels of tension at various points during the child-rearing years that are disproportionate to the demands. Various stresses contribute to this tension, but the principal reason for it is the parents' insecurity about coping with the challenges.

The increased responsibilities and uncertainties bring out each parent's insecurity. One way this manifests is in each reacting more intensely than in the past to the other's needs, fears, expectations, and distress. For example, feeling unsure of her ability to be a good mother, a wife wants more attention and support from her husband. He feels pressured by this, but tries to meet expectations. Because children do not grow up overnight, the sustained pressures and expectations erode each parent's tolerance for the other's reactions. The wife feels increasingly overwhelmed and that her husband is not doing his part. He feels increasingly harried and that she is too demanding. She gets more critical and pressuring; he gets more defensive and oppositional. Tension escalates. This is only one of a number of scenarios that can play out between parents and escalate tension.

Tension is one thing, but how people manage it is something else. A key point for this discussion is that *if the parents do not address the difficulties they are having dealing with each other, their child is vulnerable to filling this breach in their relationship.* Addressing the difficulties means that parents keep their needs, fears, unrealistic expectations, upsets, and immaturity focused on each other. This keeps them in emotional contact. Ideally, it takes the form of talking productively about problems, but arguing unproductively maintains contact also and keeps a child out of harm's way! The alternative is emotional distance. People may distance quietly, with each parent acting as if things are fine, or they may distance emphatically, with each one knowing that things are not fine but avoiding dealing with the issues.

The usual way that marital distance places a child in harm's way is that the mother focuses less energy on her husband and turns to the child to gratify desires for a comfortable emotional connection. In the process, the child becomes so important to her well-being that he easily triggers her worries as well. This mix of needs and fears cements a powerful connection. The father invests much of his energy in work and is usually less entangled emotionally with the child. However, he participates equally in the child focus by playing his part in the marital distance and getting anxiously entangled in his wife's relationship with the child. The parents may draw closer around concerns about the child, but that is not the same as dealing with their relationship problems. The pattern of an overly involved mother and distant father tends to occur even if both parents work outside the home. Furthermore, a father can be an active presence in the home, but still fairly distant emotionally from the child.

The firstborn child is not necessarily the one that fills the breach. It can be any member of a sibling group and may involve more than one child. It is determined primarily by the emotional state of the family when a child is born. For example, parents may cope more successfully with the addition of the first child than they do with the addition of a subsequent child. Even if a child is born with a defect, how well the parents cope in face of it usually has a greater impact on the child's emotional development than the defect itself.

A parent being overly involved with a child is harmful because *the ongoing emotionally intense interactions over the years of his development program the child's well-being and functioning to depend heavily on relationships*. The child actively participates in this emotional programming by automatically reciprocating the mother's involvement with him. Like a moth drawn to a bright light, he becomes preoccupied with her attention, approval, expectations, and distress. His mood and motivation become linked to how she and others view him. Being ensnarled in the emotionality constrains the child's instinctive urge to develop his individuality.

*If one child fills the breach in the parents' relationship, his sibling is relatively off the hook*. The parents expend their needs and fears on the overly involved child. It enables them to be more relaxed and at their best with his sibling. The sibling's reality needs rather than their anxiety largely govern their interactions with him. Developing in a less intense emotional climate, the sibling tunes into social cues, but without being programmed to overreact to them. Less entangled with mother, he is available for a fairly even relationship with both parents, he can develop other relationships inside and outside the family, and he can energetically explore the world around him. Learning about life in many domains fosters the development of his individuality.

The depth of a mother's over-involvement with a child may be difficult to discern in the early years because it can be seamlessly woven into meeting his reality needs. The relationship is generally harmonious. In other cases, the sensitivities between an overly involved parent and child erupt in ferocious power struggles early on. Intense periods of conflict and distance may persist throughout the child's development. The tone of an overly involved attachment does not affect the degree of relationship dependence that the child develops. For example, an oppositional child may be just as sensitive to attention, approval, and expectations as a compliant child.

Differences in functioning between an overly involved child and his sibling are evident in the preschool years. For example, one child is easily bored and looks to mother for direction. The freer sibling finds things to do. In elementary school, one child feels excluded by his peers and his ability to learn depends on the interest the teacher takes in him. Relationships are less of an issue for the other child and he can learn from most any teacher. The overly involved child is the one prone to rebel in adolescence. He rebels with a vigor that parallels his difficulty being an individual. The freer sibling navigates adolescence more smoothly. The overly involved child may function fairly well until stumbling badly in trying to make the transition into adult life. At whatever point problems surface, the parents intensify their focus on the child in an effort to fix him. This further escalates the tension, particularly if the child does not respond.

Leaving home does not resolve the emotional attachment to the parents. This is evident in the overly involved child's insecurity in adult relationships. He looks for someone to replace the original dependence on the parents. His partner seeks the same thing. Their mutual insecurity makes it difficult to sustain a close relationship. They are so reactive to each other's needs and fears that it becomes too intense to manage. His unresolved attachment also manifests in difficulty defining and pursuing life goals. The emotional turmoil that is associated with relationship disruptions and the absence of a life direction render him vulnerable to serious clinical problems. Tensions with the parents may eventually result in cutoff from the family, which aggravates his difficulties.

The life of the freer sibling is a contrast. His relationship to the family is more resolved by the time he leaves home. He is secure in adult relationships and selects a mate like himself. The couple is able to face life's challenges with only modest tension levels and upheaval. The freer sibling takes full advantage of educational and work opportunities and, consequently, his life is productive and orderly. He, his spouse, and their children usually have few serious clinical problems. The mature relationship between him and his parents makes cutoff from them unlikely. The ongoing connections with extended family further enhance his life adjustment.

Bowen theory, of course, does not explain everything about how differences in the life adjustment of siblings develop. However, by explaining what transpires in the mother–offspring relationship in the context of the family unit, it expands our understanding of the forces shaping human development. I have covered only a few ideas in the theory, but have tried to describe them in enough detail that the reader could recognize them as relevant to his or her life and family. That is how I got attracted to the ideas thirty-five years ago.

By the time I heard about Bowen theory, my impaired brother had already received a psychiatric diagnosis. A diagnosis is supposed to facilitate treatment, but it made things worse in my family by reinforcing the view that my brother's problems were the principal cause of the family turmoil. We were certain that if he could change, our family would be happier. This view reflects the cause-and-effect model that has long dominated medicine.

A systems model does not assign the cause of a disturbance in a group to one or a few group members. Hearing this was a breath of fresh air! It helped me not to see my brother as a psychiatric case, but as someone deeply dependent emotionally as well as financially on my parents. He had not separated from them and they had not separated from him. The interdependency existed long before his serious problems surfaced. It was refreshing to see that we all played a part in the problem. No one caused it. This view seemed accurate and fair.

One dividend from applying these ideas to my family was that I could see that my mother's anguished and subjective view of my impaired brother had powerfully influenced my own view of him. She did not force her view on me. It was shaped by my sensitivity to her approval, expectations, and distress. Seeing the world through her eyes connected me to her, but it interfered with my ability to think for myself. I was less relationship dependent than my brother was, but relationship dependent nevertheless. The ability to observe relationship processes and one's part in them more factually is referred to as *emotional objectivity*. It is a necessary step toward being able to be present in an anxious family without one's thoughts, feelings, and actions being governed by the powerful relationship currents. If one person can get more objective about how family interactions contribute to the difficulties and change his part in those interactions, it calms the system and opens up new options for problem solving. Paradoxically, being more of an individual in a system promotes closeness and cooperation.

The discoveries from family research and the new systems model of human behavior have policy implications. One implication derives from the research finding that the child who is most vulnerable to developing significant problems is the one with whom the parents have been overly involved emotionally. The finding challenges a prevalent attitude in society, namely, that one of the main reasons children develop emotional, behavioral, and other problems is that their parents are *inadequately involved* with them. This notion is that the parents are not providing enough attention and support, nor are they monitoring the children's activities sufficiently. The frequently heard caution about mothers working outside the home reflects this attitude.

The policy implication is the need to reconsider the wisdom of education policies implemented in recent years that seem to have been influenced by the attitude that parents are not doing enough. The policies have been developed in response to schools being flooded with a growing percentage of students that are having major learning, behavioral, emotional, or other problems. The trend has generated pressure on teachers, administrators, and other officials to develop programs to fix the problems. Some programs that have been implemented are replicating at an institutional level the family relationship processes that have created the youngsters' difficulties in the first place! To understand how this replication has occurred, it is necessary to examine what has been happening in society.

Societies, like families, can undergo long periods of heightened anxiety that impairs their functioning. Many societies around the world have been experiencing anxious times for several decades. The factor that may contribute most to societal anxiety is a gut-felt sense that our species is jeopardizing its relationship to the planet and no solution for it is in sight. This societal anxiety affects many families by intensifying their child focus. For example, unnerved by what they experience around them, many parents overprotect their children more than they would in a calmer and safer environment. The impact of the intensified focus is to funnel more children with significant vulnerabilities into the schools.

Policies have been implemented in response to this trend that pressure the schools to invest more time and energy to support, organize, and motivate students that are having difficulties. This is what families do when their overly involved child begins to have problems, namely, more of what they have already been doing. People often feel better if they "do something to help," but the "help" can compound the problems by parents and teachers taking too much responsibility for the child's functioning. Consequently, the child does not seriously reflect on the long-term consequences of his actions.

A second policy implication of a systems model addresses a dichotomy that arises in the minds of many parents and teachers when dealing with a chronically underachieving or misbehaving youngster. The dichotomy is thinking that *either* the child's behavior is willful *or* he cannot control it. Feeling that it must be one or the other, but being uncertain which it is, a parent or teacher often applies a smorgasbord of approaches over time, including lecturing, prodding, criticizing, praising, threatening, coaxing, structuring, bribing, and backing off from the child. The results tend not to impress.

Systems thinking views both poles of this dichotomy as accurate within limits. On the one hand, a youngster may not think about his decision, but he does decide to behave in the way that he does. It is willful in that sense. On the other hand, automatic emotional reactions to others powerfully affect his behavior. It is involuntary in that sense. The child reacts to a family system of emotionally driven interactions that each member, including the child, helps to create. Every member creates the system, therefore it is untenable for someone to blame the system or for the system to blame anyone. One and all are accountable for their actions.

It is unnecessary for a father to ruminate about *why* his daughter rebels. Alternatively, he can change how he negatively affects her functioning. This could involve several changes, such as engaging his wife more directly, getting off the daughter's back, and no longer acceding to the daughter's sense of entitlement. If he can change in relationship to his wife and daughter, they will predictably change too. They change because he has played a part in how they have functioned. This type of scenario can play out in a school setting. For example, if the leaders and policy makers are clear where their responsibility to teach ends and the students' responsibility to learn begins, it calms the system and improves its overall functioning.

One final policy implication concerns research priorities. A systems model enables researchers to track not only the complexity of human interactions, but it also makes it possible to track how these interactions affect what is occurring at physiological levels as basic as the genes. This has enhanced the ability to communicate across disciplines and to integrate facts drawn from fields as basic as molecular biology to as broad as the study of human societies. This means that interdisciplinary research projects merit more support than has traditionally been the case. Studies of the psychological and biological functioning of individuals *in the context* of their important relationship systems, such as the family, the workplace, and the larger community are particularly important ones.

In conclusion, Bowen family systems theory offers a new lens for studying human beings in the context of their important relationship systems. Murray Bowen commented that it is like moving from a seat on the sidelines to the top of the stadium to watch a football game. One appreciates the intensity of the game on the sidelines and appreciates the broad patterns of movement from up in the stands. Both vantage points provide critical facts about the functioning of the whole.

SUGGESTED READINGS

Bowen, Murray (1978). *Family therapy in clinical practice*. New York: Jason Aronson, Inc.

Kerr, Michael (1988). Chronic anxiety and defining a self. *The Atlantic Monthly* 262: 35–58 (can be obtained through the Bowen Center website).

(2003). *One family's story: a primer on Bowen theory*. Washington, DC: Bowen Center for the Study of the Family (www.thebowencenter.org).

Kerr, Michael, and Murray Bowen (1988). *Family evaluation: an approach based on Bowen theory*. New York: W. W. Norton.

Papero, Daniel V. (1990). *Bowen family systems theory*. Boston: Allyn and Bacon.

## 22  A dynamic systems approach to understanding family and peer relationships: implications for effective interventions with aggressive youth

*Isabela Granic*

George is fourteen years old and has begun to have serious problems at home and at school. When George was younger, he and his single mother sometimes argued but, more often, they played together, did chores cooperatively, and shared secrets with one another. Although George had no close friends during his childhood, he was still a relatively happy child. George began high school last year and things seemed to deteriorate from that point. Over the last year, George and his mother can't seem to agree on anything. Although they still turn to one another for support and affection on rare occasions, most of the time they are arguing furiously. Almost any topic of conversation seems to trigger another angry outburst. George often ends these fights by storming out of the house and his mother is left frustrated, hurt, and worried about his safety. At his new high school, George has recently been getting into physical fights with classmates. He's been suspended for his aggressive behavior and his grades have dramatically declined. Except for two other teenagers who have also been suspended, most of his peers have rejected George. As a result, George spends most of his free time "hanging out" with these two other troubled youths.

Why has George suddenly begun to act aggressively? Some psychologists would suggest that his testosterone levels have peaked now that he's reached puberty. Others would speculate that something in his genes has just started to become expressed. Still others may argue that he has always been an angry boy and his physical growth has given him the confidence to challenge his mother and peers more overtly. Or perhaps George is just going through a typical stage of adolescent rebellion. Although reasonable hypotheses, each of these common explanations attempts to pinpoint the cause of George's problems within George himself.

In our research, informed by dynamic systems principles, we take a very different approach. From our perspective, the emergence and maintenance of George's aggression can best be understood in the context of his relationships and how those relationships develop over time. Instead of studying individuals, we study parent–child and peer relationships. We examine how these relationships grow, change, and stabilize over development.

There are three principles taken from dynamic systems thinking that have particularly profound implications for intervention and policy development. In the present chapter, I will focus on each of these principles in turn: (1) Individuals develop in the context of relationships that can be best understood as systems with properties irreducible to each individual's behavior, (2) flexibility (as opposed to rigidity) in relationships is a key factor for healthy development, and (3) transition periods in development are pivotal phases during which there is an increased potential for both positive and negative changes to occur.

### The parent–child system

The study of dynamic systems in scientific fields as diverse as biology, physics, and astronomy is the study of systemic wholes that emerge from the many interactions of their parts. Researchers using dynamic systems principles study, for example, the complex organizational structure of the bee hive that grows out of the millions of interactions among bees or the evolution of an ecosystem like the Amazon jungle that comes from the multitude of interactions among flora, fauna, and various animal species. Along these same lines, in our research, we study relationships as complex wholes that emerge from repeated interactions among members of those relationships (for example, the behaviors, emotions, and cognitions of parents and children or peers). In fact, we go so far as to insist that relationships (like bee hives and ecosystems) are important to study in their own right, without focusing on each individual's behavior in that relationship. In other words, at the heart of our research program is the old adage: the whole is greater than the sum of its parts.

Studying the "wholes" in development means that we are interested in identifying *relationship patterns*, patterns that cannot be "blamed on" or explained by the behavior of any individual member in a relationship. The relationship itself has its own developmental history. For example, although I am a mature adult with reasonably high self-esteem, when my mother asks me if I *really* want that extra piece of cake I immediately become defiant and tell her to mind her own business. She, in turn, gets angry and we are suddenly in the same old argument about my sensitivity and her lack thereof. Both of us believe the other started it, both of us vow each time never to repeat the dumb argument, but both of us seem drawn by some invisible force beyond our control to repeat the same type of interaction. Especially in our family relationships, most of us can readily identify interaction patterns that feel like forces beyond our control. This invisible force is what we are studying when we study the behavioral patterns of relationship systems.

It is also important to recognize that relationships cannot be characterized as just one "type" (e.g. hostile or supportive). For all normal relationships, a multitude of behavioral patterns stabilize over development. Early in their relationship, George and his mother could be warm with one another, they could play together and they could also argue. Now, as George enters adolescence, there are far fewer types of interactions that characterize George's and his mother's interactions. We are most interested in how relationship patterns change over time, what types of interactions become rigidified and cause difficulty and how to introduce new, more healthy patterns into the relationship repertoire.

### Flexibility in parent–child relationships

As we study healthy and problematic relationships, and try to identify what distinguishes the two, we are guided by one central hypothesis: Flexible relationships are healthy relationships. This expectation is consistent with dynamic systems thinking and evolutionary science. Organisms are considered optimally healthy when they can readily adapt to changes in their environmental context. Similarly, when interpersonal interactions are rigidly repeated no matter what the context, problems seem to arise.

Going back to our example of George and his mother, their relationship was quite flexible early on – they were often cooperative and intimate with one another, but they also had occasional arguments. In different contexts, they engaged in different emotional interactions. Later on, however, George's relationship with his mother became much more rigid – almost any interaction would end in an angry fight.

One way we have tested the general flexibility hypothesis has been to look at relationships that are particularly troublesome and assess rigid patterns of interaction that may have developed over time. We have observed hundreds of parents and their prosocial and aggressive children interacting with one another while they engaged in different types of activities (e.g. playing games, trying to problem-solve a recognized conflict, cleaning up a mess, sharing a snack). We videotaped these interactions and found that aggressive, antisocial children and their mothers are indeed more rigid in their interaction patterns.

Instead of expressing many kinds of emotions, and controlling those emotions when the situational demands changed, aggressive children and their parents remained stuck in one or very few emotional states. For example, it was common for families to become angry in the problem-solving interaction and then remain angry when asked to change activities (for instance, play a game). But it was just as common for these families to show neutral or closed emotional states across all activities. It wasn't so much the content of the emotions that indicated future problematic behavior. Rather, it was the inability to experience a range of emotional states as the context shifted.

Why would it be important for a child's healthy development that family members display a variety of emotional states with one another? We might expect that a task such as conflict-resolution would produce anger and frustration in most families. Playing a game or sharing a snack are more likely to elicit positive emotions. Sometimes it is appropriate to be anxious and hesitant, other times to be excited and spontaneous. We believe that, without the opportunity to experience a range of emotional states in family interactions, children do not develop an adequate ability to regulate (i.e. adjust, control) their emotions. They become entrenched in particular emotional habits that feel inevitable, and they lack the skills for shifting from one state to another when it might be advantageous to do so.

### Effective interventions promote emotional flexibility

Understanding the role of emotional flexibility in parent–child relationships has implications for studying the effectiveness of clinical interventions with distressed children and families. We have been particularly focused on treatments that target antisocial behavior in children because the problem is so complex and affects not only the child and his or her family but society as a whole as well. Among the most effective treatments for aggressive children is Parent Management Training (PMT). PMT was developed at the Oregon Social Learning Center by Marion Forgatch and her colleagues (a number of other researchers have developed similar programs using the same intervention principles). The intervention directly targets negative emotional family interactions and attempts to replace hostile and aversive parenting practices (e.g. yelling, hitting) with mild sanctions (e.g. time-out) that contingently target children's misbehavior. PMT also promotes positive parenting practices such as skill encouragement, problem-solving, and monitoring. Several studies have examined the impact of PMT on children's aggressive behavior and have confirmed its general effectiveness.

In our work, we partner with well-established community mental health agencies who provide PMT. When we first began working with these agencies, we were astonished to find how little was known about the processes of change that support successful treatment outcomes for aggressive and antisocial youth. Research had shown us that PMT *does* work on average, but *how* it worked and *for whom* it was most effective was still a mystery.

We've known for a long time that certain types of parenting relationships have a huge impact on children's aggressive behavior. In the past, researchers who have studied the outcomes of treatment with these children have generally assumed that treatment works by getting rid of negative, angry parent–child interactions and replacing them with happy, positive patterns. From our dynamic systems perspective, this assumption may not only be simplistic, but also wrong. When families and children benefit from treatments like PMT it may not be because they are no longer angry, sad, anxious, or disengaged, but rather because they acquire the emotion–regulation skills necessary to move in and out of these states voluntarily. This process can be thought of as *relationship repair* and is another way of thinking about flexibility in family relationships.

We have begun to test this hypothesis in our research. We videotape aggressive children with their mothers before treatment begins and then again after it ends. In these interactions, families are asked to pick a topic of conflict that gets them angry and that they have difficulty resolving. Then we ask them to try to talk about this issue for six minutes. At the end of the six minutes, we interrupt them and ask them to switch to talking about a positive topic that we provide for them (for example, what they would do if they won the lottery).

Before treatment begins, most parents and children express anger, anxiety, and sadness during the conflict discussion. When they switch to the positive topic, their emotional states remain unchanged. They seem to be stuck in their well-established negative emotional habits. When treatment is over, we collect information from parents, teachers, and clinicians about the extent to which children's aggressive behavior has improved. Those children whose problem behavior did not improve show the same pattern as before: they get stuck in angry and anxious interactions with their parents, beginning during the conflict discussion and continuing through the positive topic. Those children whose problem behavior did improve still show negative emotions during the conflict discussion. But when they and their mothers switch to the positive topic, their emotions shift accordingly, toward interest, happiness, and mutual care. It seems, then, that children whose level of aggression is decreased through treatment have learned, in cooperation with their mothers, to pull themselves out of their negative emotional interactions when they need to. Instead of remaining enslaved to their old reactive impulses, they develop a new capacity to modulate their emotional responses. They flexibly repair their conflicts rather than avoid negative emotions altogether.

## Transition periods in development

As developmental psychologists, we are always trying to keep in mind how different developmental phases bring about unique capacities and challenges for children. As a result, we are concerned with identifying the optimal windows across development during which prevention and intervention efforts are likely to have the strongest impact on problematic parent–child patterns. To pinpoint these developmental periods of opportunity, we have found the dynamic systems concept of a *phase transition* very useful.

Phase transitions are relatively short periods of time during which a system becomes more chaotic. For all living systems, periods of developmental stability and relative predictability are punctuated by abrupt transition periods. After these times of flux, developmental systems re-stabilize and settle into new habits or styles of interactions. It is during these periods of instability that systems are most open to change (both positive and negative).

In our work, we have studied early adolescence as a prime example of a phase transition in human development (others have identified infancy and early childhood as similar transition periods). But unlike most researchers, we don't think of this period as transitional only for the youth. Again, we study the parent–child system as one integrated system and, as a result, we believe that it is the entire relationship system that undergoes massive reorganizations.

Of course, the beginning of puberty and the accompanying enormous biological changes including hormonal and physical changes are clearly happening "inside" the youth. But given that adolescents essentially develop an entirely different body during this period, these changes have profound influences on how mothers and fathers interact with these new "beings." George's mother no longer can pick her son up and soothe him after a disagreement and he is physically stronger than her now, making her feel more vulnerable. George may also start physically resembling his father, leaving his mother with ambivalent feelings and perhaps misplaced anger towards her son.

In addition, George's thinking capacities have grown. He now has the ability to think more abstractly. As most parents will attest, these new cognitive powers bring with them an arsenal of novel demands, platitudes, and cries of injustices. The parent's and youth's roles and responsibilities need to be renegotiated and the relationship will need to become realigned to represent a more egalitarian balance of power. And so, in all these ways and more, it is the parent–child relationship system as a whole that is in transition.

Another important characteristic of phase transitions is that, during this period of flux, small changes in the child's or family's context can have a huge impact on the developmental system (what many people refer to as the "butterfly effect" described in chaos theory). Whereas George was content to have no close friends during his childhood, once he entered high school, one irritated word from a peer or being left out of a team in gym class may send George into a rage. Although these slights may have been completely overlooked by a younger George, the shame that may be triggered by peer rejection now has the potential to have an enormous impact on George's future development.

Our research and others' has shown that aggressive children who are rejected begin to seek the company of peers who are more like themselves. New peer relationship systems develop from antisocial youths' mutual need to feel accepted and admired. Now, in the context of these peer relationships, seemingly small incidents such as George accepting the first joint that is passed to him or agreeing to be a bully's "right hand man" can have disastrous developmental consequences. These relatively minor incidents may make George finally feel accepted and even powerful, increasing the probability that he will continue to associate with similarly troubled youth. In turn, these new antisocial friends are likely to be the source of increased parent–adolescent conflict. The various relationship changes, beginning at the time of a phase transition, are likely to lead George on an aggressive, antisocial developmental path.

As much as developmental transitions provide hotbeds for negative influences to become amplified and adversely affect developmental outcomes, this period of instability also provides tremendous opportunities for positive changes. During phase transitions, the system is much more open to environmental shifts and seemingly small changes have the potential to radically alter the trajectory of relationships. As a result, prevention and intervention efforts aimed to strengthen family relationships and promote healthy friendships may have their maximal effect during these developmental transition periods.

### Clinical and policy implications

In this final section, I summarize the three main dynamic systems principles that can dramatically change the way we understand and intervene with distressed families, particularly aggressive youth and their parents. Below each principle is a list of recommendations for developing innovative interventions that address the complexity of childhood aggression.

1. Individuals and their behavior cannot be separated from the relationship systems through which they develop.
   - Instead of focusing on directly changing individual children's behavior (for example, through anger-management programs), change the systemic/relationship factors that promote and maintain childhood aggression (for example, unhealthy parent–child relationships, access to antisocial peers in unsupervised neighborhoods). A child who changes in a treatment setting and then returns to an unhealthy home and community environment will immediately revert back to old problem patterns.
2. Flexible systems are the most adaptive and healthy.
   - Promote emotional flexibility by teaching children and parents to repair, not avoid, their negative emotions.
   - All families have a range of emotional interaction patterns in which they can engage. Teach families to amplify and elaborate positive emotional states and the frequency of negativity and conflict will necessarily decrease.
3. Transition periods in development are short-lived windows of opportunity for both positive and negative changes.
   - Increase educational and mental health funding for programs that target youth in unstable developmental periods (for example, early childhood and early adolescence). It is during these periods that small changes can dramatically influence the rest of a child's life trajectory.
   - Clinical interventions should trigger a major reorganization. Support groups that do not radically shift family interaction patterns are less effective in the long run than interventions that challenge and confront the family system. Families that benefit from these latter interventions will likely go through a period of

flux or variability during which circumstances get worse rather than better, but this may be the only route towards a re-stabilization into new, more productive family patterns.

## SUGGESTED READINGS

Granic, I., and T. Dishion (2003). Deviant talk in adolescent friendships: a step toward measuring a pathogenic attractor process. *Social Development*, 12, 314–334.

Granic, I., T. Hollenstein, T. J. Dishion, and G. R. Patterson (2003). Longitudinal analysis of flexibility and reorganization in early adolescence: a dynamic systems study of family interactions. *Developmental Psychology*, 39, 606–617.

Lewis, M. D., and I. Granic (2000). *Emotion, development, and self-organization: dynamic systems approaches to emotional development.* New York, NY: Cambridge University Press.

Reid, J., G. R. Patterson, and J. Snyder (2002). *Antisocial behavior in children and adolescents: a developmental analysis and model for intervention.* Washington, DC: American Psychological Association.

# 23    Prenatal substance exposure and human development

*Daniel S. Messinger and Barry M. Lester*

Robert was small and slightly underweight at birth. He had been exposed to drugs while his mother was pregnant. His cries sometimes sounded high-pitched, and he was often tense and rigid. Robert's mother moved twice before he was two years old. First she moved in with her mother; then she moved out again. Robert was not quite as quick as other children at learning new words. He was not good at sorting blocks and learning to pick up beads. Robert had a new sister, a half-sister, when he was three. There were not many books or magazines at home. When Robert began kindergarten, he had trouble learning the letters. Sometimes, he seemed a little tuned out and apathetic.

Neighborhood poverty and family disorganization contributed to Robert's delayed developmental course – as did the prenatal insult of Robert's mother's substance abuse. In our society, prenatal drug exposure is a major public health problem. Many drugs used during pregnancy travel freely through the umbilical cord and cross the fetal blood–brain barrier. What kind of effect would such drugs have on Robert's development? A developmental systems model suggests that the interplay of many factors influenced Robert's development. The impact of drugs on the fetus during the pregnancy depends on the timing of use, dosage, level of prenatal nutrition, and individual differences among mothers, some of which may be heritable. The impact of maternal drug abuse on subsequent child development is even more complex and multidetermined. It is part of an ongoing array of familial, cultural, and social institutional processes within which the child is nested and in which the growing child participates. Nevertheless, exposure to specific drugs is associated with different types of developmental problems.

What drugs was Robert exposed to? Robert was prenatally exposed to nicotine from the cigarettes his mother smoked during the pregnancy, exposed to alcohol from her drinking, and exposed to cocaine from her crack use. All of these are forms of prenatal substance exposure. Let us first consider prenatal exposure to alcohol and nicotine, which are especially frequent. Prenatal exposure to alcohol affects one in four births, with one in twelve mothers reporting binge drinking during the pregnancy. In America, alcohol and tobacco are the most common drugs of abuse during pregnancy. Alcohol impacts prenatal development by impairing and altering the development of fetal brain structures. Extensive alcohol use during pregnancy is associated with the altered facial characteristics, reduced growth, and severe cognitive deficits of Fetal Alcohol Syndrome. Alcohol effects are dose-dependent. This means there are readily apparent relationships between the quantity of alcohol consumed by the mother and subsequent deficits and problems in the child. Less obvious effects of alcohol exposure include reductions in general intelligence and verbal learning as well as problems with social functioning. Attention problems, memory deficits, and motor skills problems have been associated with habitual social drinking by the expectant mother throughout the pregnancy. It is not known if there is a minimum safe quantity of alcohol that may be consumed during pregnancy, nor is it known whether cultural factors, such as attitudes toward drinking, impact the association between alcohol use and developmental difficulties.

In the United States, alcohol use and tobacco use during pregnancy are associated. One in five women reports using tobacco while pregnant. The association between smoking during pregnancy and adverse child outcomes is well known. Prenatal exposure to cigarettes is associated with premature birth, low birth weight, and irritability in the newborn. Tobacco exposure is associated with lower intelligence scores and higher risk for attention deficit disorder in school-age children.

But what about the impact of illegal or illicit drugs? Approximately 3 percent of pregnant women report using illicit drugs during their pregnancies, though actual numbers are likely greater. A developmental systems perspective suggests we attend to the social context of drug use and abuse. Illicit drug use is higher among nonwhite than white women, higher among women who have not finished high school, and higher among poorer women. Women who use illicit drugs during a pregnancy are much more likely to smoke and drink during the pregnancy than women who do not use illicit drugs. This is referred to as polydrug use. Because of polydrug use, it is difficult to isolate the impact of specific illicit drugs on the developing child.

Cocaine accounts for 10 percent of illicit drug use, affecting about 45,000 births per year. Prenatal cocaine exposure has subtle effects on infant and child development. Robert's mother used crack cocaine while she was pregnant. Crack is a smokable form of cocaine and is highly addictive. Initially, crack was thought to do irreparable harm to the fetus. Crack was thought to lead to insurmountable problems in behavior and in cognitive development which would make exposed children unteachable. However, scientifically rigorous research found that cocaine effects were subtle.

Cocaine-exposed infants are born slightly earlier and lighter than non-exposed infants. Some of these cocaine-exposed babies show slightly elevated levels of irritability at birth – but the majority do not. In the first months of life, cocaine-exposed infants sometimes show signs of emotional under-arousal and negativity. But in most cases there is nothing to distinguish these infants from other infants in their communities. We still do not know if there are subtle deficiencies in the cognitive performance of cocaine-exposed infants. But we do know that in an entire population even subtle effects can increase the proportion of children who need later special education services in school.

Both legal and illegal drugs contributed to Robert's apathy, problems in school, and difficulty with learning. Does that mean there are no differences between legal and illegal drugs? Drug molecules are chemical structures. Bonds between atoms in the chemical structure of the molecule determine the physiological properties of a drug. The chemical structure of a drug does not determine its legality.

The issue of dosage underscores the difference between legality and developmental impact. Both cocaine and the nicotine contained in cigarettes are stimulants. There are similarities in how the two drugs impact the fetus. Both cigarette use and cocaine use during pregnancy are associated with low infant birth weight and premature birth. But consider the differences in typical usage of these drugs. Cocaine use is considered high when it occurs three times a week or more. Smoking cigarettes three times a week, on the other hand, might be considered low usage. Cigarette use often occurs multiple times daily, increasing the developing fetus' exposure to the nicotine and other toxic substances contained in cigarette smoke. Issues of dosage have been a focus of the behavioral teratology perspective on prenatal drug exposure.

A behavioral teratology perspective has dominated research into the effects of prenatal drug exposure on development. This perspective posits a linear model of the relationship between exposure and outcome. The behavioral teratology perspective searches for associations between exposure to a particular substance and a specific behavioral outcome at a given age. The perspective asks what levels of exposure are safe and what levels affect outcome. The perspective has asked what level of exposure to various substances (from lead to PCBs to alcohol) can impact the developing child and to what degree. However, the behavioral teratology perspective does not focus on the impact of social risk factors such as poverty and family instability on child development. Robert must cope not only with prenatal drug exposure but with the corollaries of poverty and exposure – potato chips and pop for lunch, roaches in the apartment, second-hand cigarette smoke in the air, and frequent moves between none-too-pleased relatives and friends.

A developmental systems model is emerging in studies of prenatal drug exposure in children. The developmental model incorporates indices of social risk and family environment into the study of prenatal drug exposure. Current investigations of prenatal drug use from all perspectives focus on infants of mothers who are as similar as possible. They differ – insofar as is possible – primarily with respect to drug use during pregnancy. These infants and mothers are frequently from inner-city neighborhoods and are typically poor and poorly educated. A high proportion are from ethnic minority groups. The good news is that infants who are cocaine exposed show only subtle deficits compared to infants who are not exposed. But this finding is overshadowed by the bad news.

The bad news is that on standardized tests of early development and later tests of cognition, both exposed and non-exposed groups perform poorly. All the children in these samples perform below age norms, placing them at substantial risk for difficulties in school. Whether or not children such as Robert are drug-exposed, poverty and poor parental education place them at risk for deficits in verbal development, difficulties with abstract thinking, and subsequent problems in school.

The developmental systems model seeks to understand how prenatal and social factors interact. Prenatal drug exposure tends to occur among impoverished families. This presents children like Robert with a double whammy. Subtle effects of drug exposure might have negligible impact in environments of optimal stimulation, safety, and educational resources. But the impact of prenatal exposure may be especially detrimental in situations in which mothers are less attentive to their child's cues and provide them with fewer resources for cognitive stimulation. One common problem for children whose parents have low levels of formal education is a deficit in the quantity and complexity of the parental language they hear.

Different aspects of Robert's developmental history are likely to influence his development in different ways at different times. The developmental systems model seeks to understand how prenatal and social factors impact children to different degrees and in different ways at different points in development. The impact of poverty on cognitive development may become more pronounced as children spend more time in an impoverished environment, while the impact of being born underweight declines in importance as children catch up with their peers mentally as well as physically. Little is known about the impact of prenatal cocaine exposure on older children, but subtle deficiencies associated with cocaine exposure may also grow larger as children encounter difficulties with more complex work in school.

The practical implications of the continuous mutual influence between infant and mother are especially salient in the case of prenatal drug exposure. On the one hand, maternal actions cause prenatal drug exposure. On the other hand, the pregnancy itself is often a primary and effective motivation for women to stop or cut down on drug usage. After birth, infant behaviors and predispositions continuously impact mother and family. A slightly premature and perhaps more irritable infant places more emotional demands on its parents. A less sensitive and less involved mother places increased demands for self-regulation on the infant.

The developmental systems model can also consider real-time social processes and their impact on development. During face-to-face inter-actions, both cocaine-exposed infants and their mothers show tenden-cies toward disengagement. It may or may not be meaningful to ask whether infant or mother brought such tendencies to the interaction. The important point is such tendencies are likely to be mutually reinforcing, creating a developing infant–mother pair with real, con-tinuing, and perhaps growing difficulties.

### What can be done?

In asking what can be done, we must consider the social reality of drug abuse. The social consequences of drug abuse by a pregnant woman vary from state to state. In some states, drug abuse during the pregnancy is regarded, ipso facto, as child abuse and, so, as grounds for criminal prosecution. In other states, civil action by the state can be initiated based solely on the presence of drugs in fetal urine. But it is simplistic to argue that prenatal drug exposure determines the infant's develop-mental outcome.

Prenatal drug exposure appears to be linked to a range of outcomes. An infant may be unaffected. An infant may experience subtle effects that do or do not increase with development. Alternatively, an infant may appear clearly affected. Only assessment of the infant can deter-mine the degree of impact. Only assessment of the infant and his or her family can determine the need for referrals for drug rehabilitation and intervention. How should we confront the issue of crack babies? We should remember: it's not the crack – it's the baby!

Fortunately, there may be increasing awareness that drug exposure by itself is not sufficient grounds for termination of parental rights. A developmental systems perspective considers the infant's drug-using mother as part of the system. Illegal drug use is associated with psychiatric problems and childhood histories that often involve physical and sexual abuse. Drug abuse exists and is maintained within interlocking familial, cultural, and social matrices involving poverty, discrimination, and familial instability. Its effects may be lessened by the impact of religious and other community affiliations.

Addiction may be viewed as a social and neurophysiological black hole in the landscape of life. This black hole is known as an attractor in dynamic systems theory. Once the user becomes addicted and metaphorically enters in orbit around the black hole, it is very hard to escape its pull. Like contact with a black hole, addiction is frequently devastating. Crack, for example, is well known for its ability to destroy lives. As drug users are drawn near the black hole of addiction, they are increasingly under the sway of the drug. Their lives are consumed by activities to obtain the drug. They neglect social obligations and their role as parents is distorted. Infants are frequently left in understimulating environments, are often neglected, and are sometimes exposed to the violence that often accompanies hard-core drug use.

Nevertheless, drug use during pregnancy should not be criminalized. Criminalization takes a complex system, assigns a causal role to the abuser, and seeks punishment. Criminalization represents a dichotomous (right vs. wrong) orientation, which does not help make things right for children. Ten states consider substance abuse or prenatal infant exposure to be forms of child abuse. The women prosecuted under these statutes are typically poor and black. These prosecutions typically do *not* lead to convictions. Criminalization drives pregnant women from the health care system. They are wary of mandatory reporting and the possibility of losing custody of their child. Criminalization leads to inadequate prenatal care and the possibility of accompanying nutritional and health problems for the mother and developing fetus.

Drug use during pregnancy is a question of public health. Maternal drug use and addiction should be recognized as an illness. Like alcoholism, addiction to illicit drugs is characterized by a syndrome of behaviors. A systems perspective suggests that changing these behaviors requires comprehensive treatment at the biological, behavioral, and social levels. Here the idea of the dynamic attractor (the black hole) is useful. Even when out of the immediate vicinity of the pull of addiction, contact with objects, places, and people associated with prior drug use is like re-entering the gravitational pull of the drug. The addict can be quickly drawn in once again. The gravitational well of addiction exerts its influence even when the user is in remission and is not using. Drug addiction is a chronic illness with rates of relapse similar to those of other chronic illnesses. Recognizing addiction as an illness does *not* remove responsibility from the mother. It simply confronts the severity of addiction with insistence that the addiction be treated. And treatment involves mother taking responsibility for her use. A substantial number of states are now providing for or even mandating treatment programs or coordination of services for drug-using mothers.

A developmental systems perspective indicates we be aware of infant, mother, and community simultaneously. These forces can facilitate drug use, but they can also facilitate recovery. Maternal mental illness, for example, is often associated with drug abuse. Treating either the mental illness or the drug abuse – without treating both – may offer little benefit. Systems perspectives emphasize the mutual interconnectedness of infant and mother. Intervention with one partner – particularly the mother – is likely to have multiple cascading positive consequences for the infant. The social support available to the mother in her role as non-drug-using mother is particularly important for her prognosis and child outcome. After intervention, mothers are frequently drawn back into social circles that support or enable their drug use. The ability to escape communities wracked by poverty and legal and illegal drug activity is one predictor of positive outcome for both mother and child. The systems perspective suggests that escaping the gravitational pull of drug abuse can require a radical change or perturbation in the system.

Sometimes parental rights of drug-abusing mothers must be terminated to protect the child. This is a last-ditch measure taken when the current and future safety of the child is clearly at-risk. The Adoption and Safe Families Act of 1997 makes the safety of the child the pre-eminent concern of child welfare actions. It aims to make foster care a temporary solution and makes planning for permanent placement an immediate goal of the child welfare system. These changes follow from a scientifically based concern with articulating the importance of secure, permanent relationships to healthy development. Although reunification with a parent is ideal, in cases of abuse and abandonment, adoption by relative caregivers or a non-related family may be in the best interests of the child.

Whatever the final family constellation, early intensive intervention has shown a significant impact in samples of at-risk infants including those prenatally exposed to cocaine and other substances. Such intervention is most effective when it provides a structured routine to children that includes developmentally appropriate activities and the opportunity to develop warm bonds with child-care providers. Provision of a network of social service referrals is also essential to supporting the family unit as they negotiate obtaining needed services. Obtaining multiple services for family members integrates a developmental systems perspective with common sense. Transportation to a single location that offers both child-centered intervention and, as necessary, referrals to the parent for substance abuse treatment, mental health services, financial assistance, and medical care are important elements of successful programs.

## SUGGESTED READINGS

Claussen, A. H., K. G. Scott, P. C. Mundy, and Lynne F. Katz (2004). Effects of three levels of early intervention services on children prenatally exposed to cocaine. *Journal of Early Intervention*, 26(3), 204–220.

Hart, B., and T. R. Risley (1995). *Meaningful differences in the everyday experience of young American children*. Baltimore, MD: Brookes Publishing.

Jacobson, J. L., and S. W. Jacobson (1996). Methodological considerations in behavioral toxicology in infants and children. *Developmental Psychology*, 32(3), 390–403.

Lester, B. M., L. Andreozzi, and L. Appiah (2004). Substance use during pregnancy: time for policy to catch up with research. *Harm Reduction Journal*, 1(5), online at www.harmreductionjournal.com/content/1/1/5

Lester, B. M., L. L. LaGasse, and R. Seifer (1998). Cocaine exposure and children: the meaning of subtle effects. *Science*, 282, 633–634.

Messinger, D. S., C. R. Bauer, A. Das, R. Seifer, B. M. Lester, L. L. LaGasse, L. L. Wright, S. Shankaran, H. Bada, V. Smeriglio, J. C. Langer, M. Beeghly, and K. Poole (2004). The maternal lifestyle study (MLS): cognitive, motor, and behavioral outcomes of cocaine exposed and opiate exposed infants through three years of age. *Pediatrics*, 113, 1677–1685.

Tronick, E. Z., D. S. Messinger, K. Weinberg, B. M. Lester, L. LaGasse, R. C. Seifer Bauer, S. Shankaran, H. Bada, L. L. Wright, K. Poole, and J. Liu (in press). Cocaine exposure is associated with subtle compromises of infants' and mothers' social emotional behavior and dyadic features of their interaction in the face-to-face still-face paradigm. *Developmental Psychology*.

*Part V*

# Conclusions and outlook

# 24   A dynamic systems approach to the life sciences

*Alan Fogel, Stanley Greenspan, Barbara J. King,*
*Robert Lickliter, Pedro Reygadas, Stuart G. Shanker,*
*and Christina Toren*

Each of the chapters in this book points to expanding our understanding of the multiple and complex relationships that surround development through the lifespan. In this chapter, we as the organizing committee of the Council for Human Development give a brief description and overview of the science of dynamic systems that is exemplified in the other chapters in this book. The goal of this chapter is to help people see how dynamic systems research helps us to understand human development and how it can assist in creating relevant policies and funding priorities.

The dynamic systems approach is fundamentally different from existing ideas about simple cause and effect. It begins with the realization that the living world is too complex for any one factor to have a significant effect on an outcome in the absence of many other competing and cooperating factors, all of which change over time. Dynamic systems scientists, such as the authors of the chapters in this book, seek to understand certain aspects of this constantly changing network of mutual influences according to their focus of study. The core of the notion of "system" is that it shows the relation of the "whole" and its "parts." To think about dynamic systems means that we have always to consider the history of how the system under study – be this a single child with autism or an inner-city neighborhood – changes over time.

In a few rare cases, a prior condition, or the combination of prior conditions, can be said to be a direct cause of an outcome. Hitting the "s" key on a keyboard causes "s" to appear on the screen; hitting the same key while holding down the shift causes "S" to appear. This is *sequential or linear causality*. In nature, however, instances of linear sequential causality are the exception rather than the rule. In many cases, illustrated by some of the chapters in this book, factors affect each other in mutual and simultaneous ways as they resonate and synchronize with each other. We call this *systems causality*.

Take, for example, the case of an automobile accident, which would seem to exemplify linear causality. Even in this case there are complex factors that conspire together to create the outcome. To be sure, we often highlight a single critical factor, such as that the driver was drunk or the road was slick. But injuries depend upon many sudden, dynamic, and concurrent events surrounding the accident; on whether drivers wore seatbelts; on the type and condition of the automobile, and the like. Even in this apparently simple example, systems causality is operating.

A legislative policy debate is another example of systems causality. As speakers are presenting their "point of view," they are always adjusting their words, gestures, and body postures in relation to what they perceive to be the emerging responses of the opposition. In order to get legislation passed, the sponsors of the policy need to construct their argument in terms of what they think will convince the other side. Even before a floor debate occurs, each speaker is influenced by systems causality in seeking to create a mutual, shared, compromise position. While the debate happens on the floor of the legislative body, aides and constituents are simultaneously talking and negotiating. What goes on at the same time outside the chamber is just as important as what happens inside. Nothing in the process is linear or direct. This is even true – in fact, especially true – in cases where legislative bodies repeatedly find themselves unable to reach any consensus, even though individual members desperately wish for such an outcome.

How would a scientist, such as one of the authors of this chapter, seek to understand this complex, systems causal legislative process where important decisions and turning points take place unexpectedly, in the heat of the moment, without anyone being able to trace a clear linear sequential pathway to how the decision was made? And how would such an understanding enable the actors involved to overcome the impasse in which they find themselves? By the end of this chapter, we will return to this question.

In reality, all social and biological processes are as complex and dynamic as what happens in a policy-making body. For example, how can we address the long-standing and apparently insoluble persistence of poverty in society? Taking a linear sequential view of causality has not worked. Increasing funding for welfare assistance in and of itself, while providing an important safety net, does nothing to address the root problem of poverty and its long-term negative effects on children and families. Addressing the presumed cause of the problem, the lack of money for basic needs, does not of itself produce the intended effect of eradicating poverty.

The knee-jerk response to this failure has been to look for further causes which, when combined with each other, lead to poverty. The goal here is to identify all of the critical causes and the weight that each of them has in causing the phenomenon. Even in the most sophisticated statistical models that study the interactive effects between factors, the assumption remains that causes can be broken down into a number of independent variables that operate together in linear and predictable ways. There is no sense in these models of how the multiple factors involved influence each other in mutual and simultaneous ways.

According to a dynamic systems approach, there is no linear sequential cause or combination of causes of poverty and therefore no linear sequential solution for it. Rather, poverty is *dynamically sustained* in a society by a complex set of systemically causal relationships, both political and economic, that keep it in a steady state. Lack of money is associated, at the same time, with increased psychological stress. Simultaneously, not after the fact, stress and low income drain the person's ability for working, learning, and growing. Even when access to educational resources is available, education may be forced into a low priority by the combined effect of these pressures.

Poor neighborhoods are usually unclean and unsafe, so there is no easy escape, even temporarily, from the stress: for parents and children alike, it is constant and ongoing, not a prior sequential cause. The neighborhood may be embedded, simultaneously, in a network of gangs, weapons, drugs, death, and disease. These mutual and simultaneous influences serve to sustain the status quo and to thwart the best intentions to induce change. There is, it seems, no way to exit from the continual cycle of stress, loss, fear, and disenfranchisement. This is the down side of systems causality: the stable maintenance of undesirable situations through cycles of mutual influence.

We of the Council of Human Development (CHD) take the view that understanding the complex processes of developmental change requires a science of dynamic systems. So too does the path to understanding how to eradicate poverty, disease, war, and other social ills, as well as how to raise happier, healthy children in a nourishing environment in an educational system that promotes the creativity and achievement of each and every child. Some of us are concerned primarily to research and explain what it is to be human, while others of us are focusing on how our research can be used to create effective interventions. All of us know that dynamic systems research is not meant to uncover simple causes, because in truth they rarely exist except in the imagination. Systems scientists do not seek the kinds of over-simplified statements that cater to a media looking for "sound bites." Instead, dynamic systems research:

- seeks primarily to probe the systemic and simultaneous linkages in the network of relationships that sustain particular patterns of development over time;
- aims to uncover the possible pathways that lead to changes in certain undesirable patterns;
- attempts to discover the processes required to sustain and foster the development and maintenance of a healthy developmental trajectory, or a more desirable network of relationships needed for effective decision-making and positive social change.

Dynamic systems research, in other words, sees change in terms of systems causality. So those of us concerned to make practical use of our research know that systems don't get "fixed" or "cured" with a simple formula. Rather, the "bad" system must be allowed to transform slowly over time, systemically, into a "good" system. *In dynamic systems science, we seek to understand the laws of transformation.*

## What is a dynamic system?

A dynamic system is a network of overlapping relationships that exist simultaneously. We could see the whole world of living things as just such a network, but as dynamic systems scientists concerned with understanding human development, we take as our focus particular aspects of this massive network. At the same time, we recognize that the demarcation of domains of study is a matter of research convenience because, as systems scientists know, these systems are bound to inform one another.

The *intra-personal system* takes account of relationships between the various systems of the body and mind, such as between genes and their cellular environment, between brain and behavior, between muscles that act together to perform an action, or between emotion and intellect.

The *inter-personal system* includes social relationships such as, in many organisms, those between parent–child and close companions; and in humans, the same types plus teacher–student, supervisor–employee, therapist–client, romantic partners, business partners. Relationships between humans and their physical environment are also in the interpersonal system. When we relate to, and care for, the animals with which we share our planet, and in some cases our homes, we build interspecies relationships.

The *socio-cultural system* contains all the relationships within and between groups of people with intersecting histories; it takes in relations of international peace or conflict, systems of kinship and religion, of politics and economics, institutions of education or medical care, systems of government and law.

The working groups of the CHD (Anthropology of Human Development, Biology and Development, Ecology of Human Development, Evolutionary Perspectives, Geo-Political Contexts of Development, and Mental Health and Development) encompass all these systemic relationships. There are specific research methods that apply to each domain of relationship and that are used by scientists in each of the working groups. Understanding gene action within the cellular environment requires very different techniques (see Tim Johnston's chapter, part I of this volume) than those used by the anthropologist who tries to grasp relationships within a large group of people and their ideas about the world around them (see Christina Toren's chapter, part III of this volume). This chapter, however, discusses some of the more general notions of dynamic systems science that could potentially apply to all these areas of investigation.

Most research in the life sciences has tended to use linear sequential models of cause and effect that are statistically manageable and conceptually straightforward. These models are of the form: A precedes and causes B to occur. Taking a particular drug is thought to lead to a cure for a disease. Teaching more mathematics and reading skills is thought to improve standardized test scores. Increased welfare assistance (or creating more jobs, or providing basic skills training, or something else) is thought to lead in a linear causal way to the alleviation of poverty. While these linear causal ideas often serve as a first approximation to the way nature works, they do not take account of the "big picture." As Gilbert Gottlieb and Carolyn Halpern point out (part I of this volume), a dynamic systems approach emphasizes "relational" causality. Traditional methods of observation and experimentation are based on the idea of holding everything in a situation constant except one factor, which is allowed to vary. However, factors do not act in isolation. Gottlieb and Halpern emphasize that what makes developmental outcomes happen is the relationship between two or more factors, not the factors themselves.

Dynamic systems research principles can be used by scientists to get closer to the "big picture." What's in the "big picture"? *The "big picture" contains a description of the complex relationships between parts of a whole system, and how that system functions in real situations.* The "big picture" also shows how systems transform over time. How do relationships early in life transform into emotional well-being or mental health problems? How do situations of international conflict transform into states of war or eras of peace? The "big picture" helps us to understand how complex systems of relationships change over time so that we may come to know the factors that regulate systemic change toward particular outcomes. The focus is on systemic causality – how the whole system transforms – rather than on simple fixes.

As Michael Kerr shows, this approach has had a dramatic impact on family research. In this case, taking the "big picture" means seeing the family, not as a collection of psychologically autonomous individuals, but as an entity or "organism" in its own right. That is, all of the members of the family are bound together in a highly interdependent relationship system. This discovery has enabled family systems therapists to answer long-standing questions that could not be explained on the old linear causal models, such as, why we see such disparities between siblings in a family (Kerr, part IV, this volume).

## Traditional research about linear cause and effect

As Stuart Shanker describes in his chapter, our thinking about mental health and mental illness have long been and continue to be governed by a philosophical picture that assumes that mental disorders are the direct effect of linear causes (Shanker, part II, this volume). The result is a pronounced oversimplification of the complexity of mental disorders. As Stanley Greenspan highlights in his chapter (part IV, this volume), among the oversimplifications has been a tendency to focus on the genetics or genetic susceptibility to different mental illnesses without adequate understanding of the experiential and environmental factors or even metabolic factors that influence genetic expression.

To appreciate the significance of this point on a larger sociological scale, suppose we want to know the effectiveness of an educational program meant to alleviate the effects of poverty in an inner city neighborhood. The goals of the program are to help people to understand their options, seek educational resources for self-improvement, and reduce stress so that they can focus on self-improvement instead of simply fighting to stay alive.

A traditional research approach would be to measure indices of achievement – such as income, employment, stress levels, completion of educational training programs, etc. – both before and after people's attendance in the program. How does the traditional approach draw its conclusions from these measurements? This is done using statistics that show whether the group as a whole increased their levels of income and achievement after the program was completed compared to before. This seems like a perfectly reasonable metric and indeed it is the currently and widely accepted way to do research on program effectiveness.

This, however, is not the whole story. In fact, from the perspective of a dynamic systems scientist, this is a highly limited and in some cases even a misleading story. To understand why, we will first look at the meaning of these particular statistical methods for inferring program success. Second, we will look at what else would be important to know in evaluating this program.

The statistical methods used in the traditional research approach are statements about averages. Thus, one could say that *on the average*, people who attended the program improved. But how much, *on the average*, did they improve? Perhaps there was not enough of a change to make a contribution to their lives over the long run. Traditional statistical methods seek universal statements. Dynamic systems methods focus on individual difference and variation. Just to say that people improved does not tell us what that improvement means to them, nor does it say how much of an improvement is enough to make a real difference for them. Dynamic systems scientists would seek to preserve for study and analysis the measures for each individual, rather than losing information about individuals by computing a statistical average. All too frequently, however, it is just such simple statistical statements that justify the investment of large sums of money from government and private sources into programs whose ultimate effectiveness is not well understood.

Improvement of people *on the average*, however, is also a problematic way of thinking about human and social change. *On the average* means that some of the people improved more than others. In fact, it could mean that some of the people did not improve at all and some actually became worse off after the program than before. A handful of people who benefited a great deal could raise the average, making the program seem more effective than it actually is for most of the people who attended. This is why statements about averages can be highly misleading, and why systems scientists endeavor to keep track of individual change, for example, by computing how many individuals improved and how many did not. Another approach is to form sub-groups of individuals – say a group that improved a great deal, a group that improved moderately and a group that did not improve – in order to better understand how these groups may differ.

The fact is that in every program seeking change, some people will do better than others. Some children are academic stars in school while others are seen as failures or drop-outs. Some families will rise above their poverty with or without a program while others make little or no progress even with a great deal of resources given to them. It seems important to understand how these individuals and families progress through the program: at what point do they excel or fall behind? Are there particular program features that work for some people and not others? Dynamic systems scientists would want to make frequent measurements on people throughout the program. They may use the same measures as the traditional scientist but assess them more frequently, to show the ongoing progress of change and to preserve information about how each person changed, for better or for worse.

The traditional research methods cannot address these issues of change processes in part because they focus on averages and in part because they often fail to observe people while they are actually in the program, relying instead on "before" and "after" snapshots of their lives. This is not to deny the importance of the valuable research that has been done on the relationship between socioeconomic status and various aspects of child development. Rather, this relationship should be the subject of much more detailed research. In other words, large population studies are not an end in themselves, but alert us to the need for the focused lens of systems analysis.

Another fact about social or educational programs is that the professionals who deliver them will never teach identically the same program twice. Professionals always adjust their teaching or consulting to the needs of the particular group. What's more, even in the same group going through the same program at the same time, the professionals are likely to treat each person a little differently. These small differences may make a big difference for particular people, whose success in the program may depend on whether they trust or respect that professional. Dynamic systems scientists would want to assess the changes in behavior and attitudes not only of the program participants but also of the program providers. A systems approach which focuses on relationships would assess the way in which the participants relate to the providers, not only before and after but at many points in time during the program. Because traditional research does not study the program and its changing implementation over time, focusing instead on measurements taken before the program begins and then after its completion, there would be no way of knowing how that particular program affected each different participant or how the program staff made adjustments to each person.

The same point applies to education. The effective teacher adjusts her teaching to the needs and abilities of every individual child. But when classrooms are too large to allow for this sort of individualized attention, it invariably happens that those children who may need the most attention end up getting the least, as is reflected in the overall class averages measured by the standardized tests mentioned above. The linear sequential response to this result has not been to enhance the teacher's ability to meet the individual needs of her pupils, but rather, to remove any variability in teacher performance by carefully scripting how teachers should deliver their lessons (in extensive marginal notes in the teacher's textbook). Far from curtailing the poor results observed in schools in many lower income areas, this strategy has actually exacerbated the problem by further reducing the creativity of teachers who were already feeling overwhelmed by the constraints in which they are operating.

### Traditional research cannot provide a complete scientific basis for policy decisions

Thus, there are indeed many ways in which the traditional approach to research gives us limited and sometimes even misleading information. Yet policy-makers in government and private settings may only have this *on the average* information at their disposal. The traditional research is used in so many different settings that it may seem to be the only available and credible source of scientific evidence. Private and government funding agencies often assume that their approach is integrative, capable of taking all complexities into account, just because multiple measurements are used to assess change. They may even assume that the traditional research method *is* science, the only meaningful form of doing research.

Traditional research is used, for example, when testing the effectiveness of drugs for treatment of mental illness. Results of such tests are stated in terms of averages and percentages. A certain percentage of people are said to "improve" on the drug. But what constitutes "improvement"? In the case of clinical depression, improvement might be measured in terms of the subject's eating and sleeping patterns, with no thought given to their overall sense of well-being, their ability to form meaningful relationships, take pleasure in their job, etc. In other words, what constitutes a "successful" treatment is reduced to terms that are commensurate with the sorts of changes that can be produced by the drug in question.

Or consider how a certain percentage of people have serious side effects to a drug. How does a person decide if he or she might be the one who might have a serious side effect? Traditional research can't say because it does not typically study how particular people with particular characteristics fare with the medications. The National Institutes of Health in the United States have only recently begun to study the effects of certain medications on women and children. In the past, dosages and effects have been determined largely from samples of adult men.

Interactions between one drug and another are not sufficiently known since only one drug at a time is typically investigated.

Traditional research is also used when school programs are tested for their effectiveness using standardized tests. What makes an achievement test standardized? Items are selected for the test in such a way as to allow for half the children to score above average and half below average, the so-called "bell curve." In other words, the test itself actually manufactures an "average" student who only "exists" by virtue of the way the test is constructed. Aside from this, all the same problems that we saw for poverty programs exist for interpreting the results of the standardized tests in relation to the effectiveness of an education program. What we really need to know is how each child does in school. Why does one method of instruction work only for some children and not for others? What does each child need to optimize his or her learning potential? As Ken Richardson (part I, this volume) points out, the interactions between social structures and regulations and personal histories is the source of the amazing mental diversity found among people. *On the average* research can't help us here. There is another kind of social and behavioral research that is also scientific and which provides a powerful tool to answer these questions: dynamic systems science.

## Dynamic systems science provides a picture of the real-world that can facilitate policy decision-making

There are some major and important differences between the traditional scientific methods and scientific methods based on a dynamic systems approach: We examine these differences and discuss the implications for making policy decisions based on dynamic systems research. Though our examples focus on programs, the same principles apply to understanding processes through which groups of humans (or other animals) spontaneously cooperate to solve some task, develop skills of communication or language, and so on. A strength of the methods we discuss here is their broad applicability, as reflected in the diverse chapters in this book.

## Dynamic systems research principle 1: focusing on particular cases rather than averages

Dynamic systems research focuses on relationships within and between particular organisms, persons, groups of people, and populations. In the example of the poverty program, above, dynamic systems scientists would assess the relationship between participants and program providers, and the relationship of the participants with each other. This could be done by interviews, questionnaires, or direct observations of how each person related to the others and how that relationship affected their participation and achievement. Dynamic systems research is based on case studies rather than the "average" person and the focus is on how that particular person understands, interacts with, and utilizes what is made available in their relationships with the staff and other program resources. In the poverty program research, for example, it is important to understand how each person was affected by their participation.

In other words, systems analysis provides us with the sort of focused lens that is needed for discovering vital relationship *patterns* that a larger lens will not detect. As Beatrice Beebe and Joseph Jaffe describe it, dyadic "microanalytic" research operates like a microscope, identifying in detail the instant-by-instant interactive events which are so fast and subtle that they are usually lost to the naked eye (ear), and operate largely out of awareness. Their own work illustrates how microanalysis uncovers aspects of nonverbal communication that the unaided human brain simply cannot report (Beebe and Jaffe, part IV, this volume). Similarly, George Downing describes how video microanalysis gives an access to the nitty-gritty of what is going on in relationship disorders, which is difficult to achieve by other means (Downing, part IV, this volume). In fact, by building on Beebe and Jaffe's approach to therapy, he has been able to show that such "video microanalysis therapy" can provide us with a remarkably rapid and effective way to change what is happening between parents and infants, or parents and children.

To think in terms of patterns of communication, of social processes, or of life, therefore, is a defining characteristic of dynamic systems thinking. Patterns permit abstraction in science without eliminating difference, variation, and the uniqueness of particular human beings.

Suppose, to take one example, that poor single mothers who had the support of the child's grandmother are more likely to reach higher levels of education or job training at the end of the program compared to single mothers who did not have family support. An immediate policy implication is to fund alternative child care for single mothers who do not have family child care as an explicit part of the program. This additional program component is likely to enhance the effectiveness for those particular mothers, which then makes the program as a whole more successful.

This increased program success could be measured using the traditional before–after *on the average* approach, but that does not take account of systems causality. From a dynamic systems perspective, an increased number of success stories that emerge *during* the program is likely to influence all the participants, even if they do not fall into the single mother category. Because of systems causality – the simultaneous and spontaneous emergence of mutual effects – a kind of "critical mass" of enthusiasm may be achieved that boosts everyone's involvement with and commitment to the program. Dynamic systems research would more easily capture this phenomenon because it would have assessed each person's relationships with others on a frequent basis, so that the researchers can track the changes in mutual enthusiasm, or for that matter mutual conflict, as they unfold during the program.

*Dynamic systems research does not focus on single measures of each person but rather on the whole person and the relationships and conditions that inform their life.* People cannot be characterized by a simple set of numbers. It makes an important difference whether a single mother has good child care or not. This difference cannot be captured by a simple index of her success or failure. A dynamic systems scientist is likely to obtain measures not only of a person's success or failure in the program, but also of their general well-being, hopefulness for the future, and impacts on other family members. More detailed systems analysis may consider changes in the family, neighborhood, and community to consider how the program's effects may or may not "spread" into the larger social system.

On a much smaller scale – or much larger, depending on how one looks at it – this approach can, as Stanley Greenspan outlines, have an extraordinarily powerful impact on one's understanding of an individual child's developmental disorder, and how to best treat it (Greenspan, part IV, this volume).

*Scientific validity and power is achieved by comparing and contrasting different case histories with each other.* Careful study of each case individually and then together can begin to reveal the similarities and differences more clearly. Scientists using this approach can come to a general conclusion that applies to many people, but this conclusion comes from the hard work of observing each person individually and then looking for common factors and processes.

This method of comparing and contrasting takes into account that no single set of either research methods or research findings applies equally well to all human populations. People's experiences and understandings of the parameters under discussion here – what they embrace, what they avoid, what they admire, and what they aspire to in their lives – differ in structured and patterned ways as a function of each person's history. This personal history is one aspect of the history of a particular family and its relationships with other families, which are themselves embedded in the history of relationships between much larger social groups.

Dynamic-systems anthropologists, for instance, can learn about the factors that a person considers important in their own history and family history by talking and listening to, and living with, people "in the field" – whether in New York City or Tokyo, the mountains of Papua New Guinea, or rural China. When they come up with a set of findings for one population, they do not automatically assume it applies to another.

Further, within any population, exceptions to the general rule always occur and the scientist can use this case comparison method to better understand differences between people so that more effective interventions and policies can be tailored to meet everyone's needs. No person need be left behind because this type of research considers the whole person, rather than aiming for a particular test score or outcome measure.

### Dynamic systems research principle 2: making multiple observations of the way in which each particular case responds to changing circumstances rather than only one observation before and one observation after

Dynamic systems research seeks to observe particular cases all during the process of change: before the program, during the program, and after the program to better understand who succeeds and who falls behind, when, and why. Typically, this is done by making multiple observations on the same cases. Let's suppose the program lasts fifteen weeks. Instead of just two observations (before and after the program) in the traditional approach, a psychologist might observe people weekly, beginning before the program starts and continuing until after the program is over. With eighteen or twenty observations on each person, one can get a much clearer sense of their progress through the program, their ups and downs, when, and why they occurred. An anthropologist might even join the program herself, observing others from the position of participant and deriving a near-continuous account of change over time, supplemented by before–after interviews.

Continuing the example from the poverty program, the dynamic systems scientist armed with multiple observations on each person, as well as multiple observations on the whole group during meetings or classroom discussions, can create a real-life picture of how each person changed over time in relation to the events that took place in the group sessions. This is a way of fine-tuning our understanding of what works and what does not work for each person. Elements introduced early in a program may have a greater impact if they are introduced later.

Experiments can be done by creating variations on the program differing in sequence or timing of components.

From a policy perspective, it is considerably more cost effective to adjust components of a program and the way in which individuals interface with those components, than to reject programs summarily that fail to show an effect *on the average*, or to continue funding poor quality programs that do show an effect *on the average*. Contrary to the assumption that has guided policy-making over the past fifty years, *on the average research* is not a sufficient tool for making informed policy choices when funding is limited and needs are great. *A fine-tuned, case-based documentation of the real-life histories of change over time for the people in the program, in the hands of a dynamic systems scientist, can give a policy-maker a much more sensitive tool for allocating precious resources.*

### Dynamic systems research principle 3: accounting for how a whole system of relationships changes over time, focusing on this whole system and its transformations, rather than on an idealized average individual, who by definition has no history

Dynamic systems research takes account of the fact that the features of the program will change as the people who deliver it and the people who take the program mutually and simultaneously adjust in their relationship to each other over time. *This means that the "program" is changing over time, not a static entity that either works or does not work.* Dynamic systems research is based on the notion of a web of interrelations. It also means that change may occur "in the moment" as a result of a shared and simultaneous convergence or divergence between people, rather than as the result of a step-by-step pre-planned sequence of events.

Everyone knows that teachers, parents, supervisors, counselors, therapists, and other service providers are not machines that stamp out identical replicas of themselves each time they repeat what they do. Everyone also knows that the most effective leaders are those who can dynamically and creatively adjust to each individual circumstance while still applying their set of skills and accrued wisdom. And if our teachers are not allowed any scope for freedom and creativity because of the introduction of the sorts of rigid teaching tools described above, or even worse, a shift from personalized teaching to classroom situations that rely primarily on computerized forms of instruction, how can we expect their students to develop the sorts of creative, reflective thinking skills that will be needed to address the challenges of this new century?

So, whenever scientists who study programs use the before–after *on the average* approach, they may be missing these creative moments that could make or break a program. They are reducing real-life to the simplification that the "program" is static, fixed, a product to be delivered, exactly the same each time. Social and biological systems are simply not machine-like. They are alive and they grow with experience.

Money and resources don't just go to programs but to people who participate in those programs. Dynamic systems research can inform policy-makers about these human characteristics that enliven a program. Policy-makers need to know whether program administrators allow for flexibility, creativity, sharing, and growth in the program staff. Is there a team spirit that wants to make things better for providers and participants? Does the program provide for training and development of project staff? Are there ways for staff to seek advice and new ideas for what they may encounter each day? If the assessments of the program are based on people's perceptions and evaluations of their relationships within the program, then all of these dynamic processes may be documented for further study.

*Dynamic systems research is based on the possibility for spontaneous emergence of new discoveries.* This means there is something that can only happen "in the moment" when two or more people are fully engaged with each other: the sparking of new ideas, thoughts, feelings, and ways of acting. Co-creativity cannot be planned in advance, nor is it the result of step-by-step linear sequence of events. Co-creativity is a product of systems causality that can only happen via simultaneous and shared commitment. A dynamic systems scientist taking this point of view can use observations and self-report measures for judging whether relationships are creative or whether creativity is hampered. These measures of opportunities for creativity may reveal a great deal more about the origin of desired outcomes than any specific characteristic of the individual or the program.

### Dynamic systems research principle 4: including the scientist as part of the changing environment of the system being studied rather than assuming that the scientist does not in any way affect that system

To say that the scientist affects the system is not the same as saying that the scientist is biased or that the scientist deliberately acts to change the outcome of the research. Rather, it is another instance of recognizing the complexity of the real world. According to international guidelines governing research on humans and other animal species, scientists are obliged to obtain consent to do research whenever possible and to protect the safety, rights, and privacy of their research subjects. So, it is impossible for a scientist to be unobtrusive and without any effect at all on the system being studied because participants know they are being observed.

But the scientist's involvement with the system being studied is much more rich and complex than just obtaining consent. There is a myth in society that scientists – who people imagine always wear white coats and carry clip boards – are dispassionate, objective, and emotionally cold. Nothing could be further from the truth. A study of the lives of the most famous scientists – Galileo or Einstein in the past, Jane Goodall or David Suzuki in the present, for example – reveals that they all have an emotional connection to what they study: they care about it enough to invest their careers and lives in that work. Scientists are also part of the social, political, and religious factions and controversies of their time.

Dynamic systems scientists accept the humanity of the scientist as part of the complexity of the system being studied. They do not try to be detached "objective" observers. Once this leap of acceptance is made, however, it creates an entirely new meaning of the word "scientific." *To be scientific means to find a way of engaging with the real world and at the same time to describe explicitly and openly how that world is concurrently being affected by the scientist's engagement with it.* The scientist becomes part of the system to be observed and as such may become part of the systems causality.

To apply dynamic systems research methods, it is often the case that extended participant observation, in which the scientist actually becomes a living and working member of the system, is essential. This is often the case in anthropology and sociology, as we have seen. The scientific discipline of writing the field notes made by the participant observer is capable of revealing to the scientist what the scientist may take for granted. In such a case, to be able to lay bare what is taken-for-granted and to ground one's analysis there requires, for example, systematic data on the way that relations between people are projected into their lives and made concrete in the rhythm of the day as this is lived in the context of the particular program or process being studied.

Scientists often work together in teams so that each different scientist's perception of the world being studied is itself a case study. Similarities and differences between each scientist's point of view become part of the process of understanding the whole system from the perspective of how different human scientists relate to it. The result is in fact a much more accurate view of reality because it is holistic and not based on the viewpoint of one privileged observer who has all the power and authority to make judgments about the "correct" view of reality.

Rather than ignoring one's effect on the system in the name of objectivity, the dynamic systems scientist is highly trained to be constantly exposing his or her judgments and biases in order to be critically examined by self or others. Collaborative scientific work is not very different from the policy-making process in a legislative body. Dynamic systems thinking considers that we are able better to understand nature and human problems, but we do not think that our knowledge is the last word. There is always an open door for indetermination, innovation, and new levels of complexity and precision in the process of scientific discovery. Just as what happens in any dynamic system is a co-creation as people interact and change over time, science is living and breathing, changing and being created, until some kind of convergence is reached about the nature of a process of change, or about the life of a particular individual or group being studied.

## Conclusions

We now return to the example of how policies are made in a legislative body. In the traditional approach, we could simply do a straw vote of the members before the negotiations begin and compare that to the actual vote on the floor at the end of the negotiations and debates. We could see how many minds were changed and whether the policy was or was not approved. This type of information has a certain utility in the news media and certainly the vote matters to the lives of those affected by the policy.

But from the perspective of the policy-making process, the traditional approach says virtually nothing. Each legislator personally learns something valuable from each debate and each vote. No matter which side they took, each person learned a little more about how to better present their position, about who could be counted as an ally, about how to use constituent and advocate input, about when in the process of negotiation it is better to act and when it is better to remain silent, and the like. What the legislative body is really about is the ongoing and dynamic relationships between these different groups and finding, for each particular legislator, more effective ways to maneuver. In their learning process, each legislator is implicitly using dynamic systems methods of research and not traditional scientific methods.

Dynamic systems scientists combine a similar sensitivity and respect for how the real world operates in all its changing complexity with the tools and training of a research scientist. Dynamic systems scientists may use statistics that describe how individuals change over time rather than statistics based on averages. As scientists, it is their job to fully get to know how the members of any system – in a chimpanzee group in Tanzania, a Canadian family, or a rural village in Madagascar – behave, think, feel, and act. Dynamic systems science is as messy as the real world. The scientist, however, is trained to see patterns that emerge out of that complexity after a long period of observation and personal engagement with the particular system under study.

Dynamic systems research is a more costly investment in the short run. Because the focus is on multiple observations of particular cases and examining multiple factors that make up the whole system or whole person, relatively few cases can be studied at any one time. Funding dynamic systems research is placing a bet on quality over quantity. The dynamic systems scientist may work more slowly but the yield is detailed information that is highly meaningful to the making of policy decisions. Over the long run, dynamic systems research can build a complete picture of the human transformational process that will give us a better understanding of how each human life is lived, the environments that optimize each person's growth and development, and the most effective ways for policy-makers to allocate precious resources.

### Basic principles of dynamic systems science

- The living world is too complex for any one factor to determine an outcome in the absence of many other factors, all of which change over time
- In the living world, multiple factors influence each other in mutual and simultaneous ways
- The manner in which living phenomena function and develop cannot, therefore, be explained by trying to isolate specific causes that operate in linear and predictable ways
- To understand how living phenomena function and develop we need to understand:
  - the complex relationships between parts of a whole system and how that system functions in real situations
  - the history of how the system under study changes over time
  - the systemic and simultaneous linkages in a network of relationships that sustain particular patterns of development over time
- Dynamic Systems Science (DSS) focuses on how a whole system of relationships changes over time, rather than on an idealized average individual

- In place of the sophisticated statistical methods that traditional research uses to arrive at generalizations about *population averages*, DSS focuses on individual difference and variation
- General conclusions that apply to many people are made on the basis of careful study of each case individually which, together, can begin to reveal similarities and differences
- This sort of fine-tuned, case-based documentation of the real-life histories of change over time is critical for making informed policy decisions
- DSS aims to uncover the possible pathways that lead to significant changes in highly entrenched patterns
- In practical terms, DSS attempts to discover the processes required to sustain and foster the development and maintenance of a healthy developmental trajectory, or a more desirable network of relationships needed for effective decision-making and positive social change
- DSS recognizes that the scientist is part of the changing environment of the system being studied
- The DS scientist is trained to see patterns that emerge out of complexity after a long period of observation and personal engagement with the particular system under study

SUGGESTED READINGS

Bergman, L., R. Cairns, L. Nilssom, and L. Nystedt (2000). *Developmental science and the holistic approach*. Mahwah, NJ: Erlbaum.

Fogel, A., A. Garvey, H. Hsu, and D. West-Stroming (2006). *Change processes in relationships: relational–historical research on a dynamic system of communication*. Cambridge University Press.

Granott, N., and J. Parziale (2002). *Microdevelopment: transition processes in development and learning*. Cambridge University Press.

King, B. (2004). *The dynamic dance*. Harvard University Press.

Moustakas, C. (1994). *Phenomenological research methods*. London: Sage.

Shanker, S., and King, B. (2002). The emergence of a new paradigm in ape language research. *Behavioral and Brain Sciences* 25: 605–626.

Toren, C. (2002). Comparison and ontogeny. In A. Gingrich and R. G. Fox (eds.), *Anthropology, by comparison*. London: Routledge.

# Index